The Beginner's Guide to
Property
Investment

The ultimate handbook

for first-time buyers

and would-be property

investors

TONY BOOTH

howtobooks

Subscribe to www.propertyhotspots.net for up-to-the-minute
information on property hotspots, property prices, rental yields,
property search, estate agents, letting agents, auctions, 100%
mortgage providers, buy-to-let mortgage providers, portfolio
management and much more.

First published in 2004 by
How To Books Ltd, 3 Newtec Place,
Magdalen Road, Oxford OX4 1RE. United Kingdom.
Tel: (01865) 793806. Fax: (01865) 248780.
email: info@howtobooks.co.uk
http://www.howtobooks.co.uk

British Library Cataloguing in Publication Data
A catalogue record for this book is available from the British
Library

Cover design by Baseline Arts Ltd, Oxford
Produced for How To Books by Deer Park Productions,
Tavistock
Typeset by PDQ Typesetting, Newcastle-under-Lyme, Staffs.
Printed and bound by Cromwell Press, Trowbridge

NOTE: The material contained in this book is set out in good
faith for general guidance and no liability can be accepted
for loss or expense incurred as a result of relying in particular
circumstances on statements made in the book. The laws and
regulations are complex and liable to change, and readers should
check the current position with the relevant authorities before
making personal arrangements.

The Beginner's Guide to
Property Investment

If you want to know how...

Buying and Selling Your House

Build Your Own Home
*The ultimate guide to managing a self-build project
and creating your dream house*

How to Get on the Property Ladder
*The first-time buyer's guide to escaping the rent trap
and owning your own home*

The Buy to Let Handbook
*How to invest for profit in residential property
and manage the letting yourself*

Buy to Let Property Hotspots
Where to buy property and how to let it for profit

howtobooks

Please send for a free copy of the latest catalogue:

How To Books
3 Newtec Place, Magdalen Road,
Oxford OX4 1RE, United Kingdom
email: info@howtobooks.co.uk
http://www.howtobooks.co.uk

Contents

List of illustrations

Preface

The sense of achievement gained from buying a first property is tremendous. It is a momentous occasion, filled with pride and contentment, and one that almost 70% of the entire population achieve at some stage in their lives (national census statistics).

In 1971, only half the population were owner-occupiers, but this increased year on year as more people came to realise the financial and autonomous benefits of getting a home of their own. The economic stability of individuals and the greater combined income of working partners produced widespread affluence and a consequential desire to invest in bricks and mortar. Buying property is no longer the exclusive domain of smug thirty- and forty-somethings – the wings of prosperity have spread far and wide, bringing the potential to capitalise on an investment within the reach of many.

The first property purchased is likely to be a principal and independent abode – a place to call home! But the concept of investment, rather than just habitat, is more widely appreciated these days and the 'first-buy' can just as easily be a dwelling uninhabited by the owner. For example, those pursuing a career may need the flexibility that rented accommodation might offer, enabling them to move from place to place quickly and easily. But the need for mobility does not prohibit them having aspirations to buy property. This group of speculators could opt to 'invest' in a dwelling, rather than live in it, to get their first foot on the property ladder.

While there is a growing trend and an ever expanding ability to buy property, there is associated with it a mounting capacity for critical mistakes. For the homebuyer these errors can spawn a millstone that becomes increasingly difficult to manage. For the investor, it could lead to a burdensome venture, financial ruin and lost opportunities.

This book is intended for savvy investors who wish to evade such errors. Although it mainly offers guidance for the first-time homebuyer, it also examines and explores the many alternative areas of property investment. These include buy-to-let, renovation, buying property abroad, self-build and self-employed business enterprise, for example, buying a shop or cafe to run as a going concern. This is the ultimate guide for all fledgling investors striding into the property world for the first time. For parents whose children are about to leave home and place their feet on the property ladder, this is essential reading: a step-by-step manual of the things to avoid and a map of the best route to follow. As a parent or guardian, this book may contain the most beneficial practical advice you will ever provide for your children. It will set them on the right course, supplying indispensable and easy-to-follow instructions to help them achieve long-term financial security and independence.

This guide does not advocate cutting corners, taking unnecessary risks with money or forging ahead blindly with a desired purchase. Indeed, by reading this book in a logical, progressive and methodical manner, you will recognise the advantage of self-assessment and careful planning. You will also gain access to generous amounts of inside information and well-kept trade secrets. We will explore why it is that estate agents yearn to make contact with first-time buyers; what constitutes a 'sound investment'; why buy-to-let has boomed; how to maximise your borrowing potential and create a golden credit profile. We will look at the extraordinary volume and range of mortgages and suggest the most suitable for your circumstances. In short, this book will progress you along a beneficial learning curve and propel you towards financial freedom. Moreover, it will not only help ensure you profit from the property you buy, but also save you money in the process.

If you aspire to invest in property but are uncertain how to proceed or think the market is out of reach, reading this book will disclose opportunities you may not even be aware exist. There are property investment prospects, products and plans for every conceivable situation and all incomes and circumstances. Gone are the days when those on a low income were excluded from buying their own home or when tenants were unable to become owner-landlords. Although it might be easier for those in work to identify and get a competitive mortgage, it does not preclude others less fortunate from investing in property. There are solutions to every problem and alternative methods of funding available even for those in the direst financial situation.

Property investment means many things to many people. For some, the prime aim is to supply a sanctuary for themselves and their family. For others, it may be essential to conduct business, pursue a long-term goal or create an asset for the future. Many believe that buying the right property in the right place at the right price and selling it at the right time is all down to luck. But the lucrative nature of property investment is not dependent on luck alone. Those relying on 'good fortune' operate under the serious misconception that providence and destiny are virtues bestowed upon them. Being in the right place at the right time by coincidence is one thing – but *planning* to be in the right place at the right time is a desire rarely satisfied.

Luck has no place in the formulae that experienced investors use to calculate profit from a property they have bought. Income and capital growth from *all* 'bricks and mortar' investments are quantifiable – they are tangible assets with a potential revenue identified at the outset by the person buying them. In other words, all residential and commercial buildings have an income-generating or capital growth potential; it is the time and attention buyers give to assess this potential, before committing themselves to purchase, that secures a more favourable and profitable outcome in the long term. This basic rule governs all property investment, whether you are a millionaire about to buy another block of London apartments to add to your portfolio or a first-time buyer preparing to leave the parental home.

An investor's ability to recognise the potential for profit occasionally fails because of temporary blindness – they simply do not see what is staring them in the face. Others fail to distinguish the crucial difference between what they want and what they need or can afford. Yet more become so stubborn in their determination to buy, they forget to consider the long-term financial consequences. A major part of this book relies on the reader having an open mind and being prepared to look honestly at themselves and their situation. By conducting a thorough personal assessment, investigating properties worthy of purchase and exploring all the alternatives, they will buy a dwelling that meets their immediate needs *and* one that provides financial security for the future.

This book represents the accumulated knowledge and experience gained over many years as a professional investor, estate agent, letting agent and author of other property related books. If only it had been available when I bought my first home, it would have prevented me making the mistakes I made then. If you follow the advice and absorb the information in its pages, buying your first investment will be easier and more financially rewarding than you could ever have dreamed possible.

Tony Booth
E-mail: *firsttimebuyer@tonybooth.info*
Website: *www.tonybooth.info*

Acknowledgements

With ever changing property regulations and new financial packages always entering the market, this has been a mammoth book to research, compile and write. Special thanks go to all those who have helped by advising and providing information – you know who you are! Thanks also to my proofreader, Chris Park, who manages somehow to identify every inappropriate hyphen, full stop and comma, and tells me when a paragraph makes no sense whatsoever. My thanks to James Jones and everyone at Experian Limited for supplying the mock credit file report contained as an appendix. Finally, thanks to Nikki Read, Giles Lewis and all at How To Books for their continued support and encouragement.

1

Why Buy?

As with most things in life, the *practical* aspects of buying a property pale into insignificance when compared against *deciding* to enter the owner-occupier market. Although there are always going to be physical and monetary matters to influence this, it is the psychological rationale behind it that remains most significant.

Make no mistake – buying property is a life-changing decision and one that can affect you for years to come. If the foundation is sound and based on realistic goals, the outcome is likely to be beneficial and rewarding. But when a purchase is hastily undertaken or intended to resolve a problem, such as family discord or frustration at work, the anticipated 'freedom' gained from investing might go unrealised. The judgement must be pragmatic, if it is to succeed. This decision-making process requires a level head and credible objectives. Above all, you must be ready to appraise your situation, personal qualities and finances, with guileless and dispassionate candour.

Rather than secondary concerns about how, what and where you buy, it is the *reason* for doing so that produces enduring success. All other matters will slot into their rightful place. Financial problems will be overcome and practical complications will be resolved, as long as the incentive for investing at the outset is realistic and sustainable.

BUYING VERSUS RENTING

The dilemma about buying or renting is the foremost consideration faced by all first-time movers. It is also of significance to those seeking commercial space, such as business premises, to carry out a trade or conduct some other form of self-employed activity.

The traditional concept that renting is just 'dead money' no longer applies, because people have come to recognise the value of flexibility – a quality afforded by renting but largely prohibited through buying. Rather than 'throwing money down the drain', renting provides the tenant with speed, simplicity, mobility and a virtual 'catch-all' expense regime. It produces a financial harness to restrict cost and liability. These are widely acknowledged as valuable and quantifiable assets among the investing community and particularly those with concerns over making long-term personal, legal and financial commitments. Figure 1 shows the average move-in and ongoing costs involved when renting property. It is useful to note that the initial costs are negligible when compared with buying; particularly when you consider that the deposit element is refunded once the tenancy ends.

We will explore the advantages, disadvantages and incentives to buying property throughout the remainder of this chapter. In the meantime, these are some of the persuasive factors involved when considering renting residential accommodation:

First-time renting expense elements	Start of tenancy costs (£)	Routine monthly living costs (£)
Deposit (usually one month's rent equivalent)	525	–
Rent	–	525
Letting agency application and referencing fee	50	–
Bank reference	2	–
Home contents insurance (with £10,000 cover)	–	12
Van hire for diy removal for one day	60	–
Gas for heating and cooking	–	40
Electricity for lighting and power	–	25
Council tax (based on average Band 'C')	–	80
Water	–	15
Television licence	–	10
Land-line telephone (initial connection plus monthly costs)	75	40
Savings (for a basic annual holiday, item of furniture, etc.)	–	75
Essential living costs (food, entertainment, clothing, etc.)	–	250
Keeping and running a vehicle (petrol, servicing, etc.)	–	150
Total	**722**	**1222**

Note: This is a typical example and should be considered a rough guide only. Rent levels vary considerably according to the size and location of accommodation.

Figure 1. Table of average tenancy expenses

◆ With a wide range of houses and apartments available to rent, there is a choice of style and space to suit all pockets. Most accommodation is available part- or fully-furnished and this reduces the immediate move-in costs of those with meagre savings or restricted incomes.

- Contractual assured shorthold lettings *can* be taken for a 'term-certain' as little as one month, though most landlords ask for at least six months. This is a 'secured' period and, as long as tenants observe the conditions of tenancy, they cannot be evicted during the start and finish dates written into the agreement.

- Once the fixed term has expired, many landlords allow the tenancy to lapse legally and automatically into what is termed a 'statutory periodic tenancy'. This increases the flexibility of contractual terms, as it operates from month to month according to when the rent is due. The tenancy can be ended with due notice at any time by either party (though common sense dictates landlords with good tenants will not usually exercise their option).

- The rent paid often *includes* the supply of furnishings, service-charge payable to a management company (where applicable), general repairs, fair wear and tear and, in most cases, building insurance. This means that major outgoings are covered in one payment, except for gas and electricity, water, council tax and other less substantial household costs.

- If the agreement includes a 'break-clause', the tenant can bring the tenancy to an early end without incurring the usual financial penalty (for example, being liable to pay the entire fixed period of rent). This affords tremendous flexibility and allows the tenant to move cheaply, quickly and easily from one location to another.

◆ Because most repairs and replacements are the land-lord's responsibility, there will be no sudden or unforeseen demands made on the householder's monthly income. Budgeting is thus much easier, particularly for those inexperienced in life's financial ups and downs.

◆ Those moving to an unfamiliar area are wise to consider renting, even if only for a temporary period. It gives time to accumulate knowledge about the neighbourhood and explore the various facilities and amenities contained within it. If the location proves to be as attractive as was first thought, the option to buy can be taken up once the tenancy ends; but if it is found disappointing, the lack of legal and financial commitment makes moving to another area a simple and straightforward task.

GETTING ON THE PROPERTY LADDER

There is some truth in the theory that the earlier you step onto the property ladder, the sooner you can climb it, and delaying this process means an equal period of opportunity is lost for capital growth. But success also relies on having enough funds to finance necessities, such as surveyors' and solicitors' fees, paying a deposit and the ongoing monthly loan instalments. This equation becomes more complicated by adding move-in and running costs, such as furnishings, general repairs, insurance and utility charges (gas, electricity, and so on).

Figure 2 describes the average cost of expenses for a small two-bedroom house purchased for £100,000. The data is not accurate for a given location and so cannot be relied on for specific cases; it is supplied as an example and should only be considered a rough guide.

In short, there can be no financial gain made from property investment without first acquiring an asset; but once it *has* been acquired, it must be remembered that it also then becomes a liability. There are those who say, 'never wait for the ship of opportunity to dock – swim out to meet it instead.' The only word of caution I would add is that you must first make sure you are (financially) fit enough for the task. The desire to invest should be balanced with an equal degree of prudence.

LEAVING THE PARENTAL HOME

At some stage, most children develop an urge to leave the parental home. This is usually born from a natural desire for independence – a yearning to stand on one's own feet and become a responsible adult.

However, when there has been an argument at home, the decision to leave is more often a gesture of adolescent defiance. In these circumstances, moving out lacks the essential support that parents might provide and the venture will probably fail as a direct result. The young person is ill equipped, financially and emotionally, for the roller-coaster-ride entering the big wide world for the first time inflicts. Without adequate planning and support, vacating the parental home can be a traumatic and frightening event in which young adults experience sudden isolation, poverty, hunger, agoraphobia and depression. The big adventure can descend into a living

First-time buyer's expenses elements	Point of purchase cost (£)	Routine monthly cost (£)
*Deposit of 10% of purchase price	10,000	–
**£90,000 25-year mortgage (5 year fixed-rate at 4.64%)	–	507
*** Mortgage arrangement fee	200	–
*** Lender's administration fee (often charged if the lender's own insurance policies are not taken)	50	–
*** Mortgage indemnity guarantee premium	900	–
Mortgage valuation fee	115	–
Lender's legal fees	200	–
Surveyor's report	300	–
Solicitor's fees	500	–
Local authority searches	75	–
Land registry	200	–
Stamp duty	1,000	–
Buildings insurance	–	12
Home contents insurance (with £10,000 cover)	–	12
Van hire for DIY removal for one day	60	–
Gas for heating and cooking	–	40
Electricity for lighting and power	–	25
Council tax (based on average Band 'C')	–	80
Television licence	–	10
Water	–	15
Land-line telephone (initial connection plus monthly costs)	75	40
Essential furnishings (bed, seating, fridge, oven/hob, etc.)	2,500	–
Savings (for a basic annual holiday, item of furniture, etc.)	–	75
Essential living costs (food, entertainment, clothing, etc.)	–	250
Keeping and running a vehicle (petrol, servicing, etc.)	–	150
General maintenance and repairs	–	80
TOTAL	6,175	1296

Note:
* Increasing the amount of deposit will reduce the amount borrowed and therefore lower the monthly payment.
** Interest rates can vary considerably according to the economic climate and individual products available.
*** Denotes a cost that *can* be included within the mortgage, but this usually results in a higher monthly payment.

Figure 2. Table of average homeowner expenses

nightmare. Hasty decisions usually result in the teenager returning to the sanctuary of the family home, tired and hungry, with their tail between their legs. It is a tough lesson in life and one that can so easily be avoided.

The transition from child to adolescent and finally into adulthood does not occur overnight. Children tend to react badly to parental boundaries, restraint and control, by stamping their feet and screaming. Adolescents rebel against authority and yearn for their freedom, but lack the maturity and funds to sustain this goal. Young adults, on the other hand, recognise the meaning of responsibility and structure their actions (and reactions) in a more calm and considered manner.

If you are in this situation, the question you must ask yourself before you walk out of the family home is this: are you a child or are you an adult? Answer honestly and you will know whether you are ready to take the plunge!

To be successful, leaving the family home needs to be a measured act, conducted with amicable parental support. With adequate preparation and a financial safety net established – and a realistic view of what lies ahead – the aspiration for 'freedom' *can* be realised and independent living enjoyed. The first part of this process is to recognise the pecuniary implications involved and adopt an early savings plan. This allows familiarity with an expense-driven routine – one that will flow into mortgage and other household payments when income rises to accommodate the financial leap. Start by analysing your income, regardless of how small the sum involved might be. It could, for example, be a salary from full- or part-time work or simply be pocket money given by parents or earnings from a student evening job. The amount of money or how it is earned is inconsequential at this stage.

Next, be prepared to save as much and as often as possible. It is worth noting that a homeowner's 'spending money' usually takes up a tiny fraction of income, with the greater part being entirely consumed by expenses. Test your determination and ability by saving 80% of what you receive over the next six months, after deducting unavoidable expenses (these do not include trips to the local pub or buying music CDs).

By fulfilling this regime, without lapsing, you will accomplish two important measures. You will prove to yourself and others that you have the ability and dogged fortitude to meet a regular payment schedule; *and* you will have accumulated a small or perhaps even a substantial nest egg for the future. This is a simple but worthwhile exercise to test your resolve and endurance. If you fail in this task, it simply means you are not yet ready to move out of the family home. To proceed regardless would therefore be reckless, irresponsible and doomed to failure. Take a break and start again and again until you overcome defeat.

THE 'RIGHT' TIME TO BUY

There are five crucial elements that together identify the most desirable moment to buy property. These are:

1. **When (regular) income is stable and secure.**
   Most mortgage providers will not consider an
   application unless there is evidence of regular
   income. Ordinarily, this means full-time fixed-con-
   tract employment. It is possible to get a loan without
   these conditions, but this usually involves less favourable terms and having to pay a larger deposit. The
   'buy-to-let' market is a rare exception to this rule,
   because rental income from property purchased is
   taken into consideration, over and above revenue from
   another source. However, this is not a remedy for
   those who intend becoming owner-occupiers at the
   outset.

2. **When savings have grown to an adequate level.**
   A buyer needs a financial safety buffer to thwart
   unforeseen events, which will invariably conspire
   against them during the first few years following
   purchase. Such events might include interest rate rises,
   resulting in higher mortgage payments; prolonged
   sickness or an injury, resulting in time off work and a
   consequential loss of overtime and bonuses; or an
   unavoidable property repair or installation. This fund
   is in addition to money required for the deposit and
   other immediate expenses incurred at the point of
   purchase.

3. **When interest rates are at their lowest.**
   There was a time when interest rates were unpredictable. They spiralled out of control because they were
   manipulated by government intervention, rather than
   as they are now, through the Monetary Policy

Committee (MPC) of the Bank of England. Government tended to adjust the rates for political reasons, whereas the MPC assesses the need for change with greater impartiality. As a result, rates are generally more favourable and much more stable. Adjustments are inclined to be in small degrees, up and down, and so do not jeopardise mortgage payers' finances with the ferocity they once did. As long as the national and world economies remain settled, interest rates should not swing dramatically one way or the other.

Buyers who apply for a mortgage while interest rates are low can enjoy the benefits of a fixed-rate product. For example, a five-year fixed-rate mortgage provides the first-time buyer with predictable monthly payments and protection against interest rate rises for a limited period. However, the starting interest rate offered by the lender may be slightly higher than other non-fixed rate products and, if the rate drops during the period, the mortgagee will not benefit from the change.

4. **When the property market is sluggish.**
   This occurs seasonally, as mid-autumn approaches, and continues through winter until early February. It can also rise spontaneously, because of a saturated local market and other influencing factors. When property sales are sluggish prices drop, because vendors keen to sell become more desperate and accept offers they would not otherwise consider. The first-time buyer can pick up a real bargain and maximise their investment potential, if they exploit the opportunities presented at this time.

But it is vital they understand and appreciate the reason for falling property prices. It may, for example, have nothing to do with seasonal influences or an oversupply and instead be due entirely to planning approval for a new factory nearby. Buying under these circumstances would *not* be wise, as property values would probably continue to deteriorate.

5. **When outstanding County Court Judgements or adverse credit conditions have been discharged and all debts settled.**

   County Court Judgements (CCJs) and a history of late or unpaid credit instalments, severely restrict people's ability to access new loans at competitive rates. Although it *is* possible to get a mortgage under such circumstances, it will almost certainly be one with a high interest rate, compounded by harsh terms and conditions. To gain access to the widest range of products, first-time buyers should settle outstanding payments, clear CCJs *and* create a 'clean' 12-month credit history.

   Interestingly, no history at all is treated the same as an unfavourable payment history. Mortgage providers will look at an individual's 'credit score rating', among other criteria, to assess the risk involved when considering an application. If there are no records of credit being taken out, there will be a resulting lack of information about payments. The individual's credit score is thus likely to be low and most lenders will reject an application under such circumstances.

These five rules of thumb are not concerned with the potential or investment merits of a specific property. They simply describe the elements that, when combined, create the most advantageous opportunity to buy.

A MAIN OR SECOND INCOME

Although most first-time investors are homebuyers whose sole intention is to create a family residence, there is a rapidly expanding group who recognises the potential for residential property to generate wealth. Indeed, there are those who deem buying and selling as a highly specialised and lucrative first career choice. The investment bricks and mortar market has opened up in recent years and is now accessible to anyone with enough acumen, enthusiasm and will-power to succeed. Having vast capital at the outset does not guarantee prosperity or a favourable outcome – the key is having the ability to seek out, recognise and exploit opportunities.

Property has always been used as a route to greater affluence but, previously, it involved waiting for years while values increased by tiny amounts. Realising a profit was often more to do with luck than know-how, people just happened to buy the right home in the right place at the right time. Today, things are very different. Buyers are more aware of the characteristics and elements that create profit and consider such qualities before investing. In a buoyant market, those possessing enough skill and insight can realise capital gains within months. Some sit tight, do nothing and sell as market conditions improve; others spend time and funds making the right property improvements, thereby intensifying profit at the point of sale.

Property investment *can* produce a comfortable second income or be a fast way of acquiring a bigger and more luxurious home. Those willing to invest time, expand their knowledge, develop new skills and take calculated risks with the funds they accumulate, might find it leads to a new career. We will explore some of these opportunities in more depth later in this book.

A NEST EGG FOR THE FUTURE

Property has long been accepted as one of the safest forms of investment and consistently outperforms bank and building society savings accounts (see Figure 3). History proves the point: take any five-year period from 1930 to the current day and there has been a steady return provided by property acquisition. In some cases, where buyers have undertaken comprehensive local research and negotiated hard to get the price down, the return was substantial and realised within a much shorter period.

Over the last 72 years, there have been only seven occasions when average annual house prices have fallen or remained static, and most of these were before 1955. These facts support the premise that property speculation is a reliable means of protecting capital against inflation and a simple way of building a nest egg for the future. Interestingly, at a time when pension funds and other traditional share plans and portfolios are suffering setbacks, property values have continued to grow. Wise investors wanting to create security and prosperity for later life are turning increasingly to bricks and mortar – the term 'a second home' has come to mean 'a pension scheme' for many. Our graph shows an investment gain

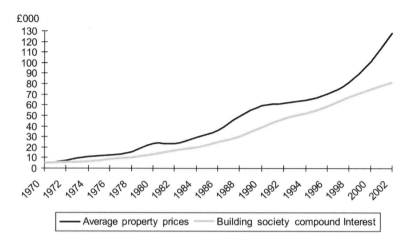

The graph above shows the estimated performance of an initial investment in property of £4,975 in 1970, compared with the same sum invested in a simple building society savings account. By necessity, property prices are taken from average UK house values (source: ODPM). They are not location- or type-specific and do not account for mortgage interest payments, other expenses, tax and variables. Bank base rates were extracted from published data (source: Bank of England) and averages compounded to reflect gross savings account interest rates.

Figure 3. Property investment versus building society compound interest

between 1970 and 2002 of roughly £46,500, for money spent buying property over placing the same sum in a simple building society savings account.

The beauty of a property-based nest egg is that it can be cashed in and enjoyed at any time, though most profitably during periods when values are at their highest. It is also satisfying and reassuring to know you possess a valuable and ever rising commodity that can be used in an emergency. Owning property is probably the best insurance policy you will ever have against financial shortfall in the future. It offers the promise of economic consistency in a progressively more inconsistent world.

Recommended websites

www.checkmyfile.com
This is a superb site that will tell you everything (you probably already know) about your credit rating, that is, your personal risk factor when applying for a loan. The good thing about the *free* assessment offered by *checkmyfile* is that it puts it in black and white, which means you can no longer wear rose-coloured spectacles when planning an investment. A much more comprehensive report can be obtained for a reasonable fee.

www.citytradingpost.co.uk/calculators.htm
This site offers a specialist calculator, which helps first-time buyers understand how much mortgage they will need to buy a house and what costs they will face in the house-buying process. There is also a calculator that illustrates how much they will be able to borrow based on current income. The site offers lots of good advice and information and is well worth a visit.

www.moneyfacts.co.uk/savings/charts/savings_regular.htm
Before you start putting regular savings away in preparation for a future investment, find out who is offering the best interest rates and the most flexible accounts. *Moneyfacts* also has a wide range of other information pages, including advice on credit card companies, unit trust funds, mortgages and business bank accounts.

$$\left(2\right)$$

Assessing Circumstances

This chapter asks you to look closely at yourself, your aspirations, your responsibilities, your support network, your current standard of living and your capabilities. By assessing your circumstances and organising your life according to priorities, you can ensure the investment route chosen is cleared of obstacles that could otherwise severely hinder your progress. Nothing worth achieving is ever attained without effort and you will need bags of energy, perseverance and enthusiasm to pursue and realise your goal. It *can* be done with greater ease, if you are prepared to make some essential early lifestyle changes and sacrifices.

PERSONAL RELATIONSHIPS

If you are involved in an emotionally-based personal relationship, it is important you consider the effect it will have on your investment strategy. For example:

◆ Has the relationship survived the test of time?

◆ Can you rely on your partner for financial and emotional support?

◆ Is the investment going to be fully shared in terms of outlay and reward?

◆ Do you both have common aspirations and a single goal?

◆ Are you both prepared to meet the financial, physical and emotional effort required?

◆ Are you planning a family and, if so, have you considered the additional financial implications?

◆ Are you both prepared to make the same short-term sacrifices to obtain long-term rewards?

◆ Is the investment going to be a contractual joint purchase or solely owned by one partner and, in making a decision, have you explored the tax implications?

◆ Have you considered the worst-case scenario – what would happen to the investment if your relationship failed?

◆ Who makes the decisions in your relationship and how are they arrived at? Is the decision-making process a confrontational exercise and, if so, can a better method be identified, agreed and adopted?

◆ What roles will each partner play in looking for and buying a property and improving or maintaining it afterwards?

◆ Do you believe that investing in property will solve some existing relationship problems? If so, is this realistic or a hypothesis based on hope?

Personal relationships can either make or break a property purchase. At worst, they multiply problems and cause them to grow into major financial and emotional issues, lacking any potential for compromise and leading to an unrewarding and burdensome investment experience. Conversely a strong, time-proved relationship, based on mutual respect and a philosophy of shared aspirations and decisions, will always overcome any early practical and financial difficulties.

The true test of a personal relationship is how it deals with external influences and problems. Success depends on the strength of the bond keeping the two parties together; it is not so much *how* they are coupled and more about *why* they are, that matters. Just as with a house, a strong and level foundation meticulously installed and of an adequate depth, allows the structure set upon it to remain steadfast and unyielding. If the elements forming the base of your relationship are sturdy and resolute, your investment strategy will have the quality of support it needs to achieve success.

BUSINESS RELATIONSHIPS

A business partnership should never be entered into lightly and particularly when capital assets, such as property, are involved. It may seem simple and straightforward at the outset to agree on matters involving a share of the workload, skill and expertise contribution, start-up capital injections and profit-sharing percentages, but these elements almost always lead to jealousy, annoyance and resentment over time, causing new decisions and negotiations to become difficult and protracted. When a partnership deteriorates, so does the business, and the very reason for combining skills and finances in the first place becomes lost in the resulting conflict. Two heads may always better than one – but only if they continue talking with the same voice, maintain the same aspirations and are both prepared to compromise!

The reasons for having one or more business partners are varied, but it is commonly believed that it would be impractical for the venture to get off the ground without them. In return for a share of the profit, a partner might contribute:

◆ All or a portion of funds to buy property and equipment or finance an initial period of high expense.

◆ A particular skill, expertise or knowledge, without which the business could not survive.

◆ A time-developed network of clients and contacts.

◆ An eagerness to 'get involved' in the day-to-day running of the business by devoting a set amount of time to it.

Quite apart from the obvious considerations over degrees of trust, reliability and commitment to the endeavour, it is the ability to 'get on' with the proposed partner that really matters. Like all relationships, there will be periods of friction and discontentment and it is how the root-causes are resolved that improves the likelihood of success. It is often better to have set procedures in place right at the outset, so each side have an agreed path to follow.

Although no one wants to discuss the terms of divorce before a marriage has taken place, it is always wise to consider what will happen if the partnership fails. How will the capital assets, including property and equipment, the profits (if any) and debts, be dealt with? The partners are usually severally liable (though the rules differ when a business is incorporated or is a limited company) and, despite any contrary agreement, a creditor can hold both or either partner fully responsible for the entire debt. This might occur when one is known to be a more financially viable target. The answer to this and all other potentially disastrous financial and legal complications is to have a written 'partnership agreement', drafted by a solicitor and in place before the business begins.

The agreement can define clearly how conflicts are resolved, assets divided and debts paid. It can also rule in the situation where a creditor uses their option to sue one of the partners for the entire debt, making the other partner legally liable to reimburse the one who is out of pocket. Fixed agreements act as a continuous guide, a set of procedures that can be relied upon when disputes arise. They should be employed in *every* partnership situation, including those where the most trusted friends and family are involved.

CURRENT EMPLOYMENT
It is not just a person's salary but also the quality and status of their employment that can make a huge difference to the type of mortgage acquired. Quite simply, the more confidence lenders have about your ability to repay a loan, the wider the choice of products there will be and the better the terms.

Figure 4. The component elements of a partnership agreement

Consider carefully how you might improve the current standard of employment and salary *before* you apply for a loan. Are there prospects for career development? Are you due for a promotion? Can you extend your hours? Would additional training or a night school course help further your career?

It is also important to realise that lenders usually disregard or accept only half of the value of vulnerable salary elements when calculating a mortgage advance. Such elements may include regular overtime, productivity and sales commissions, unsocial hours payments and bonuses that are not guaranteed as part of your standard wage. To prevent these becoming an issue, consult your employer in advance to see if regular additional payments can be incorporated into your salary. If this proves impossible to achieve, resist the temptation to enter them on any mortgage application, unless there is a section specifically designed for them.

By considering improvements to your employment status and planning a loan application months or even years in advance, you can greatly improve the potential of acquiring the best mortgage terms when the time is right for you to apply. The things you do now will significantly benefit you in the future and your quality of employment and salary are primary influencing factors. Do whatever you can *now* to enhance your prospects.

CAREER PLANS

Existing career plans will impact considerably on any proposal to invest in property. If you are in the early days of career development, study courses may prevent you from working full-time and income will therefore be severely restricted. In turn, buying property may have to be a long-term goal. But, if you have yet to properly determine your career, you can devise a strategy that supports both a chosen occupation *and* your investment proposals at the same time. For example:

◆ A career in the hotel and leisure industry or in catering will provide essential knowledge and useful contacts, if the intention is to eventually buy and manage a bed and breakfast property or small hotel.

◆ Learning to become an estate agent, letting agent, a local authority housing or university accommodation officer, will harmonise perfectly with personal plans for a buy-to-let investment. The knowledge acquired from occupational training can be directly applied to the investment, saving a small fortune in agents' fees and commissions.

◆ A career in accountancy and bookkeeping generates valuable skills that can be deployed in any small business.

◆ The legal profession involves acquiring and developing an in-depth theoretical and practical appreciation of housing and contract law. This insider know-how can be applied to any property purchase, sale or investment scheme.

◆ By learning to become a plumber, electrician, joiner or builder, the trade can be utilised in any renovation project or self-build venture.

When planning your career or occupation, consider the type of long-term property investment intended, and then examine which compatible skills could be advantageously transferred from one to the other. Bear in mind that every service you can provide yourself will reduce your immediate expenses and increase the ultimate profit of your project.

A DESIRE TO SEE THE WORLD
The desire to visit far-off countries and experience different cultures is stronger in some people than it is in

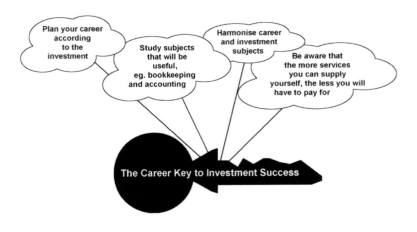

Figure 5. Career key to investment success

others. An adventurous spirit is more often satisfied during the days of youth or older age, simply because these are the periods in our lives when time is plentiful and finances are less restricted. Anyone who is considering buying an investment *and* has a desire to see the world needs to identify his or her priorities and seek to compromise on the time and costs involved. Both *can* be achieved, but when and how are crucial issues. Remember that fulfilling one may be an indulgence that causes the other to be postponed for years to come, so think long and hard before making your choice.

FAMILY SUPPORT

The support of family members is important, because they are likely to provide you with encouragement, advice and also a financial safety net if things get really tough. Never dismiss their help, even though what they say may not always be what you want to hear. Take it on board and consider it carefully, then weigh up what others have suggested and what you already know before making a judgement. The more information and opinions you have, the easier it will be to make a balanced decision and one you can ultimately depend on.

Seek guidance from someone you have always trusted and respected. This could be a parent or guardian, a brother or sister, aunt, uncle or grandparent. Ideally, it should be someone who has already experienced buying and selling property several times or who has been involved in the type of investment being planned. Their familiarity with the subject should provide you with enough helpful insight to prevent you making common errors.

You don't have to accept everything they say, nor do you necessarily have to act on recommendations given. After all, mortgage products and practices may have changed considerably since they were last involved in your chosen area of investment. At the end of the day the decisions you make must be your own based on research and good judgement, but you should always be prepared to receive other people's advice with due respect, recognising that they probably have your best interests at heart.

FAMILY INTERFERENCE

Despite the best of intentions, some family members can become overbearing and attempt to steer you in directions you don't wish to go. You will need ample amounts of self-control and a strong willpower to resist this degree of interference, without offending or antagonising them.

The easiest way to deal with such situations is to undertake comprehensive research about your chosen investment route. By becoming fully armed with factual, dependable information that supports your intended plan, it should be easier to silence those who challenge your point of view. However, bear in mind that their worries and concerns may be the result of an adverse experience they had themselves and, rightly or wrongly, they are only trying to protect you.

STARTING TO SAVE

Without doubt, the best course of action for everyone intending to invest in property in the future is to start saving as early as possible. This has a three-fold benefit:

♦ It creates a pattern of thinking in which putting sums aside from limited means becomes less demanding and more routine. This can pay dividends in the future when earnings have to be apportioned for all of life's expenses, including having to pay monthly mortgage instalments. The earlier that regular consistent saving becomes the norm, the easier it will be when income levels increase and the temptation to spend intensifies.

♦ It creates an expanding pot of gold you can employ later for putting down a deposit on a property, buying essential furnishings and paying professional fees. If you allow your savings to accumulate in a high-interest account over a few years, without withdrawing from it, your funds should triumph over inflation and increase considerably in value. You can also take advantage of some of the exceptional tax-free accounts and enhance your eventual spending power even more.

◆ It helps boost your financial profile. Lenders will assess your ability to meet payments when they consider offering you an advance. If you can prove you already have some funds available and have arranged your budget with saving as a priority, they will regard you as a sensible and prudent individual and take your application more seriously.

If you are not currently taking saving for the future seriously, start doing it now. If you *are* already putting money aside, explore the potential for increasing the amount and undertake thorough research to place it in the best interest-paying account or scheme available.

SACRIFICING LUXURIES

Just about everything you do on a day-to-day basis will reduce your potential to invest in property. This is because, quite simply, it costs money to do them. Every pound spent is one less for the investment pot. Although there are many living expenses that cannot be avoided, there is one that certainly can, if you have enough willpower. Extravagance in buying material goods is an overindulgence you should resist, if you are to realise your dream.

Before protesting profligate innocence (a natural response when someone's financial wisdom is questioned), try keeping a diary of your spending behaviour for one month. Write down everything, including minor purchases – and above all else, be honest in what you record. You may be very surprised at the results. Ask yourself how much of what you acquire is bought on impulse? Do you really *need* these items or are they obtained to satisfy another purpose, for example, boredom? Are you competing with friends who have larger disposable incomes? Are you spending yourself into debt by using credit cards and store accounts that you cannot actually afford? What percentage of your income do you *save* every month compared against the percentage *spent* on luxuries?

By addressing these issues and reducing the amount spent on unnecessary goods to a bare minimum, you will maximise your ability to save and increase the potential to invest profitably in the future.

TAKING ON THE RESPONSIBILITY

There is a significant degree of freedom bestowed on those who continue residing in the parental home beyond their teenage years. Many forego their rights to full independence and in return receive a level of security and financial liberty that is inaccessible to property owners, particularly during the first few years. Despite contributing towards household expenses, the amounts older offspring pay parents for their accommodation rarely comes anywhere near the real cost of living. This provides many in their twenties and early thirties with an extended period of saving, greatly improving the opportunities available to buy property when the time is right.

In reality, the 'right time' for stepping onto the property ladder is different for everyone and does not depend on financial stability alone. Some never achieve the level of maturity required; others may not be prepared to commit themselves to mortgage instalments; and many shy away from the maintenance and repair work so often involved in property ownership. There are also those who simply don't see it as the 'cool' thing to do!

Taking on the responsibility of investment means being prepared to pledge time and money over a prolonged period. The desire for independence must therefore be matched with an understanding and acceptance of what ownership entails, good and bad, otherwise property will be bought for the wrong reasons and at the wrong time of life.

CREATING A GOLDEN PROFILE

A 'golden profile' encourages lenders to provide a wide choice of products with good terms and conditions. If they believe you are a responsible individual who is willing and able to pay off a loan and will meet instalment demands on time and in full every month, their faith will be reflected in the type and amount of mortgage offered. To assess the level of risk, they will examine your credit history and the *current* state of your financial health. The problem is that your profile may have been adversely affected by:

- something you have done yourself;
- something someone else associated with you has done; or
- something that was done at the property address you now live at.

To make matters worse, some bad credit problems can remain on your record for six years or even longer if the outstanding debt continues to be unresolved.

Creating a golden profile allows you to reap financial rewards for years to come. Take the following 'Three Step Credit Challenge' to improve your rating with lenders:

1. *Assessment*
   Regardless of whether you already know about an undesirable credit history problem or not, it is worth confirming the situation. You can access a copy of your credit file from a reference agency for a nominal charge (currently just £2). This will show any broken credit agreement or any outstanding County Court Judgements (CCJs) against you *and* it will also identify any debt-related problem attached to your name or address, but created by someone else (typically another family member or prior occupiers of a property you have lived in). See 'Recommended Internet websites' at the end of this chapter for details of the three reference agencies you can consult for a copy of your credit file. There is also an example of a fictitious credit file in the Appendix at the end of this book.

2. *Rectifying problems*
   Once you are aware of the number and nature of problems involved, you can undertake measures that resolve them. The most logical *first step* is to pay the outstanding debt. This could be something as simple as the final balance on a hire-purchase agreement or a bill you disputed but never settled. When paying off a debt direct, always seek confirmation beforehand, in writing, that the creditor will remove negative

information from your credit file at the point of payment.

Adverse credit information may, however, be something slightly more complicated. For example, it may be the result of credit card fraud, where someone has used your identity to covertly acquire credit and purchase goods. Alternatively, you may have shared a rented property with a group of friends and, having vacated early, assumed the remaining tenants would pay the rent to the end of the term. But if they failed in this obligation, you may have acquired a bad debt record by virtue of being named on the original tenancy agreement. These scenarios may involve more protracted correspondence before they can be settled, but persist until the goal has been achieved.

If a CCJ has been paid *after* the usual time limit of one month (if it is paid within this time the courts will automatically remove your name from the bad credit reference database), you should contact the county court that originally issued it and ask for a 'Certificate of Satisfaction', which costs £10. This doesn't remove your name from the database (it will remain on it for six years regardless), but it does record the debt as having been paid. At the same time, you can add a 'Notice of Correction' to your file to explain the reason for the debt arising, such as prolonged illness or unexpected redundancy. This is useful as it partly legitimises the debt to those viewing the record.

If you identify a problem on your file that you believe has been documented incorrectly, you should challenge it with the credit bureau. They are legally bound to investigate your complaint and, if the record *is* found to be inaccurate, it must be removed from your credit file immediately. Where the debt is due to a member of your family with the same surname and address, you can ask the reference agency for a 'Disassociation'. This does exactly what it says – it severs the (financial) connection between you, your relative and the property address by adding updated information to the file.

3. *Enhancing your profile*
   Removing adverse data from your credit file is the most effective method of improving your profile. The next step involves arranging personal finances in such a way that it enhances your credit worthiness. A healthy credit score is not only determined by your bill-paying history and the amount of credit you have access to, but also the amount of money you have coming in and how you manage it.

A person may have high limits on their various credit cards, giving the illusion that they are credit worthy by default. However, if they buy goods and services up to their limits each month they will have very little 'available credit' left on their cards and, if they are also frequently late in paying routine bills, their rating may in fact be very low. On the other hand, those who always pay bills on time and only use a small amount of their available credit are likely to have a high credit rating. So, the answer to creating a golden profile is to:

- Always pay bills on time.
- Never use all the available credit on your credit cards.
- Keep the number of hire purchase and concurrently running loan accounts to a minimum.
- Manage your finances properly so you never spend more than you earn.

Recommended websites

www.clickdocs.co.uk   *www.compactlaw.co.uk*
www.netlaw.co.uk

All of the above supply standard partnership agreements of varying quality, flexibility and price. At the time of writing costs were between £30 and £45.

www.callcredit.plc.uk   *www.equifax.co.uk*
www.experian.co.uk

These agencies all have access to your credit file. Contact any of them to obtain a copy.

www.insolvencyhelpline.co.uk

This site has been created by the credit industry and is a reliable source of information on repairing an adverse credit history. It also contains a wealth of advice on redundancy, the effects of divorce, leaving and moving home, long-term illness and an anticipated reduction in income.

$$\boxed{3}$$

Daydreams versus Reality

Having explored your current personal and financial circumstances and having made changes to improve them, you should now be in a good position to initiate an investment strategy. Jumping in with both feet is not the answer. Buying property is best conducted cautiously and with a clear idea about the type of investment you wish to acquire. Throughout this chapter we will look at whether your aspirations are matched by your abilities. If they are, you can proceed with confidence; but if they are not, you will need to identify an alternative course of action.

ONE STEP AT A TIME

It is important for first-time buyers to recognise that the ideal home rarely exists, even for those with substantial income and resources, which is why many people either relocate several times in short succession or choose to build their own home (20,000 a year in the UK alone). There is always a compromise that has to be made and most investors realise that one gainful element is usually counteracted by the loss of another. In other words, what is it you are looking for in a property and what are you prepared to sacrifice, so that some of your main priorities can be satisfied?

For example, if you are planning to buy a holiday home to use for part of the year yourself, whilst letting for the remaining period, the *ideal* may be a spacious property right on the beach. However, if the ideal is too expensive, you could choose to forfeit one in favour of the other, but the decision about which to choose needs careful analysis. A smaller property might restrict the number of people who could occupy it, thereby reducing the potential income; whereas a location some distance from the beach might restrict the volume of enquiries received. In this situation, a balance between the two would probably be better than going 'all out' for one or the other. A moderately sized property within walking distance of the beach assures the best possible outcome.

The expectations of first-time buyers tend to be greater than the opportunities delivered in the real world. This often involves an initial period of disappointment for the yearning homeowner – a crash-course during which the practicalities of independent life and property investment are quickly learned. It is sometimes difficult to accept that it is impossible to *jump* up the property ladder; it requires climbing instead – one step at a time. By assessing priorities and limiting your search to the kind of properties your finances will allow, the road ahead will be easier and the speculation process much more rewarding.

APARTMENT OR HOUSE?

This is the first hurdle presented to homebuyers and those intending to venture into the buy-to-let or holiday home market. Most will have already determined whether to buy an apartment or a house, but this is usually an impulse based on lifestyle aspirations, rather than on the actual physical and financial constraints involved. It is wise to undertake thorough research before making any firm decisions, because it is only by gathering *all* the facts and comparing the merits of each kind of property that an accurate assessment can be made. Much will depend on:

◆ **The kind of person you are.** For example, a house with a garden is ideal for those with green fingers and a desire to create their own personal external recreation space. Gardens are also advantageous and safe areas for families with young children or pet animals. But private grounds take time, money and effort and not everyone may be prepared to take on the responsibility. An apartment with a balcony and communal garden areas, maintained through service charge payments, may adequately fulfil some people's needs.

◆ **Where you wish to live.** Apartments dominate the bulk of accommodation in inner cities, whereas rural settings tend to have more houses. This has nothing to do with people's desire and everything to do with land availability and the cost of plots. So, deciding *where* you wish to live is likely to influence the kind of dwelling you are able to acquire.

◆ **The function of the dwelling.** Is it intended to be a bustling family home where space will be needed for teenage children or just somewhere to rest your weary head at the end of the day? Do you envisage a single open-plan area or separate rooms on split-levels? Does modernism and fashion have priority over practical issues? Will you need a separate room to entertain guests, such as a dining area or a second reception room? Where will each of the family members' vehicles be kept (apartments often have only one designated parking space and sometimes none at all)?

If the property is to be let, bear in mind that apartments are generally easier and cheaper to maintain, resulting in higher profit margins; and if the occupiers are going to be elderly, infirm or disabled, an apartment on the tenth floor is unlikely to be either practical or popular.

◆ **The amount of time you have available.** Houses often eat into the free time people have available simply because they comprise more space which involves more decorating, more routine repairs and maintenance and more areas that will need cleaning. In addition, a house owner is usually responsible for the upkeep of the exterior of the dwelling and any garden area associated with it. In contrast, apartment owners generally occupy less space and the exterior aspects are more commonly maintained under a service charge arrangement.

◆ **The quantity of funds you have.** Apartments are not only cheaper to buy but more economical to run too. The equation is fairly straightforward – the more space there is the more it will cost to heat, light, decorate, furnish and maintain.

OLDER PROPERTY OR NEW-BUILD?

The kind of investment you choose is likely to be determined by the amount of funds available, rather than just on preference alone. Older property tends to be less expensive than new-build but, interestingly, a *very* old property with 'character' can cost much more than its new-build equivalent.

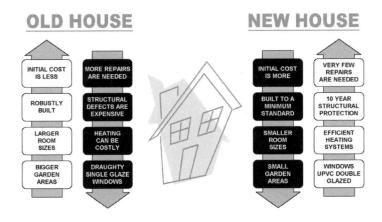

Figure 6. Advantages and disadvantages of old versus new homes

An 'investment' property in need of modernisation may cost considerably less to buy, but the repair outlay will be substantial during the months and years that follow. A newly-built home is less likely to suffer structural problems and, even if it does, these should be covered by the developer's guarantee or indemnity insurance. But recent surveys have disclosed that many people are dissatisfied with the build quality of new homes and find that floorboards start squeaking, plaster walls show signs of cracking and the joints of timber door and window frames swell. In addition (and to keep the price down), builders install soundproofing to the minimum standard required, rather than to a quality desired, which means most new homeowners suffer at the hands of their neighbours.

There is really no easy rule that applies when deciding upon the age of property to buy. Each must be considered on its own individual merits. Taking the investment potential aspect in isolation, new-build often relies more on the quality of location and how the wider area matures and develops; whereas the profit performance of older property depends largely on what improvements can be made to the immediate exterior structure and interior space.

LOCATION, LOCATION, LOCATION

The value of property is intrinsically linked to a dwelling's geographical position, which means the quality of the neighbourhood has a major influence on both the initial price and capital growth performance. It is not just the particular town or city that dictates the price – it can just as easily depend on the street or even the dwelling's position along the street. In addition, locations are volatile and an area that is 'in vogue' today can quickly become unfashionable tomorrow.

When viewing property, remember that while interior aspects can be moulded according to personal taste and desire, exterior aspects are usually beyond a buyer's control. You can change things inside – but the views from windows, orientation of the building and the neighbourhood will remain the same.

The problem for many first-time buyers is that they become blinkered by fashion and fail to recognise that a region's popularity can decline just as easily and quickly as it developed. A 'must have that property' state of mind and a desire to 'live the dream', commits them to a course of action that is often naïve and shortsighted – and one that will cost them dearly over time. The key to a sound investment is not to purchase a property that is in fashion today, but instead buy something you predict will be in fashion tomorrow. It is the basic concept for all forms of selling: buy when prices are at their cheapest, then mark it up and sell it on!

Meticulous and systematic research is of paramount importance. The following points may help you devise a suitable strategy:

- Consult local estate agents, neighbours and shop-keepers. They possess a unique insight into an area and will inform you whether it is gradually improving or rapidly deteriorating.

- Visit the local council and ask to speak to a planning officer. Find out where major redevelopment is due to take place and any areas that have been identified for regeneration. Ask to view recent planning application lists and seek advice about any major renewal programmes.

- Pay close observation to particular streets. The sight of scaffolding and skips tend to indicate people are making improvements to their property. Conversely, peeling exterior paintwork and overgrown gardens are signs of apathy and evidence of an area that is spiralling into decline.

- Explore proposed changes to the infrastructure, new

amenities being planned and any anticipated expansion to existing facilities. A good example of how these factors can influence prices occurred in Manchester, when the Metrolink Tramway System expanded to include other routes through the region. After operating for a few years, the first route proved to be efficient, fast and popular with the travelling public. When new routes were announced, there was a high demand for property close to boarding stations and prices increased accordingly.

◆ View the area at different times of the day and imagine what effect a change of season might have. For example, a trendy coffee society area by day might descend into a land of lager-louts by night; a picturesque riverside location in the summer could suffer frequent winter flooding; an open landscape of fields viewed in November may be inundated with caravans and tourists by June.

NEED VERSUS GREED

Priorities change as we grow older and the needful things we believe are essential to life in our teenage years, quickly become insignificant and irrelevant with the passage of time. Although there is youthful vibrancy and enthusiasm associated with property investment, it needs a clear and calculating mature head to maximise the profit potential. The heading 'need versus greed' relates to the change in attitude you may have to undergo, if your investment strategy is to succeed.

Sacrificing luxuries should be seen as a means to an end – a method through which you can achieve your objective.

Giving up the latest innovation in mobile telephone technology and using the model you already own will save you money that could be put towards property speculation. Going out to the bars and clubs once a week instead of every other night will allow you to bank a small fortune over the coming months. Recognising that you already own more clothes than you will ever have the opportunity to wear will prevent you from stockpiling even more.

Realising what is wasteful spending and seeing the long-term value of economising is crucial during the early years of any property-related venture. Buying (and reading) this book shows you already possess the necessary and intrinsic ability to adapt. All you need to do now is make the physical and psychological changes to your spending habit. By progressing beyond this stage, the adjustments you make will create immediate and lifelong benefits.

It is also useful to apply the 'need versus greed' concept when considering the type of property you intend to buy. Overstretching your budget by proceeding to acquire spacious or fashionable properties is certain to invite disaster. Keep these aspirations where they belong – in the future – when capital and income will match the expense. Be aware that all good things take time and effort before they materialise and property investment is best taken step by step. Identifying *attainable* goals provides for continuous forward movement and reduces the likelihood of disappointment.

GETTING HELP AND ADVICE

I have already mentioned that experienced and respected family members are a useful source of advice. Banks and building societies can also be helpful and most produce free guides for would-be investors. Take time to procure the information available from a range of institutions and not just those you are a customer of, because products and rates vary considerably.

Finally, read everything you can lay your hands on about your preferred type of investment, because the more information you have the more accurate your future judgements and decisions will become. How To Books produces a wide range of easy to read self-help books covering every conceivable form of business, including an array of financial and property investment subjects. Contact them for a free catalogue (publisher details are on the cover of this book).

PLANNING A STRATEGY

If you have absorbed and acted upon all the information and advice provided so far, you should be in a position where you can answer 'yes' to all of the following questions:

- ◆ Have I reduced my spending to the bare necessities?

- ◆ Am I saving the most that I can and on a regular basis?

- ◆ Am I putting my savings in the best interest-paying account available?

- ◆ Have I explored all possible ways of improving my income?

- Have I dealt with any known debt management problems?

- Do I know my credit score?

- Have I taken steps to identify any previously unknown credit problems?

- Have I explored all avenues to improve my credit score?

- Do I know what amount I can borrow, according to my earnings?

- Are my current aspirations to invest in property realistic and attainable?

- Have I researched my chosen investment subject, so that I know all the advantages and disadvantages involved?

- Have I examined my career and identified aspects of it that will benefit my investment strategy?

- Am I good at taking advice and willing to learn from those around me?

- If I need a business partner to fulfil my objectives, have I assessed the implications thoroughly and drafted a partnership agreement?

- Have I considered the alternatives to buying property (such as renting)?

- Is this (financially and personally) the right time for me to buy property?

- Have I discussed my intentions thoroughly with my partner and does he or she support my aspirations?

- Am I prepared to forego life's luxuries in the short term to provide benefits over the long term?

- Do I know when I expect to have enough capital saved to initiate my investment plan?

- Have I identified things I can do now, such as take up a night school course to provide myself with accountancy or bookkeeping services, thereby reducing my eventual investment scheme expenses?

Don't panic if you were unable to answer 'yes' to the aforementioned questions, it simply means you are taking things seriously enough to be truthful about existing weaknesses. This exercise in self-assessment is designed to concentrate your attention on the issues that need effort and action. It is the first step in devising a strategy that will eventually prevail. Remove obstacles that may be in your path and deal with any areas of deficit as best as you can, before moving on to the next chapter.

Recommended websites

www.first-mortgage.info
This is a good place for first-time buyers to get basic information about mortgages, assess how much they will be able to borrow and what it will cost them.

www.firsttimenerves.co.uk
Here is a great little site for first-time buyers from the Skipton Building Society. It is full of simple straightfor-

ward tips and advice about viewing, assessing and buying property.

www.thisismoney.com/savings_rates_saving_deals.shtml
Find the best interest-paying savings accounts available. This site differs from many others insofar as the accounts recommended are devoid of complicated conditions and limitations. It also excludes those that promote high interest return rates dependent upon the receipt of annual bonuses.

Your First Independent Home

This and the next six chapters deal with popular avenues of property investment – the *most* popular being a home purchased for the sole purpose of living in it. These chapters provide only brief guides to the subjects (each has details for further reading, as well as a few useful Internet addresses) and should assist your initial exploration of the possibilities available. The remainder of the book deals with searching for suitable property, surveys, negotiation and purchase issues, in much more detail.

The first independent home should be considered as a launching pad for the novice investor to enter the property ownership market. If it is approached with sufficient care and underpinned with a sound financial strategy, the venture will not just provide a home, but an asset that will rapidly increase in value as well.

STAYING EMOTIONALLY DETACHED

Developers and estate agents endeavour to present first-time buyers with 'dream homes' that match their aspirations. This invariably fires *desire* and leads to the worst possible situation for amateur buyers: an emotional attachment to material things. Most of us are aware that when you fall in love, all other matters become secondary – including logic, rational thought and financial common sense. Some realise the obvious shortcomings but pursue an unrealistic goal nonetheless and, in doing so, risk losing what they have spent so much time establishing.

The designers of show homes aim to create 'wow' factors. A sumptuous bathroom with glistening taps and fluffy white towels; a spectacular kitchen bursting with cupboards and drawers that beg to be opened; bedrooms fitted with gentle lighting and lavish tie-back curtains; bright living rooms adorned with sofas so soft and inviting you cannot resist sinking into them. Be aware that this is nothing more than window dressing – when all you intend buying is the window itself!

Developers are rarely subtle in the way they stage their show homes and, once you know what to look for, seeing through the façade is really quite easy. The removal of internal doors allows each room to appear that much bigger; carefully placed mirrors expand depth and create light; undersized furnishings give the illusion of space. When you next visit a new development, go armed with enough insight to look beyond the obvious, because you will then assess the true fabric of the dwelling, rather than the designer's smokescreen. The same basic rules should be applied to all the properties you view, regardless of whether they are new-build or existing homes on the resale market:

♦ Keep focussed on the qualities a property *must* provide and don't become distracted by desire or the promise of a presently unattainable lifestyle, which may be associated with some dwellings being sold.

◆ Find the true cost (not the advertised 'from' price) of properties in advance and only view those within your budget.

◆ Identify *exactly* what is being offered and ignore furnishings and fittings that are not included in the price.

◆ Look for faults – they *will* exist! Estate agents and vendors won't tell you where or what they are, it is up to you to find them by asking appropriate questions and peering into every nook, crack and crevice.

◆ Be aware that show homes are an example only of the structural style and design elements a property on a new development *might* include. Show homes typically have feature lighting, specially designed furnishings, alcoves, tiled floors, top of the range kitchen fittings and equipment, additional storage cupboards, plush curtains, deep pile carpets or superior timber flooring, extra wide power-shower cubicles and sumptuous bathroom fittings – *none* of which can be assumed to exist in the standard homes the developer has built for sale.

PATIENCE IS A VIRTUE

Buying a first home is an exhilarating but daunting experience. Younger readers of this book may have the stamina but lack the endurance that maturity naturally brings – and this deficiency can be costly. An enthusiastic, inexperienced and impatient buyer is an estate agent's ideal customer because they make frequent and sometimes critical mistakes. Typically, they become fixated on purchasing a particular property without viewing all the other alternatives that might be available. Many also shy away from negotiating, settling instead for an insignificant reduction or none at all. The vendor is happy – the agent is happy – and for a while at least, the first-time buyer believes they have been successful in securing the home of their dreams.

Unfortunately, the passage of time has a habit of bringing realisation and disappointment to buyers who are impulsive and naïve. It can all too soon become apparent that the original property price was inflated and the structure in a state of such disrepair, it will take all of their savings and more just to bring it up to its original market value. Having patience can truly pay a huge dividend because it allows time to:

◆ Examine a wide range of properties.
◆ Undertake thorough research.
◆ Identify a shortlist of 'best value' homes.
◆ Have a comprehensive survey conducted.
◆ Negotiate the price down to a competitive level.
◆ Complete the legal work and mortgage application process.

THE MORE YOU LOOK, THE MORE YOU WILL SEE

Obtaining agents' property brochures and conducting viewings during weekends and evenings, can initially seem an interesting, stimulating and productive way of spending time. Unfortunately, the task soon becomes monotonous and transforms into a loathsome and laborious chore. First-time buyers can quickly lose their motivation and, as a direct result, their observation skills too. Each property starts to look much like another and, after a while, the original goal to find the ideal home fades into oblivion. It is a dangerous phase when buyers will consider accepting *anything* rather than having to continue the process. Giving in to this temptation is, of course, just about the worst thing they could do.

The answer lies in reducing the workload to an acceptable level and, to achieve this, potential buyers need to adopt a methodical approach to the mission. The starting point is to identify the 'must have' attributes a property should possess before it can be considered worthy of viewing. These are likely to fall into the following general categories:

- size (number of bedrooms, room sizes, etc.)
- location (close to useful amenities, transport links, etc.)
- age (established or new-build)
- type (house, apartment, etc.)
- condition (fully refurbished or in need of modernisation)
- orientation (aspect to the sun, views from windows, etc.).

Property descriptions rarely provide full details and a follow-up telephone call to the estate agent may be needed to confirm certain facts. This procedure should quickly and easily eliminate most of the properties, leaving just a select minority to view. The next stage is to decide, in advance, set days to undertake viewings. Most vendors will be happy to meet your suggested times, given a little warning. By firmly restricting the days you look at properties, you will feel less compelled to meet other people's demands and feel more in control as a result. In addition, by giving yourself a period of at least six months to find a suitable property, you can undertake viewings at a gentle pace and alternate weekends spent socialising between others spent inspecting potential homes.

These simple measures will strengthen your resolve and sustain your enthusiasm. They will encourage you to continue searching until you find the most appropriate property available and prevent you from being tempted by something unsuitable or overpriced, simply because of frustration and fatigue.

ASPIRATIONS FOR LIFE, LOVE AND LIBERTY

Life, love and liberty are inspirational elements that encourage young people to leave the parental home and buy a property of their own. Unfortunately, they can also create problems to frustrate this process. These are powerful human emotions and when an opportunity arises to fulfil them, very few have the strength of character and gritty determination to resist it. This can lead to an earlier priority, such as buying a house, falling out of favour while another is considered (temporarily) more important.

There is no easy way of combating events that, by their very nature, involve complex emotions and occur unexpectedly. It may help to recognise that the intention to invest in property needs continuous appraisal and affirmation. If you want something badly enough you will eventually achieve it, despite the obstacles that life has a habit of putting in the way. Maintaining some degree of flexibility should allow for the occasional distraction and, given time, you can assess whether breaking your original plan is likely to be a temporary hiccup or something more permanent.

CALCULATING THE COST

We have already dealt with the elements that make up the initial purchase and running costs of an owner-occupied property and we will explore these in even more detail later. For now, it is worth reiterating two important facts:

- Unless you undertake thorough research and acquire accurate expense data in advance, any calculations you make are likely to prove unreliable and could become the root cause of a future financial catastrophe. Careful estimating is one thing – but pure guesswork is quite another and should always be avoided.

- Paying the largest possible deposit has considerable advantages, which is why saving on a regular basis and from the earliest feasible opportunity is imperative to the success of any investment plan. The more you can put down at the outset, the less you will have to borrow. This not only reduces ongoing monthly payments but also the total amount lost in interest over the term of a mortgage.

Deposit	Total amount borrowed (£)	Monthly repayment (£)	Total cost over 25 years (£)	Total saved by higher deposit (£)
Nil	140,000	902.02	270,606	Nil
5% = £7,000	133,000	856.92	257,076	13,530
10% = £14,000	126,000	811.82	243,545	27,061
15% = £21,000	119,000	766.72	230,015	40,591
20% = £28,000	112,000	721.62	216,485	54,121

Figure 7. The advantage of paying a higher deposit

The data in Figure 7 is based on a property bought at £140,000 with an interest rate of 6% and a mortgage term of 25 years. This is an example only and, in reality, interest rates are likely to fluctuate over the period, affecting both the amount paid and the amount saved.

In the example, almost 200% of the initial deposit is saved in interest charges over the full term of the loan. Other savings can also be made, for example, with a suitable flexible mortgage, an agreed monthly overpayment of just £80 can save a whopping £23,733 or cut a full five years off the term or provide a lump sum bonus. With so many variables, terms and schemes available, a wise investor will gather a comprehensive range of details, forecast costs and assess the advantages and disadvantages of each, before submitting an application to any particular lender (see Chapter 12 for a full analysis of mortgage types).

Recommended websites

www.localestateagentswebsites.co.uk
Why trudge around town on a cold, wet and windy day
when you can register your details with local estate agents
online? The page takes a while to load but it is well worth
the wait.

www.smartnewhomes.com
If you are determined to buy a newly-built home, this may
be a good place to start your search. The online facility
allows you to identify local developments across a wide
range of builders.

www.themovechannel.com/SiteFinder/residential_sales
The Move Channel is a good source of information for
first-time buyers and the above link takes you to over 16
pages of 'property for sale' website addresses, including
the big names like Assertahome, Propertyfinder and
Fish4Homes. If your ideal home is not among these, it
probably doesn't exit.

(5)

An Investment Property

People have different ideas about what comprises an investment property. The serious speculator interprets it as a dwelling purchased below market value and with the economic potential to be improved, before being sold at a profit. The typical scenario involves run-down terraced or semi-detached homes, bought by builders who complete the repairs and enhancements themselves. In this situation, the entire venture is managed under strict business terms with the property remaining unoccupied until sold.

However, a novice entrepreneur is unlikely to have alternative accommodation available or the funds to acquire it. They will therefore be forced into using the investment dwelling as a home while undertaking the refurbishment and while selling it. This creates several emotional and physical complications that could conspire against them. It has the potential to reduce the profit gained at completion and turn the whole project into a millstone, rather than the golden chalice it was intended to be.

To avoid this, the investor must maintain a dispassionate interest in the dwelling, remembering that it is a product – not a home. By maintaining a cool head and keeping one eye constantly on the profit margin, improvements will be cautiously planned, meticulously costed and installed with buyers' needs uppermost in mind.

ASSESSING PERSONAL SKILLS

The preparation for buying an investment property should start well in advance, because it is not just the financial commitment that needs consideration but also the level of personal involvement intended. This has a substantial bearing on the amount of funds required to make improvements and the level of profit realised at completion. How much work you might do yourself entirely depends on the skills you already possess or those you can gain before buying the property. Bear in mind that each pound saved on trade and professional fees is another pound added to your end profit. But, just as important as saving money, there are *quality* and *safety* aspects to consider.

Safety is paramount and it is delivered through know-how and awareness. Gaining practical experience of how a task *should* be conducted allows you to repeat the procedure appreciating the dangers involved. This might not be so important if, for example, you are fitting a new door – but it becomes critical if you are fitting a new power socket. Ignorance, in this situation, can be fatal. There are also times when it is prudent to spend money on safety equipment and clothing. For example, hiring scaffolding to work at height is not only the safer alternative to using ladders, it also reduces the time it takes to complete the job. This is not just good common sense but also makes sound financial sense.

The *quality* of work undertaken becomes particularly relevant when selling an investment. In a recent survey, buyers quoted inferior DIY jobs as one of the main reasons they rejected certain homes. The secondary problem for some enthusiasts is, while they have the ability to undertake a task to the highest standard, the time taken to achieve it is prolonged and laborious. Time is an important financial factor because, as each month passes (after purchase) the burden of costs over profit becomes greater. For example, if a mortgage repayment is £500 a month, it might be more economical to pay a builder to install a new floor within three days, in comparison with saving the builder's fee but having the job take over a month to complete. Saving on expenses is sometimes a lower priority than reaching the stage when a task can be completed and the property sold.

Assessing your own abilities is a worthwhile exercise. It will help identify personal skills you can exploit and other aspects best left to the experts. Figure 8 is an exhaustive checklist of the skills, trades and professions involved in a major property refurbishment project. Mark each on a personal aptitude scale of 1 to 5 with 1 being the highest level of expertise. Once completed, look at the list and plan a strategy to improve or expand your abilities before purchasing a property. An evening class started now could save you a small fortune in a few months' time. The checklist will also identify the trades and professions you will need to 'buy in' and any spare time available at this stage can be used to search for capable, reasonably priced contractors, before the project begins.

Skill, trade or profession	Personal ability (scale 1–5)	Could do myself (scale 1–3)	Need to buy in (scale 3–5)
Accountancy (tax advice, bookkeeping, accounting)			
Architectural (plan drawing, building regulations, planning approval, professional advice, etc.)			
Basic electrics (fitting sockets, lighting cables, etc.)			
Basic joinery (fitting doors, windows, skirting, etc.)			
Building (constructing walls and other structural work)			
Complex electrics (installing a new or adapting an existing ring mains, alarm system or fusing system, etc.)			
Complex joinery (calculating and fitting weight-load and distribution beams for floors, ceilings, roof joists and lintels; staircase construction, etc.)			
Damp-proofing (*Note*: Guarantees issued usually require trained operators to install the damp proof membrane or injection fluid.)			
Decorating (hanging wallpaper, textured effects, etc.)			
Demolition work			
Drainage installation			
Flooring (laying carpet, ceramic tiling, laminates, etc.)			
Foundation work (underpinning, reinforcing, excavating for extensions, etc.)			
Gas installations (new pipework, flues, etc.) *Note*: Installers must be CORGI registered if property is to be let or sold under certain guarantee or indemnity policies.			
General labour (fetch and carry)			
Glazing (windows, doors, etc.)			
Guttering installation			
Hard landscaping (paths, concreting drives, etc.)			
Heating installation (storage units, central heating, underfloor, etc.)			
Interior design (fabrics, colours, space creation, etc.)			
Legal (negotiating easements, covenants, purchase and contract issues, searches, etc.)			
Painting (internal and external)			
Plastering			
Plumbing (pipework, boilers, radiators, tanks, etc.)			
Roofing (battening, felting, tiling, fitting roof lights, etc.)			
Soft landscaping (planting, turfing, etc.)			
Surveying (identifying defects, valuation, etc.)			
Tiling (bathrooms and kitchens)			

Personal ability scale
1 = Qualified, experienced, trained and competent.
2 = Highly skilled and experienced but not qualified.
3 = Some experience – possess reasonable ability.
4 = Know only a little about the subject – no experience.
5 = Completely inexperienced and no proven ability.

Figure 8. Checklist of property refurbishment skills, trades and professions

FINDING INVESTMENT PROPERTY

This is the hardest part of the process because there are thousands of speculators looking for property and only a few suitable investments worthy of purchase. It is interesting to note that an Internet website company recently set itself up in business with the sole intention of matching willing buyers with sellers of run-down property. Despite receiving widespread publicity in national newspapers and employing a proactive marketing strategy to launch the site, they discovered that while they were inundated with enquiries from would-be investors, they only had details of two properties throughout the UK to sell.

The fact is that most 'suitable' properties are hidden among the bulk of other residential dwellings on estate agents' lists and the only method of finding them is to go out and explore what is available. At the outset this might seem like trying to find a needle in a haystack, but dogged perseverance and keen observation usually prevail. The following are some of the routes you may wish to exploit:

- ◆ **Estate agents**
  Contact all local agents and get on their mailing lists. Be as specific as possible about the type of property you are searching for and the maximum amount you wish to spend. Keep a record of the agents you contact and repeat the process every month to confirm your details are still registered with them.

- ◆ **Local newspapers**
  The local press is always a good source for investment property, but you will need to be consistent in scouring

their pages to find a bargain. Independent advertisements from owners only rarely appear and, when they do, it is the expeditious speculator who succeeds.

◆ **Free advertisement newspapers**
The owners of run-down property don't want to spend what little profit they gain from a sale on an estate agent's commission or expensive advertising. The 'free advert' press such as *LOOT* and supermarket freebies are thus attractive to them, so get copies at regular intervals and study them closely.

◆ **The Empty Homes Agency (EHA)**
The EHA was set up in 1992 as an independent campaigning charity to highlight the appalling housing waste of property standing empty and unused. Its aim is to provide owners with advice so that homes can be brought back into use. The statistics speak for themselves: through figures collected by the Department of Transport, Local Government and the Regions, it was found there were more than 750,000 homes standing empty in England in 2001, of which 85% were privately owned.

Many properties are vacant simply because their condition prohibits easy or profitable disposal. Yet these are the investments you need to identify and locate, because many have potential that could so easily be realised, given enough funding and effort. The likelihood is that you walk or drive by several empty dwellings in your neighbourhood every week but, because there are no for-sale signs on display and no obvious means of contacting the proprietors, you instantly reject them as prospective investments. The EHA offer the following advice in tracing absent owners:

- Pin a note to the door or post one through the letterbox with your contact details, stating your interest in the property. Be aware that the owner might have died and the house could be standing empty while the deceased's will is being administered. The wording should be respectful and sensitive to the family or friends who could read it.

- Talk to neighbours and shopkeepers. This costs nothing and often produces good results.

- Contact the Planning and Building Control Departments of the local council. They may have considered an earlier planning application from the owner or had other dealings with them.

- In rural areas, the local parish council clerk might have the information you seek.

- If a Neighbourhood Watch Group exists (look for signs on lamp posts), try to identify the coordinator by talking to neighbours or the local police. They may be keeping a record of the owner's contact details in case the property suffers damage or is broken into.

- The District Land Registry holds information on all owners of registered land. It costs just £4 to submit enquiry Form 313, which you will need to get in advance from HM Land Registry on (020) 7917 8888. This does not always produce good results because, although you might identify the owner's name, the address is likely to be that of the empty property. If the land is unregistered, you will need to search the Land Charges Registry using Form K15 (cost £1). This will reveal the owner's details if there are charges against the property, such as a second mortgage or where bankruptcy papers have been filed. The Land Charges Registry can be contacted on (01752) 635600.

The Empty Homes Agency can be contacted at 195-197 Victoria Street, London, SW1E 5NE. Tel: (020)7828 6288 for further advice and information. See the end of this chapter for details of their website.

◆ **Property auctions**

This is a natural hunting ground for investors keen to make a killing. Property auctions contain lots from disheartened and financially strained owners whose attempts at selling through traditional means have already failed. They turn to auctioning their property as a final resolve and are sometimes prepared to accept bids significantly below the original valuation. Auctions also include dwellings repossessed by lenders, run-down inheritances, derelict or abandoned farmhouses and dilapidated property owned by local authorities.

Local estate agents know when and where auctions are to be held, so this should be your first port of call. You should also check *Yellow Pages* for details of other contacts, under 'Auctioneers and Valuers'. Local surveyors may have useful information and it is also worthwhile contacting the local council, a local landlords' association, independent building firms and developers operating in the area. Notices of forthcoming auctions are likely to appear in local newspapers, so maintain continuous scrutiny of their property and public notice pages. The Internet is also a rich source of information and the following websites are worth exploring:

www.auctionpropertyforsale.co.uk

www.eigroup.co.uk

www.halifax.co.uk

www.numberone4property.co.uk

www.propertyauctions.com

www.ukpad.com

Chapter 15 provides *essential* reading if you are considering attending an auction. Buying property in this way is quite unlike the traditional method – the most important difference being that if you bid for a dwelling and you are successful, you will have already entered a legal and binding contract to purchase the lot. Unlike the sluggish conventional process of 'offer – negotiation – acceptance – surveying – draft contract – exchange of contracts – and then completion', buying property at auction is completed within the day. For the novice entrepreneur, it can be unnerving to realise just how fast, final and legally binding the decision is, once you raise your hand!

SCRUTINISING AND INVESTIGATING

When considering the purchase of a dilapidated property, it is important to:

- Research the area and neighbourhood thoroughly to confirm it is on its way up rather than on its way down, as this will help ensure the property's capital value grows rather than stagnates (or worse, deteriorates).

- Consult the local authority to find out whether grants exist to help with refurbishment costs. The qualifying criteria for grants change from time to time and among local authorities (see 'Obtaining Grant Assistance' below). It might be worth restricting your search to designated regeneration areas, as it is customary for conditional grant assistance to be available to the owners of dwellings found in them.

- Conduct your own preliminary survey of the dwelling (see Chapter 18) to help identify major faults or concerns. The results could persuade you that buying the property and paying for an unproductive professional survey, besides other expenses, would be too high a financial risk.

- Arrange for a comprehensive professional structural survey to be conducted (if the findings of your preliminary investigations have not already discouraged you from proceeding).

- Draw up an accurate schedule of essential repairs, maintenance and improvements, then get **at least** three written quotations for each job from respected and dependable contractors. Bear in mind that it is not uncommon for a simple task to turn into several complicated ones, so add at least 10% to the estimated total. Once this task is complete, assess whether the price of refurbishment falls within your forecasted profit and outlined budget.

- Consider the time it will take to complete the works, because this will affect routine ownership expenses (council tax, energy costs, etc.) and influence the profit realised at the point of sale.

- Present the results of your survey and estimated cost of repairs to the owner or their agent (using the highest quotations obtained) and renegotiate the price down as far as possible. Forceful and dispassionate negotiators often succeed in buying property at a fraction of their former value, thereby increasing substantially their own profit margin at the point of sale.

REFURBISHING TO SELL

Most novice investors fail to achieve substantial profit at the point of sale because of one simple fact: either during the planning stage or while implementing an improvement strategy, they impose their own emotional and personal values onto the project. In other words, rather than satisfying buyers with the type of improvements undertaken, they seek to satisfy themselves. This is an expensive mistake that can place the entire venture in jeopardy. Typically:

- Higher quality and more expensive fittings and fixtures are incorporated into the dwelling than they need to be.

- General decoration is unnecessarily detailed and prolonged.

- Unimportant areas of the property are enhanced while more influential ones are ignored.

- Repairs undertaken and appliances and systems installed are above the minimum standard required to sell the property.

So, what *do* you spend money on? Most people are aware that kitchens and bathrooms are influential areas. But transforming one to the detriment of the other is not always the answer, because it will highlight problems and discourage at least one group of potential buyers. Sometimes, spreading funds among several areas to improve the appearance of each is the best all-round decision.

The location of a property and the sort of person likely to buy it also play significant roles. For example, in rural areas the kitchen remains king because preparing food and eating it are fundamentally social family events; but in cities, young childless professionals rarely cook meals and often dine out instead. For them, the bathroom is more important, being an essential space for relaxation at the end of a stressful day.

Fads and fashions change, but the main elements sought by homebuyers remain fairly constant. Figure 9 provides information on the most attractive and profitable improvement projects suggested by recent buyer surveys, respected experts and property commentators. This should only be considered a general guide, because much also depends on:

- The size and style of neighbouring property. For example, if you create a home with four bedrooms in

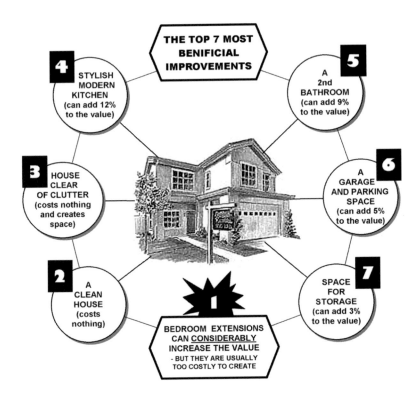

Figure 9. Improvements advised by the experts to maximise value

an area where most properties have only two, it will never realise its true 'comparable size' value. Equally, a poorly designed extension can cause the dwelling to become incongruous with others nearby and this is more likely to deter buyers than attract them. Think of 'blue stone cladding' on a terraced property and you will get the idea.

◆ How the property is likely to be used. For example, transforming a traditional home into a luxuriously appointed contemporary pad is pointless, if most residents occupying property in the area are ordinary working couples with young children.

◆ The eventual price group. Turning a standard home into something extraordinary is fine providing there is a *growing* demand for such dwellings in the region. But if the local economy deteriorates, the population's capability to buy luxurious homes will diminish. It is therefore important for the local economy to be strong and people to be confident about their earning potential, if you are planning such a project.

It is more important to undertake repairs than improvements. Basic structural defects *must* be attended to first, so that the property becomes marketable and saleable. It is also crucial you conduct exhaustive research to identify the likely buyer group and what they expect from a home, before considering which improvement projects to carry out. Matters requiring immediate attention will probably include:

◆ installing central heating

◆ fitting double glazing

◆ exterior decoration

◆ replacing cracked or unfashionable sanitary ware

◆ installing security measures such as an alarm system, new locks and exterior lighting

◆ repairing garden and boundary fences/walls

- repointing brickwork

- replacing corroded or damaged guttering

- renewing a damaged damp proof course

- reinstating damaged roofing felt and missing tiles

- removing and replacing rotting floor or ceiling timbers

- replastering 'blown' internal walls (affected by dampness or detached from the brickwork because of the passage of time).

Costing out all proposals and estimating realistic returns from a predicted growth in market value will determine the improvement projects best to invest in and those that are better abandoned. This can only be achieved by comparing 'like' property with other 'like' property in the neighbourhood. Bear in mind that all this needs to be undertaken *before* you purchase, because the best dwelling to invest in is determined by comparing the cost of works with profit potential.

GATHERING ESTIMATES

The more estimates you get for each job, the more choice of contractor you will have and the more accurately final costs can be assessed. There is no easy or quick way of achieving this – you simply have to set to it, draw up a schedule of work, pick up the telephone and book the appointments. Once you have all the estimates in, you should ask for referrals from preferred contractors to assess their quality of work and reliability. Good builders and diligent tradesmen never shy away from providing the contact details of their customers – if they are proud of their work they will be happy for you to see it. When getting estimates, confirm:

- they are inclusive of VAT (where applicable)

- you will receive them in writing

- the terms and period that work is guaranteed

- that they include *all* charges, such as the removal and disposal of debris

- the contractor's indemnity to you in the event of damage to property and details of their public liability insurance

- that the contractors are registered members of the professional or trade bodies they claim to be (this can usually be done by telephone or on the Internet)

- that the local Trading Standards Office has not had complaints about them.

RAISING FINANCE

As you begin searching for a mortgage, the early practice of saving money regularly will now pay dividends. It should not only be enough to provide you with funds for a comfortable deposit but also cover expenses for the mortgage arrangement charge, surveyor's and solicitor's fees as well. But, it is unlikely to finance the biggest problem commonly experienced by those buying run-down investment property with a traditional loan – suddenly being informed of a *mortgage retention*. The typical scenario goes something like this:

Buyer finds a property he wants to purchase at £100,000 and submits a mortgage application for 80% of the price.

▼

Buyer pays valuation and arrangement fees. The lender demands a comprehensive survey has to be undertaken.

▼

The lender receives the survey report, which identifies structural and other defects. The property value (with no defects) is assessed at £100,000. The cost of repairs is assessed at £15,000.

▼

The 80% mortgage is granted, but the lender retains £15,000 for 12 months (or until the repairs are conducted). The buyer's advance is therefore now only £65,000 and there is still £15,000 worth of mandatory repairs that need to be financed.

▼

Buyer's immediate shortfall to acquire the property (after paying the deposit) is now £30,000 (£15,000 retention plus £15,000 worth of repairs).

The buyer must make an urgent decision: do they proceed with the purchase, funding the shortfall with another loan, or abandon the project altogether? It depends on whether they have enough income to cover the monthly mortgage payment *and* the new short-term loan, or starting from scratch trying to find a more suitable property. There are several actions they could undertake that won't necessarily remedy the situation, but could ease the sting.

◆ Within two or three days of the survey being undertaken, the applicant should contact the lender and ask for the results. If a retention is likely, it is better to know about it early so more thought can be given to the repercussions. It will also give enough to time to identify and arrange a competitive loan, rather than having to scramble around at the last minute and accept a high-interest loan out of pure desperation.

◆ Armed with the survey and the retention amount, the buyer should consult the vendor or the selling agent about reducing the price of the property. A 50% reduction of the estimated cost of repairs is usually considered a reasonable compromise.

◆ If the vendor won't reduce the price, will they have the repairs done at their own expense? This is not always the best solution as the quality of work cannot be controlled and the process may cause considerable delay and uncertainty.

Perhaps a more productive alternative might be found by expanding your search of the mortgage products available. With thousands of loans on the market, mortgage brokers are a good way of reducing the time it takes to find the right product. For example, The Money Centre, telephone (01603) 428500, offers a suitable discounted product with wide flexibility. The loan is released in stages: first for the purchase and then for each major repair project. More can be borrowed as the value of the property increases and, for a one-off fee, the discounted loan can be converted into a fixed-interest rate product.

Various types of traditional mortgage and the standard application process are explored fully in Chapters 12, 13 and 14. More unconventional products are described in each individual chapter, according to subject.

OBTAINING GRANT ASSISTANCE

Getting a grant to help with repairs may seem very appealing at the outset, but funding is highly restricted and the application process is fraught with bureaucracy. Local councils administer most of the property-related grants available and they are your best first port of call for information and advice. Contact the housing or environmental health department and ask to speak to a senior officer. A face-to-face meeting always tends to be more productive, if it can be arranged. Bear in mind that grants are means-tested, they are offered on a sliding scale and usually have conditions attached.

The following types of assistance are obtainable under Part 1 of the Housing Grants, Construction and Regeneration Act 1996:

♦ **House renovation grant** – for the improvement or repair of houses or flats and the conversion of properties into houses or flats for letting. It is awarded by discretion of the local authority and is not available for second homes and holiday properties or those built within 10 years of application. Tenants or owners who have not lived in the property for at least three years are unlikely to qualify.

◆ **Common parts grant** – for the improvement or repair of the common parts of buildings containing one or more flats. The grant has restrictions and conditions and is means-tested.

◆ **HMO grant** – for the improvement or repair of 'houses in multiple occupation' (HMOs) and the conversion of existing buildings into them. An HMO is defined as a 'house occupied by persons who do not form a single household' and refers to let dwellings. Novice investors would be wise to avoid purchasing these properties, as they are fraught with legislative and management problems (see Chapter 6).

◆ **Disabled facilites grant** – to help adapt homes for disabled people.

◆ **Home repair assistance** – to help with minor repair works.

◆ **Group repair schemes** – where the local authority undertake repairs to groups of homes. The idea is that the external fabric of a row of dwellings is repaired at the same time by the same contractor, thus improving the whole neighbourhood and at a reasonable cost. Where available, the grant pays for half the works required.

◆ **Relocation grant** – to help people displaced by clearance action to buy a new home in the same area.

More detailed information is available in a free booklet from the Office of the Deputy Prime Minister, *House Renovation Grants* (product 96 HC 202C). Telephone: 0870 1226 236. Useful leaflets are also available from your local authority and from the Citizens Advice Bureau.

There is also the 'Starter Home Initiative', which is a recently introduced Government funded scheme to help key workers (mainly teachers, health workers and the police), to buy a home in areas where high house prices are undermining recruitment and retention. The scheme is available in London, the South East and housing hot spots in Eastern and South Western England. For more details visit the website at: *www.odpm.gov.uk/starterhome*

A SHORT-TERM STRATEGY

A short-term strategy is one that involves buying, refurbishing and selling a property within a year, then using the profit to repeat the entire process all over again with another dwelling and so on. This is a potent but exhausting investment plan where 'time' plays the most critical and influential part. The concept involves retaining ownership of a property only for the period of refurbishment, thereby reducing or evading altogether the financial liability for household expenses, such as council tax. It *can* produce extremely good results so long as personal enthusiasm and energy levels remain constant throughout. But there are often complications, which include:

- **Burnout**. A stage when the investor becomes so fatigued, physically and emotionally, they lose motivation for the project. If this occurs during a time-restricted restoration scheme, it can jeopardise earlier profit and the entire venture.

- **Selling at the wrong time.** Because the property cannot be held beyond the period of completion (or else it will incur profit-attacking expenses), it must be sold as quickly as possible. The problem is that national or local market values may be in a period of cyclic depression and the price achieved will thus be lower than if selling were delayed a few months.

- **Unproductive capital growth.** Most property values rise gradually over a period of years with peaks and troughs in between. Selling within a year severely restricts the dwelling's ability to realise true capital growth.

- **Living a life of chaos.** The initial excitement of moving up the property ladder in rapid succession can diminish once the reality of living life in storage boxes sets in. Constantly moving means no dwelling purchased ever has enough time to develop into a home and, with most possessions packed away, practical day-to-day existence can become miserable and intolerable. Add to this fact the relentless noise, constant clouds of dust, the invasion of personal space caused by repair works and tradesmen, long months of inaccessible leisure time – and the entire venture can deteriorate into a gruelling ordeal.

A short-term strategy should only be considered if you have stamina and tenacity in abundance; alternatively, think about taking a more restrained route to success.

A LONG-TERM PLAN

Experienced investors work on a three to five-year yield plan. Yield is the growth return on investment (profit), expressed as a percentage. Returns depends on many variables including:

◆ The condition of the local housing market.

◆ The national economic performance.

◆ The costs involved to acquire funds (loan and mortgage charges).

◆ Interest rate fluctuations.

◆ The cost of the refurbishment project.

◆ Property disposal expenses.

◆ Experience and knowledge (making the most appropriate cost-effective improvements and selling the property at the most profitable time).

Acceptable yields are those that surpass other relatively safe forms of investment such as dealing in low-risk shares, professionally managed portfolios and high-interest bank and building society saving schemes. Extending the period of ownership has many advantages and widens the scope for profiteering. For example, it may provide time for you to:

- Undertake some or all the work yourself, rather than employ contractors.

- Complete meticulous research to identify the type and scale of improvements that will boost the property's marketable qualities and increase its value.

- Carry out the works at a steady and comfortable pace.

- Spread the cost of the project over a more manageable period, allowing funds from regular income to meet expenses, rather than having to borrow money.

- Turn the finished refurbished property into an 'in-house' buy-to-let scheme, where the income gained from letting is redeployed to pay outstanding loan instalments.

- Choose to sell the property when local prices peak and competitive alternative housing supply is low.

THE ADVANTAGE OF PARTNERSHIPS

Going into partnership with a family member, a colleague or a trusted friend, can provide access to an investment opportunity that might otherwise be beyond your ability or financial reach. A partner may not only help with funds but could also have valuable skills and experience to contribute. Not only are two heads sometimes better than one, four hands can also work out cheaper and easier than two when it comes to undertaking the physical tasks involved.

While partnerships *can* be very stimulating and productive, they are not suited to all and if you *are* thinking of entering into one, consider the advice given under 'Business Relationships' in Chapter 2.

GETTING ADVICE ABOUT TAX

The best tip given to me when I began buying property over 25 years ago was 'get yourself a good accountant' and, since that day, I have always sought to pass this advice on to novices entering the investment market. Although no one is entitled to avoid tax, a professional and independent financial advisor can suggest the best way of managing assets, funds and income, to take advantage of tax rules and allowances. There is no escaping that the Chancellor will collect what he is due, but by organising your investment project appropriately, you can reduce your liability to the minimum rather than the maximum or postpone payment until a later date.

While an accountant will help with self-assessment tax returns and accounting procedures and guide you through the extraordinarily complex tax system, an independent tax or financial advisor (IFA) can show you the route to saving tax through lesser known rules and regulations. Choosing an IFA is best achieved through personal recommendation and it may be worth consulting your relatives, friends and colleagues to identify an advisor. Alternatively, The Institute of Financial Planning can provide you with a list of its fee charging members. Visit their website at *www.financialplanning.org.uk/find_planner.cfm* or telephone them on (0117) 945 2470. There is also a central register of qualified advisors kept by the Financial Services Authority (FSA) who can be contacted on (020) 7066 1000 or through their website at *www.fsa.gov.uk*

Taxation is a complex subject and liability depends on personal circumstances and an individual's specific financial arrangements, which means it is impractical to offer constructive general advice in such a short paragraph as this. However, matters worthy of further exploration with your advisor include:

- Minimising capital gains tax (CGT) by buying a *second* property jointly with a partner or spouse, thereby taking advantage of each person's individual allowance.

- Looking at the most favourable dates property is purchased and disposed of, which can have a considerable influence on CGT liability and the date it becomes payable.

- Assessing the potential of turning the investment project into a business opportunity and creating a limited company to offset expenses against tax.

- Choosing appropriate property to buy and making improvements that keep the selling price within stamp duty limits, thereby improving its marketable qualities. Stamp duty is paid by the buyer and calculated on a sliding scale according to property price.

Recommended websites

www.emptyhomes.com
Information and contacts regarding England's large volume of empty homes.

www.primelocation.com

A very slick and comprehensive property site supplying advice and information, articles and guides, search facilities and contacts, on all aspects of buying, improving and selling residential property.

www.rics.org.uk

A valuable guide to property auctions is supplied by the Royal Institution of Chartered Surveyors (RICS) in the 'public zone' of their website.

6

Buy to Let

Just a few years ago the term 'buy-to-let' didn't even exist, but in an astonishingly short time the concept has boomed and become *the* first choice for property investors. The theory is simple: buy a suitable property, let it and use the rental income to pay mortgage instalments. Although renting property is probably one of the earliest established businesses in history, many people were excluded from taking part because of how lenders once used to assess risk. Quite simply, if you weren't earning enough – you couldn't get a loan.

Everything changed when the Association of Residential Letting Agents (ARLA) proposed a new kind of mortgage product, one that would not just consider an individual's occupational income, but a newly acquired property's *rental income* as well. 'Buy-to-let' was born and after high street lenders began supplying suitable mortgages, thousands of new landlords were created.

But these were inexperienced landlords and many fell foul of the investment trap – they failed to recognise the significance of supply and demand and bought the wrong property in the wrong place at the wrong time. Some were also ignorant of the law involved in letting and found tenants they could neither get rent from nor evict. Buying property to let *can* be an extremely lucrative form of investment, but only if enough care is taken to purchase a dwelling apt for the purpose. Equally, landlords should be armed with enough knowledge about letting that they are able to distinguish good tenants from bad and offer accommodation that complies with private rented sector regulations.

HOW TO REALISE PROFIT

There are two types of profit obtained from a property purchased to let:

♦ **Capital growth** – the increase in market value of the property over time.

♦ **Rental income** – the immediate gains made from rent payments, after deducting expenses.

If all the elements involved in buying and managing the property are conducted properly, both levels of profit *are* easily realised – in fact, they happen as a matter of course and with little effort. The difficult work occurs beforehand when searching for the most suitable property to buy and while trying to identify the right tenants to accept. Everything that follows afterwards involves gaining familiarity with routine tenancy matters and property management procedures.

The whole process is like entering a marathon where you not only have the desire to take part but also want some certainty of winning. You must prepare yourself thoroughly and research the other entrants' abilities beforehand, so you know that the prospects of beating them are high. Starting the race without adequate training and with little knowledge of the other competitors' skills increases the risk of losing – once the marathon begins, it is too late and what will be will be.

Likewise, buying a property without researching its letting potential, getting tenants without checking references, having only scant knowledge about the legal implications and failing to stay aware of market forces – all add up to high risk. Like entering the marathon – once you buy the property and have let it, what will be will be. Your ability to influence the end result is largely determined by what you do at the outset. If an inappropriate property is bought at the wrong price and in the wrong location and then let to bad tenants, little can be done to counter the inevitable complications that will arise. Capital growth and profit from letting are consequential to the preparation you undertake right at the start. This should be considered *the* most crucial aspect of your investment strategy.

FINDING SUITABLE PROPERTY

The combined influence of four elements (TLCC) help identify the most suitable dwellings as 'buy-to-let' investments. These are:

Property Type

The most popular type of accommodation among renters throughout the UK is a two bedroomed apartment above the ground floor, though this varies in some regions according to local needs. For example, in a small rural town, where most would-be tenants could be couples with young children, a terraced property or town house with an enclosed small garden might be more sought after. The intention should always be to buy a property that is in high demand, because this will reduce void (empty) periods and increase the rent received for each year.

Property Location

Although it may be tempting and more convenient to buy a dwelling near your own home, it might not be the most advantageous for maximising profit. The most suitable location for let property is one that satisfies all the needs of its intended tenants – not only those of the landlord. Tenants usually look for accommodation that:

◆ is close to transportation links such as a bus-stop, train station or motorway network

◆ has good amenities nearby such as a doctor's surgery, a park or other open space, fitness centre, cinema, local pub, restaurant, newsagent, general store or supermarket

◆ is within a short drive of where they work (relevant if *the* major employer in the area is a specific company, hospital, university, college, local authority or industrial manufacturer)

◆ is close to a good primary school or nursery (if a small family home is going to be purchased).

Property Condition

A well maintained, newly decorated and spotlessly clean home will always be more popular than one with leaking pipes, crumbling plaster and damaged fittings. The standard and presentation of a property has a considerable bearing on the quality of tenant it attracts and the rent it might command. Gone are the days when accommodation could be supplied in any old ramshackle form – even today's students are far more discerning than their predecessors and have high expectations of property they go to view. Besides this, there are also minimum standards of condition that all landlords in England and Wales are legally bound to observe (see 'Legal Issues' later in this chapter).

Property Cost

The amount paid for a specific property depends largely on where and what it is, but with 'buy to let' the cost of purchase is also fundamentally linked to the yield – or to be more accurate – the size of loan required. The worst-case scenario is to borrow such a large sum that *all* the rental income is absorbed into mortgage instalments. With no margin of safety for voids, interest rate rises or emergency repairs, the landlord might experience the golden chalice turning swiftly into a millstone. The cost of the property and amount of loan required must be compared against an attainable rent, less expenses and a 15% contingency, before it can be considered worthy of buying. Getting this calculation wrong could prove financially lethal in the long term, so it is worth approaching all investments cautiously and working out the figures involved, before making purchase decisions.

In addition to the above elements, there are a variety of advantageous aspects to property that improve its appeal to tenants. These include:

◆ **Orientation** – a south-facing home always feels brighter and more welcoming.

◆ **Vehicle parking** – a garage or allocated parking space might be a priority if the applicant owns a car.

◆ **Storage space** – tenants who move frequently often require more storage for their possessions.

◆ **Balcony or garden** – access to external space is attractive, particularly during warm and dry months of the year.

◆ **Natural light** – large windows that provide good natural light into each room are a bonus. Internal rooms without windows discourage applicants.

◆ **Security** – solid doors, good door and window locks, alarm systems and external security lighting, all help reassure tenants about their safety. People also have preconceived concerns over ground floor apartments, as they believe they are more vulnerable to intruders.

◆ **Position** – occupiers of top floor apartments will not be irritated by noise created from those moving around above them. They might also have the benefit of loft space for added storage. However, the top floor position of a high multi-storey block could be discouraging, if it doesn't have a lift.

There are some properties best avoided by inexperienced landlords, because they require considerable management input and an extensive knowledge about letting. Others involve complications that could potentially restrict profit. These include:

♦ **Houses in Multiple Occupation (HMOs)**. These properties are defined by legislation as houses 'occupied by persons who do not form a single household'. The bulk of HMOs on the market are older converted semi-detached or detached houses, which are too large to let as one unit. They comprise several bedsits or studios usually with a shared kitchen, bathroom or living area. This type of property is weighed down with fire and management regulations that are too complex to describe here. Readers considering purchase should seek professional advice before proceeding.

♦ **Restrictive leases**. Most leasehold properties have clauses in the lease that prohibit letting. Although it is not usually difficult to get consent, it may involve an administrative or authorisation payment for each tenancy created and this will increase expenses and reduce profit.

♦ **Properties with a service charge**. Some residential dwellings are subject to a service charge or management fee. Typically, the charge associated with newly built properties is subsidised by the developer until all units on the estate are sold. In the second and third year, the true cost of services (communal gardening, lift maintenance, exterior painting, building insurance, and so on) are realised and the charge often has to be substantially increased. Liability for payment falls on the owner whether the property is occupied or not. Although a service charge amount *can* be built into the rent, it may cause the cost associated with letting to become uncompetitive and thus discouraging for would-be tenants.

Some estate agents don't just sell property but also act as letting agents and they are the best source of advice for novice investors entering the 'buy-to-let' market. Their local knowledge and business acumen will guide you toward keenly priced property found in areas of high demand by tenants. They will also be able to estimate the rent each dwelling might achieve and offer guidance about the type of tenant it is likely to attract.

WHAT TYPES OF MORTGAGES ARE AVAILABLE?

The 'buy-to-let' (BTL) mortgage is tailor-made for this market and available in a variety of established options, such as fixed and discounted rates (see Chapter 12). Many landlords apply for interest-only loans, which reduce the monthly payment and improve the margin of profit. However, this doesn't pay off any of the capital. There is thus a reliance on property value rising to meet the cost at the point of disposal or having enough personal resources to pay the outstanding loan by the end of the mortgage term.

The BTL mortgage is ideal for those whose employment status, income level and credit limit restrict access to traditional loans. Because the rental income likely to be gained from a property is taken into consideration alongside other sources of revenue, this product allows many more people to enter this investment arena. See Figure 10 for hypothetical typical examples of finance packages available. Interest rates quoted were accurate and competitive at the time of writing, but be aware that rates change frequently and they are unlikely to be accurate now.

There is one major downside to BTL mortgages – most providers insist on an approved managing agent to supervise the letting and this entails paying an additional fee of about 10% of rent received. There are also often agency costs for finding tenants, supplying a tenancy agreement, formal inspections and repairs, which you might otherwise have provided more cheaply yourself.

If you have no option except to go for such a product, get details from a range of lenders as interest rates and conditions vary. Also check the Internet, because it is a rich source of information on BTL mortgages (see Recommended websites at the end of this chapter). Alternatively, if your circumstances allow access to standard loans (check with the lender that letting is allowed), explore these in addition to BTL and compare the benefits of each – while the rates are likely to be similar, the conditions might be less restrictive.

USING AN AGENCY OR DOING IT YOURSELF

Hiring a letting agency might be seen as the best course of action for many. The agent's services will usually include:

Rate	APR (variable)	Monthly payment	Monthly payments at current mortgage rate	Total amount payable	Fixed rate expiry date	Early repayment/ switching charge
Variable rate						
5.59%	6.1%	£464.61 x 300	N/A	£143,431.70	N/A	None
2 year fixed						
5.19%	6.1%	£446.78 x 24	£463.51	£142,996.86	2 years from commencement	2% 1st year 1% 2nd year
2 year fixed with no early repayment charge						
5.39%	6.1%	£455.65 x 24	£464.05	£143,364.25	2 years from commencement	None
5 year fixed						
5.55%	6.1%	£462.81 x 60	£464.32	£143,554.52	5 years from commencement	5% 1st year 4% 2nd year 3% 3rd year 2% 4th year 1% 5th year

(Details appropriate at time of writing. See notes.)

Notes

◆ The example is based on a 25-year capital repayment mortgage of £75,000 (property valued at £100,000). The average maximum early repayment charge based on these examples is £3,750. There are 300 monthly repayments. The total amount payable (and APR) includes the 300 monthly repayments, an arrangement fee of 0.5% of the loan, estimated solicitor's fees of £460, valuation fee of £200 (including £60 administration fee), a £25 remittance fee and a bank's sealing fee of £75. Life assurance premiums of £10.02 are also included in the calculation. No account has been taken of interest rate changes.

Figure 10. Hypothetical buy-to-let mortgage – typical example

Loans are usually available for:

◆ £15,000 to £500,000.

◆ A single property or several properties in a portfolio.

◆ Up to 80% of the purchase price (or value, if lower).

◆ There is usually a choice of fixed or variable interest rates.

◆ Flexible options (flexible variable rate package) might include:
  − increasing monthly repayments to reduce interest payments and
    − taking a payment break of up to six months.

Fixed rate options
If a fixed rate is chosen, there may be a non-refundable booking fee payable (about £300). This secures the rate for a fixed period (about three months). As fixed rate funding is subject to availability, banks offering this facility often recommend booking early. The maximum booking for a fixed mortgage is normally around £500,000, however requests for amounts above this level will usually be considered.

Payment break option
This is an extremely useful element for any mortgage. Rules vary from one lender to another, but typically at any time after six months from the start of the mortgage or six months after a new house is bought, a payment break of up to six months can be taken. Requests for a payment holiday are often subject to satisfactory conduct of the mortgage and all other loans or overdrafts with the lender, and may not be granted if any arrears have arisen at any time in respect of the mortgage. Life assurance premium payments usually have to continue during a mortgage payment break.

- marketing the property for letting
- conducting viewings
- identifying suitable tenants
- undertaking tenant referencing
- completing the tenancy agreement
- creating an inventory of furnishings
- taking and holding a security deposit
- dealing with tenant enquiries
- arranging property repairs
- collecting rent
- checking the property for damage at the end of the tenancy.

Fees vary, but they are generally 50–100% of the first month's rent for tenant find and tenancy set-up; and an extra 10–15% a month for ongoing tenancy management (most are also plus VAT at 17.5%). Anyone can become a letting agent, as there is no formal procedure or registration, which makes finding a good one very difficult. It is always better to go from recommendation than simply plucking a name out of the telephone directory.

Employing an agent has many virtues – but these are also the disadvantages. When you provide someone else with the power to organise an investment, you relinquish personal control and access to knowledge. It is unlikely you will, for example, meet and choose the tenant or help construct clauses for the tenancy agreement. Your agent will undertake these tasks, which is fine, providing you share similar standards and they carry them out professionally.

Conversely, some landlords may want more involvement and there are extensive rewards for those prepared to spend time and effort. Quite apart from gaining confidence about the tenancy having been aptly created (by learning about legislation and regulations), the agency fees normally paid will be saved and control over the type of tenant chosen to occupy the property will be retained. Acquiring knowledge about this new primary or secondary occupation is important, even if you decide to employ an agent, because you will then have enough insight to decide whether they are acting diligently on your behalf.

I wrote *The Buy To Let Handbook* (How To Books, ISBN: 1 85703 864 9) as a detailed step-by-step guide for novice landlords. It contains a wealth of information on buying and preparing property to let and explains all the regulations and procedures involved in creating and managing a tenancy, in plain English. It is available at good bookshops or direct from the publisher at *www.howtobooks.co.uk*

DIFFERENT TYPES OF TENANT

The type of tenant you get is likely to depend on the size, quality and location of your property, which is why buying the right dwelling in the right place is so important at the outset. The easiest tenant group are established professionals; because they tend to care for the property they occupy and uphold their rent payment obligations. Novice landlords are advised **against** accepting four particular groups of tenant:

- **Those receiving state benefit** – because the benefit system is extremely complex and is fraught with payment delays and other complications.

- **Students** – whose excited first taste of independent living can lead to impromptu parties, property damage, excessive noise and rent arrears.

- **Sharers** – who collectively might be able to afford the rent, but whose funds could be stretched if one among the group decides to vacate early.

- **Non-UK citizens** – because it will prove difficult, if not impossible, to obtain authorised employment, bank and credit references.

In addition, tenants who are students or are unemployed and in receipt of benefit are likely to be prohibited by insurance policies or, at best, expenses will be higher because of increased premiums.

By targeting your property to a particular type of tenant, marketing and viewing appointments will be easier and more productive. It is crucial to remember that *all* applicants are strangers whose identity, employment status and financial history **must** be checked by thorough referencing. This should be completed before money or keys change hands and a tenancy agreement is signed. Several companies offer a fast and professional referencing service. These include:

Experian Tenant Verifier.
verifier.services@uk.experian.com
Tel: (0115) 901 6004

Leaseguard Ltd.
landlords@leaseguard.co.uk
Tel: 0845 345 1705

Letsure Ltd.
tas@letsure.co.uk
Tel: 08700 777 808

Undertaking your own tenant referencing is usually slower and details of a person's adverse credit history might be more difficult to obtain. Prices for professional reports vary between companies and according to the number of checks requested. Most reference agencies use their own tenant application form and these should be obtained from the appropriate agency in advance of arranging property viewing appointments.

ISSUES OF SUPPLY AND DEMAND

Assessing tenant demand for rented property in a given area is a difficult but essential task. The ideal (for landlords) is to have a shortage of suitable accommodation available in a neighbourhood where lots of tenants want to live. With tenants competing against each other to secure the property of their choice, landlords enjoy fewer void periods and higher rent levels. An oversupply of property with little tenant demand has the opposite effect. It reduces rents and increases the number of weeks a property remains empty between tenancies.

Evaluating supply and demand involves observing the rent levels advertised by agents and individual landlords over several months. If the levels seem to be gradually falling, there is probably an oversupply of rented property in the area. If rent levels remain static or are increasing and the same properties are not re-advertised, demand will almost certainly be outstripping supply.

LEGAL ISSUES

Legal compliance is a basic service your letting agent should provide. It is their job to ensure the accommodation you supply is adequately prepared, that essential pre-tenancy inspections are carried out and the proper safety certificates obtained. It is also usually their responsibility to furnish you with a legal tenancy agreement and inventory and administer completion of the documents.

The law is complex and unforgiving. If these aspects of letting are not conducted meticulously, the tenancy produced may not be valid or an unintended form of tenancy might be created. There are also severe penalties for offenders, which include fines and imprisonment. The repercussions that result from acting illegally can be alarming, prolonged and expensive. Crucial legal issues include:

◆ **Tenancy agreements** must conform to the requirements of the Housing Act 1988 (as amended by the Housing Act 1996). Landlords are not allowed to interfere with the tenant's right to 'quiet enjoyment' of the property. They must not harass the tenant or make any attempt to evict them (only the courts can do this after a successful possession case has been brought). A useful free booklet, *Assured and Assured Shorthold Tenancies: A Guide for Landlords,* explains the fundamentals and is available free from the Office of the Deputy Prime Minister (telephone 0870 122 6236 and ask for publication reference 97HC228B) or it can be downloaded from the Internet by going to: *www.odpm.gov.uk* (follow 'housing' links).

◆ **Furnishings** must comply with the Furniture and Furnishings (Fire) (Safety) Regulations 1988, which were amended in 1989 and 1993. Most items affected by this legislation are upholstered and have some foam content. Compliant furnishings must have a display label or a permanent label attached to them (see Figures 11 and 12). Enforcement is undertaken through the local Trading Standards Office, who can be approached for specific advice. A free guide to these regulations is available from the Department of Trade and Industry's website: *www.dti.gov.uk/ccp/topics1/ facts/furniture.htm* (follow the 'Guidelines' link contained in the factsheet). At the time of writing there was no alternative hard copy version available for non-Internet users.

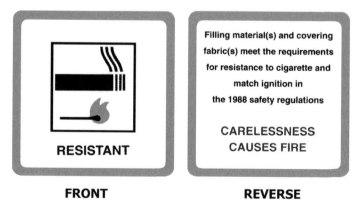

Figure 11. Example of a furniture display label

CARELESSNESS CAUSES FIRE

A N Other Ltd. AB1 2XY

AB 1234

1 March 1990

**This article contains CM Foam
which passes the specified test.
All upholstery is cigarette resistant.**

All cover fabric is cotton and is match resistant.

**This article does not include a
Schedule 3 interliner.**

Figure 12. Example of a permanent furniture label

◆ **Gas safety** is governed by the Gas Safety (Installation and Use) Regulations 1998 and the Gas Cooking Appliances (Safety) Regulations 1989. Landlords are required to have an up-to-date safety certificate for gas appliances and all associated pipework. An authorised and registered engineer must conduct the annual inspection and issue the certificate. A free guide to the regulations is available from the Health and Safety Executive (telephone (01787) 881165) and detailed information is also available on the HSE's gas safety website at: *www.hse.gov.uk/gas/index.htm*

♦ **Electrical safety** is governed by the Electrical Equipment (Safety) Regulations 1994, The Plugs and Sockets (Safety) Regulations 1994, The Low Voltage Electrical Equipment Regulations 1989, the General Product Safety Regulations 1994 and by the Consumer Protection Act 1987. These demand that appliances, wiring, fusing systems and installations are provided in a safe condition and are fitted properly. Although there is no requirement for a safety certificate, landlords are advised to have a qualified electrician inspect and test all supplied appliances and fittings annually.

TAXATION ISSUES

Landlords are burdened by taxation on two levels: they become liable for capital gains tax (CGT) when they dispose of let property (only an individual's principal residence is usually exempt); and they are liable for income tax on any profit from rent received (over and above personal allowances and after taking account of authorised expense deductions).

Your accountant will guide you toward arranging your finances and accounting procedures to take advantage of current rules and regulations. Consult him on all the following:

♦ keeping receipts
♦ maintaining account records
♦ buying property

- furnishing the dwelling
- insurance
- replacements and repairs
- professional assistance (solicitor, letting agent, and so on)
- legal documents and tenancy agreements
- postage and telephone calls
- contractors (for repairs and inspections)
- advertising
- self-employment
- starting a business (for example, becoming a limited company).

Book-Keeping & Accounting for the Small Business by Peter Taylor (How To Books) is a useful easy-to-understand manual that anyone can follow and is an ideal tutorial for new landlords. Preparing and presenting your accounts in a clear and methodical way will help you to stay organised and reduce the fees charged by your accountant. There is also a range of useful tax information available on the Inland Revenue's own website at *www.inlandrevenue.gov.uk*

INTERNET RESOURCES

The Internet is a rich and ever-expanding source of valuable information for landlords. There are free resources to find property and tenants, buy-to-let mortgage information, guides on the law and advice on how to solve common tenancy problems. The following are my personal top five favourites:

www.landlordzone.co.uk
An enormous site packed with valuable information, resources and products covering every aspect of letting.

www.landlordlaw.co.uk
This solicitor-run website, designed specifically for landlords, explains the legalities involved and provides access to tenancy agreements, forms and notices.

www.letlink.co.uk
The site of 'The Letting Centre' and 'Letting Update Journal' contains a wealth of good professional information and also supplies tenancy forms and documents.

www.lettingzone.com
Joining a local Landlords' Association is probably one of the best ways of learning about letting different types of property and keeping up-to-date with changes in legislation. This site provides contact details for Associations throughout the country.

www.themoneycentre.co.uk
A great site covering everything financial. This is a good place to learn more about buy-to-let and other mortgages and to identify the current best-value package provider. There are also links to tax resources and independent financial advisors.

CALCULATING THE COST
The cost of buying a property depends on its condition, size and location; these factors also influence the rent that can be obtained. There are other variables, such as local

supply and demand, which we have already discussed. Figure 13 is an example of the expense elements usually incurred by the landlord after a property has been purchased. The costs shown are average amounts (these will vary among different suppliers, agencies and tradesmen). Not all expenses are relevant in all situations – for example, an apartment owner obviously will not incur charges for garden maintenance – so you should draw up your own list of expenses and get competitive estimates appropriate for your own circumstances.

Income details	Annual income amount (£)	Annual income less expense amount (£)
Rent (£750 x 11 months)	8,250.00	8,250.00
Expense details	**Annual income amount (£)**	**Annual income less expense amount (£)**
2-year fixed-rate BTL mortgage (£446.78 x 12)	5,361.36	2,888.64
Letting agent's tenant-find, referencing and tenancy set-up charge (50% of first month's rent + VAT)	440.62	2,448.02
Letting agent's management charge (10% + VAT)	969.37	1,478.65
Inventory creation and checking	65.00	1,413.65
Gas and electrical safety inspection and certificate	131.65	1,282.00
Internal and external painting (£1,500 over 5 years)	300.00	982.00
Building and Landlord's insurance (legal and rent protection)	500.00	482.00
Empty period council tax (50%), gas and electricity charges	110.00	372.00
Garden maintenance while empty	20.00	352.00
Repairs and replacements	250.00	102.00
Accountant's fees	100.00	2.00
Postage and minor administration costs	2.00	Nil

Figure 13. Typical letting expenses

The example is of a property bought for £100,000 with a 75% buy-to-let mortgage. The start-up costs of furnishing and decorating have not been included. Other costs, such as exterior painting every five years, have been taken into account and divided by the appropriate period to give an average 12-month cost. Most lettings are for six or twelve months, but when there are two separate six-month lets, some costs such as additional advertising, might be doubled. The example assumes there will be at least one month each year when the dwelling will be empty. A shrewd investor will attempt to forecast these figures for every property they show an interest in buying.

While most expenses are allowable deductions against tax, it is only the *interest* element of mortgage instalments that qualify. This has a considerable bearing on the example given because, although rental income has just covered all the expenses, there remains a taxable profit resulting from the *non-interest element* of mortgage payments. Assuming all personal allowances have been taken into account, the additional income tax created from this scenario will need to be funded from alternative financial reserves. The venture might still be worthwhile if substantial capital growth can be expected over the medium term. Needless to say, the venture could conversely be disastrous if interest rates were to rise substantially, because expenses would then be greater than the rental funds being received. This example proves that care must always be taken to analyse the financial risks of an investment thoroughly **before** proceeding to buy.

Recommended websites
www.letalife.com
Free property advertising and a facility for you to find a letting agent from more than 5000 listed.

www.tonybooth.info/9.htm

This is a page from my own website and contains useful links to a wide range of free letting forms, documents and templates.

www.uk-buytolet.co.uk

An excellent site from Platinum Mortgages, who assess a range of buy-to-let products on the market (more than 40 are quoted) and find the 'best buy' for your particular circumstances. The good news is that unlike many other brokers, this service is free and independent. The site also has a section for tax advice (including a free down-loadable guide).

7

Buying a UK Holiday Home Investment

Many people aspire to own a holiday home, either as a hideaway for relaxation during the summer months or as a convenient city centre pad for occasional weekends away. Some have adequate financial resources, enabling them to retain the property for their own use throughout the year as and when required; others have to take a more pragmatic view, recognising that luxury and affordability demand large amounts of compromise.

As the stresses and strains of people's lives increase, so too does their desire to 'get away from it all', if only for a few days. Self-catering accommodation satisfies the need many have for a 'home from home', complete with familiar levels of comfort and luxury but in an entirely different setting. Property speculators have long recognised the profit potential of supplying this market and are constantly looking for new up-and-coming tourist areas where they can invest.

However, first-time buyers will need to overcome several obstacles before they can fully exploit the holiday home market. The price of property in tourist areas is likely to be the greatest of these and could be *the* deciding factor for most. The good news is there are several unique elements to holiday home investment that set it apart from other endeavours. If you are willing to make the effort and take a long-range view, your venture has the potential to develop into a highly profitable business.

THE MAIN PURPOSE OF THE PROPERTY

Investors must accept the property is primarily a business asset to be exploited for financial gain and not an exclusive leisure facility for them and their family. The choice of location, size, amenities and style, should all reflect the desires of holidaymakers rather than satisfy any personal preference. These elements change according to where a property is situated and what people expect from their holiday. Thorough pre-purchase research is essential to ensure it will be attractive to the largest number of people. By targeting the market accurately, you will enjoy the maximum number of bookings throughout the year with minimal advertising costs.

Quite apart from the financial advantage of receiving a regular income, there are also significant tax benefits when a holiday dwelling is let for more than a set number of weeks in a year (see 'Taxation' later in this chapter). The intention therefore should always be to extend the usual peak periods by adding elements and facilities that appeal to a wider audience. For example, accepting pets would encourage pet owners to use your property or installing luxurious furnishings (four-poster bed, spa bath, and so on) might attract those looking for a romantic break.

TYPE AND LOCATION OF THE PROPERTY

Financial resources and sheer practicality are likely to influence the type and location of the property that is purchased. However, major self-catering agencies have identified a sliding scale of popularity. These are:

◆ **Type**. Picturesque detached cottages come top of the list, followed by detached houses and barn conversions. Small terraced cottages, semi-detached and large terraced houses cover the mid-range; while modern bungalows and courtyard developments are less sought after. Log cabins, apartments and chalets are at the bottom of the scale, although the quality of fittings and furnishings and a fashionable location, can all help elevate the popularity of an apartment.

◆ **Size**. Size matters! The most popular of properties have two bedrooms and cater for a family with children. The bigger the holiday home the more expensive it is to buy, furnish and maintain. However, in areas where larger dwellings are few and far between, an investor can succeed by filling the void – although it may be less popular, there is also less competition and the rules of supply and demand thus come into play.

◆ **Location**. For many holidaymakers, location is just as important as the style of property. It not only matters where it sits geographically in the country, but also what views it has from the windows and the ambience of its immediate surroundings. Properties in coastal regions fare better when they are within walking distance of a beach; rural properties in high demand are likely to be found in picturesque villages or open countryside; and a suitable city centre apartment can provide all year round occupation, regardless of the weather.

During 2002, Welcome Holidays Limited supplied holiday accommodation to over 300,000 people. They are currently the fastest growing self-catering holiday company in Britain and, in their *Owner Information Guide*, they classify certain areas of the UK as 'outstanding' by demand (see Figure 14). Checking the list is a good starting point for speculators entering this market as it might help to narrow the search for an ideal location.

HOLIDAY HOME **HOT**SPOTS

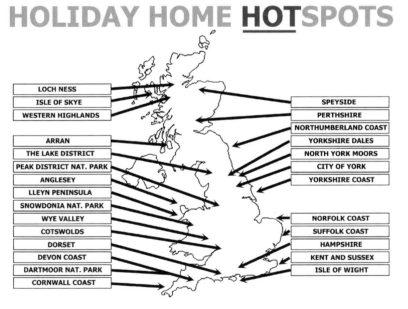

LOCH NESS	SPEYSIDE
ISLE OF SKYE	PERTHSHIRE
WESTERN HIGHLANDS	NORTHUMBERLAND COAST
ARRAN	YORKSHIRE DALES
THE LAKE DISTRICT	NORTH YORK MOORS
PEAK DISTRICT NAT. PARK	CITY OF YORK
ANGLESEY	YORKSHIRE COAST
LLEYN PENINSULA	
SNOWDONIA NAT. PARK	
WYE VALLEY	NORFOLK COAST
COTSWOLDS	SUFFOLK COAST
DORSET	HAMPSHIRE
DEVON COAST	KENT AND SUSSEX
DARTMOOR NAT. PARK	ISLE OF WIGHT
CORNWALL COAST	

Figure 14. Best locations for a holiday home

RAISING FINANCE

Raising funds to buy a holiday investment is easiest for those who already own their own home, because they can use the property as security or remortgage it, as long as the market value has increased since it was purchased. Those who already have a lump sum to invest might be wiser paying off their own home mortgage first, because they can apply for an interest-only loan for the holiday dwelling and offset payments against income tax. However, these solutions are not available to the *first time* investor.

Everything outlined in previous chapters is also relevant to the issue of raising funds for a holiday home: the amount of earnings and savings and the quality of your credit-file information will influence how successful your application for finance is likely to be. As with 'buy-to-let', the other major factor involved is the profit-making potential of the asset you wish to buy. In short, you must convince lenders that their risk is small and, to achieve this, you will need to devise an accurate business plan and present it in a confident, enthusiastic and professional manner. Matters to consider include:

- Researching the area thoroughly and gathering factual evidence of payments being made for other similar properties.

- Finding out what the most likely occupation rate will be per year and highlighting peak seasons, such as summer and Christmas, when you should be able to increase the usual weekly charge substantially.

◆ Getting written estimates of costs for management, cleaning, insurance and so on; then suggesting how these might be reduced should funding the project become difficult.

The lender will consider the worst-case scenario, that is, if all else fails, will repossessing and selling the property raise enough to cover the outstanding loan? You will need to produce evidence showing that prices in the area are rising and are likely to continue doing so for some years.

Armed with this data in presentation form, you should consult various lenders and see what they have to say. High street banks and building societies are probably easier to approach than Internet lenders, because you can meet face to face, present your documented facts and ask pertinent questions. Some may dismiss your proposals, but others are likely to see the work you have put in and recognise the enthusiasm and confidence you have for the venture. Bear in mind that typically, even if you are successful, most lenders will only offer a mortgage up to 70% of the property value, so you will still need to have considerable sums for the deposit, furnishings, legal fees and administrative charges. The quality of your presentation, validity of data and the lender's risk analysis of the venture will significantly affect the amount of loan offered.

At the time of writing, my own search of lenders identified only three that were prepared to offer residential rate mortgages to finance a holiday home purchase. These were Birmingham Midshires (BM Solution), the Scarborough Building Society and Stroud & Swindon. Birmingham Midshires were originally offering their full 'buy-to-let' mortgage range for holiday home buyers (employing the same basic principles and taking rental income into account). It was, however, complicated by the fact they required a three-year track history of how the property had been let, which meant it had to have been a holiday home prior to purchase. The product eventually proved to be too much of an administrative nightmare for building society staff and was subsequently withdrawn.

CHECKING OUT THE FURNISHINGS

Holidaymakers expect all the comforts of home while they are on vacation and it is essential for supplied furnishings and appliances to reflect this. It is false economy to provide a holiday home with outdated décor and uncomfortable furnishings, as this will only cause disappointment and discourage recommendations. Half the battle in achieving success is to build up a core of regular clients, people who will book weeks with you year after year, because they like both the property and its location.

A good tip is to spend a week in your newly furnished property as if you were actually on holiday and hiring the accommodation yourself. This test will help you identify a shortage of crockery, pots, pans, and so on; you can also try all the appliances and find out first hand how comfortable beds and seating are.

UNDERSTANDING THE LEGAL ASPECTS

There are relatively few legal restrictions when owners intend using a holiday home purely for themselves.

However, this changes considerably when the main purpose involves letting it to others. While holiday lets are outside the scope of the Housing Acts, the health and safety regulations affecting them are identical to private sector landlords. Owners must comply with the legislation to avoid severe repercussions. Specific regulations include:

◆ Furniture & Furnishings (Fire) (Safety) Regulations 1988 (as amended).
◆ Gas Safety (Installation and Use) Regulations 1998.
◆ Gas Cooking Appliances (Safety) Regulations 1989.
◆ Electrical Equipment (Safety) Regulations 1994.
◆ Plugs & Sockets (Safety) Regulations 1994.
◆ Low Voltage Electrical Equipment Regulations 1989.
◆ General Product Safety Regulations 1994.
◆ The Consumer Protection Act 1987.

Refer to Chapter 6, 'Legal Issues', for further details about these regulations. Enforcement action is allocated to the Health and Safety Executive, the local authority and Trading Standards, and these agencies are likely to become involved where a complaint has been made about the standard and safety of accommodation or the furnishings and appliances supplied. The local authority is also obliged to follow up any complaints regarding the stability and safety of the building and any dangers presented to members of the public (including food preparation and general hygiene issues). In short, the property and the items contained therein must be supplied in a safe condition. Failure to do so can result in harsh fines being imposed and, in severe cases, offenders can also be sent to prison.

It is important the occupying status of guests is verified through a formal agreement defining the terms and conditions. This will prevent any misunderstanding should possession become an issue. Holiday lets are governed by contract law and a written agreement sets out the rights of each party. Booking agents sometimes combine this with an introductory brochure and booking form and, in effect, create a contract by 'offer and acceptance'. Although this route is slightly more complex, it has the same end result. You should consult your solicitor or booking/managing agent about devising a suitable agreement. Standard holiday let contracts are also available from:

◆ Oyez, the legal stationers. Tel: 0870 7377 370.
◆ Legalhelpers Ltd. Website: *www.legalhelpers.co.uk*
◆ Law Pack. Website: *www.lawpack.co.uk*

There are occasions when it might be beneficial to switch between short-term holiday lets and long-term renting, for example, in a seasonal tourist area where the winter months are very quiet. This involves changing from 'contract law' to 'housing law' and using an Assured Shorthold tenancy agreement for the long-term let (see Chapter 6). Ground 3 of the Housing Act 1988 (as amended) provides an answer to some of the problems that can arise during mixed use. As long as prior notice (worded strictly as per the Housing Act) is given to the long-term tenant explaining that the property was previously used as a holiday letting and will be again, possession can be sought through the courts if the tenant fails to vacate.

Regaining possession of a holiday let property is usually straightforward, as the Protection from Eviction Act 1977 doesn't apply and occupiers are therefore largely unprotected. Incidents of guests overstaying their welcome are rare and even when they do occur, offenders can be treated as squatters and removed legally with ease.

UNDERSTANDING TAX LIABILITIES

Value Added Tax (VAT)

The bad news is that holiday lets *are* liable to VAT at the standard rate of 17.5%. The good news is that there is an annual turnover threshold before it becomes accountable and unless you are charging guests more than £1,000 per week and are fully booked, you won't need to charge VAT or register with HM Customs and Excise. The threshold is currently £56,000 (correct at April 2003). If you suspect your turnover is likely to exceed this limit, it is probably worthwhile consulting a business advisor or employing an accountant to establish professional invoicing and book-keeping practices.

HM Customs and Excise produce two useful guides covering holiday let situations: VAT Notice 700/1 *Should I be Registered for VAT?* and VAT Notice 709/3 *Hotels and Holiday Accommodation.* These Notices and information about current threshold limits can be obtained direct from their website at *www.hmce.gov.uk* or by telephoning the National Advice Service on 0845 010 9000.

Income tax

Holiday letting income is taxable. However, unlike other

forms of letting (which are regarded by the Inland Revenue as investment income), holiday lets are classed as a **business** under certain circumstances – and this provides owners with a considerable advantage. To qualify:

◆ The property must be 'available' for letting to the public for at least 140 days a year (it must have actually been let for 70 days and there must be strong evidence of attempts to let it for the remainder).

◆ A continuous period of letting to the same person or the same group must not exceed 31 days in any period of seven months, though it can for the remaining five months (such as in the case of an out-of-season long-let).

◆ The property must be fully furnished.

◆ Owners who use the property occasionally for themselves cannot claim tax benefits during such periods.

◆ The weekly charge must be a true market rent and not reduced to benefit family, friends or colleagues.

Subject to the above conditions, all expenses can be claimed against income tax (see 'Profit Potential' later in this chapter). Married couples can also capitalise on their tax allowances by placing ownership of the property in the name of the lower earner. This is particularly beneficial when the lower earner is in the lowest tax band and their partner is in the highest tax band.

During the early years, while a core client group is being built up, the business is likely to make a loss and this would ordinarily paralyse those whose sole income is generated through property letting. But most holiday home owners also have a secondary occupation. One of the tax benefits people in this situation can exploit is that any losses from the rental business can be offset against any other income, thereby reducing their overall income tax bill. This goodwill gesture by the Inland Revenue usually allows enough time for the business to carry on and become profitable.

Capital Gains Tax (CGT)

CGT is usually payable when a holiday home investment is sold, but because the property is recognised as a business asset, it qualifies for business asset taper-relief (BATR). This has considerable benefits over and above most other CGT liable disposals, such as buy-to-let property or investment shares, neither of which qualify for the higher relief. The difference can be substantial. For example, non-business assets must be kept for ten years to achieve the maximum level of relief and, even then, the effective rate of tax only reduces to 24% for higher rate taxpayers. Once BATR is applied, assets only need be kept for two years and the effective rate of tax drops to 10% for higher rate taxpayers and just 5.75% for basic rate taxpayers (taking other influencing factors into account).

In simple terms, if a holiday home is sold after two years of ownership and the capital gain made (current selling price less original purchase price) is £100,000, only £25,000 of the gain would be taxable. The figures quoted are accurate for 2003, but be aware that the Chancellor has a habit of changing the rules and percentages from time to time and these are usually announced in advance during his budget speech.

Holiday home owners can also avoid paying CGT by employing roll-over relief. To take advantage of this, the proceeds gained from selling a holiday home must be re-invested *within three years* in another holiday let property. This is really a 'postponement' of liability, rather than perpetual avoidance, because ultimately the tax *will* become due.

Business rates versus council tax

When the holiday property is let for less than 140 days, it is usually liable for council tax at a rate set by the local authority. However, when it is let for 140 days or more and therefore classed as a non-domestic property by the Inland Revenue, it becomes liable for business rates instead.

Unless it is exempt, every non-domestic property has a rateable value. The local authority calculates the applicable business rate by multiplying the rateable value by a figure set by the Government each year, known as the uniform business rate or UBR. So, for example, if the UBR were set at 45p and the property rateable value was £10,000, the local authority would impose business rates of £4,500. However, this is not necessarily the amount you would have to pay, because transitional or other reliefs could reduce the figure or it could be increased because of revaluations that were undertaken in the year 2000.

GETTING ADEQUATE INSURANCE COVER

Insurance is crucial for any modern business enterprise and never more so than with holiday lets. You will require:

- **Public liability** cover, should a guest sustain injury while on the premises.

- **Legal expenses** and **rent protection**.

- **Building insurance**, which will probably be insisted upon by your lender.

- **Contents** cover for supplied furnishings.

- **Employee liability**, if you employ tradesmen or labour.

Contact your managing agent or booking agent for advice on insurance policies, as they may have details or direct access to specialist 'all-in-one' packages at discounted rates. Alternatively, a preferred company you are already familiar with may be prepared to put a bespoke package together for you. If you intend relying on an existing insurance product (for example, a buildings policy), check the wording and exclusions very carefully. Most residential policies do not cover commercial or business-related property ventures.

MANAGING AGENTS

To manage the holiday let yourself, you will need to spend time every weekend welcoming guests, cleaning the accommodation, washing and ironing bed linen, making repairs and maintaining the garden areas. You will also have to deal with advertising, keep accounts and administer bookings – and you will need to live close enough to the property to undertake all these tasks. Owners without sufficient time and those who live far from the property are going to require a managing agent. Some lenders also make a loan advance conditional on an agent being employed.

Agents offer different levels of service. Some help with advertising and guest bookings only, leaving owners to sort out property cleaning and maintenance; while others deal with every aspect of the holiday letting. Charges vary according to the depth of service required, the size of the property and its location. Average fees are between 15 and 30% plus VAT and expenses. There are numerous holiday let managing agents established in popular tourist areas and it is worth getting details from all of them to assess which offers the best quality of service and value for money.

PROFIT POTENTIAL

The size, condition and location of properties determine their market value; but it is the cost of upkeep and management *and* volume of bookings that determine their profit potential. Unfortunately, *value* and *profit potential* usually go hand-in-hand – holiday dwellings with high yield prospects are invariably the most expensive to buy. It is therefore important (regardless of the purchase cost of the property) to reduce expenses, thus retaining more of the money paid to you by guests. Quite simply – the more that you can do to manage the letting yourself, the less you will need to pay for.

However, bear in mind that most expenses are tax deductible as long as the main intention at the outset is to generate profit. So, it may be worthwhile calculating cost-effectiveness against inconvenience, before making any final judgements. Expenses that can be claimed include:

◆ mortgage interest payments
◆ most legal and accountancy fees
◆ repairs to the property
◆ heating
◆ lighting
◆ power consumption
◆ cleaning costs
◆ professional management fees
◆ advertising
◆ decorating costs
◆ insurance.

It is exceptionally rare for a property to achieve full occupancy throughout the year. The average is about 65% or 35 weeks. Income therefore depends on the amount of rent received during the maximum seasonal letting periods, according to location. It is clearly advantageous to ensure your property is made available during school holidays, the warmest months of spring and summer and throughout the festive period; leaving any major repairs and redecoration for the quieter months when the dwelling is likely to be empty.

ADDITIONAL INFORMATION

There are actually very few resources to help guide UK holiday home buyers in the right direction. How To Books publish one by Wendy Pascoe, called *Making Money from a Second Home*. Having moved to Cornwall from London to set up her own property letting business, former BBC journalist Wendy wrote this practical guide to investing in holiday lets. It covers choosing the right property in the right area, how to prepare it for letting and how to manage the property, and its guests.

Recommended websites

www.cottageownersunite.co.uk
Cottage Owners Unite (COUNT) is dedicated to the needs of owners and managers of self-catering holiday properties. There are valuable contact details, information and research sections, statistical data and a wealth of professional services – all under one roof.

www.nacoservices.com
If you are contemplating a mobile or static caravan as your holiday home investment, then the National Association of Caravan Owners (NACO) is a good starting point.

www.tourismtrade.org.uk
This site for the British tourism industry is particularly useful if you want to research a particular area, contact regional tourist boards or find statistical information.

8

Buying Property Abroad

It is true what they say – the world *really is* getting smaller! Access to foreign property markets has never been easier or more affordable. Luxurious dwellings can be bought in some countries for a fraction of what they would cost at home and, although most only see the opportunity for extended holidays, others recognise the potential for making a profit.

It can sometimes seem like it's all too good to be true and, of course, it sometimes is. The mistake many make is to assume that other countries have property purchase procedures and legislation similar to the UK. In reality, nothing could be further from the truth. Foreign laws are diverse and ignorance of them can lead to disastrous financial decisions and heartbreaking scenarios. Success depends on:

◆ Taking a deliberate and cautious approach.

◆ Getting appropriate, independent and comprehensive professional advice.

◆ Having *all* the facts about the property and pertinent information about the country, such as how its inheritance and taxation laws may affect you in the future – *before* making any purchase decisions.

KNOWLEDGE, EXPERIENCE AND FAMILIARITY

There are cultural divides between countries and this is attractive to those whose only intention is to visit for a two-week holiday. But when contemplating a foreign purchase, it is important to realise that a different way of life will usually involve different laws and what may appear to be an alien way of thinking. For example, it would be inconceivable in the UK to buy a house and then be told you are also responsible for the prior owner's debts – but this *can* happen in Spain. In Italy and France, property cannot be passed on exclusively to a sole surviving spouse; it must also be spread amongst any offspring. There is a danger that these nuances of property law can evade those unfamiliar with the mechanics of a country's legal system, until it is too late.

Going on holiday to another country is not enough to gain the knowledge needed to buy property. If anything, it creates a false impression, because the favourable aspects of a foreign land blinker a holidaymaker's view of reality. Long sandy beaches, hot sunny weather and lazy days spent exploring tourist areas are alluring qualities; but they pale into insignificance compared to the practicalities of owning property in the region. You need to know about taxation laws and assess costs for electricity, local rates and service charges. Is it easy to hire tradesmen and acquire replacement furnishings or appliances? What is the weather like out-of-season? Is crime a major concern amongst local people?

Having identified a country to invest in and narrowed your interest to a specific province, you then need to undertake extensive research. This involves three levels of work:

◆ Acquiring **knowledge** by reading everything you can lay your hands on about the country in question.

◆ Gaining **experience** by visiting the country whenever possible and exploring both its positive and negative attributes.

◆ Becoming **familiar** with the customs and cultures of the country by talking to expatriate communities, that is, British people who have gained a unique insight into the region by relocating to it.

By satisfying deficiencies in these three fundamental areas you may identify previously hidden obstacles and discover ways others have found to resolve them. Walking a well-worn path is always easier than stumbling along an independent route through unfamiliar territory. The following resources might help.

◆ How To Books publish over 30 different practical guides about living, working and buying property in France, Spain, Portugal, Italy, Canada, Greece, Australia, Saudi Arabia, New Zealand and the USA. People who have actually done it themselves have written these useful references, which make them both accurate and inspiring. A free catalogue containing the titles and details of each book can be obtained by telephoning (01865) 793806 or visiting their website at *www.howtobooks.co.uk*

- *Homes Overseas* is the UK's best-selling specialist international property buying magazine. The journal is published monthly and is available from most good newsagents. It also has a website at *www.homesoverseas.co.uk* and can be ordered direct (annual subscription is £34) from Homes Overseas Magazine, 207 Providence Square, Mill Street, London, SE1 2EW.

- The Internet is a great source of valuable free information for buying overseas. The following addresses are good starting points and should help initiate a more comprehensive exploration:
  Australia – *www.apm.com.au/osbuyers*
  France – *www.french-property.com/reference*
  Germany – *www.real-estate-european-union.com/*
    English/germany.html
  Greece – *www.grecian.net/newcentury/faq.htm*
  Italy – *www.italyassist.com/property.html*
  New Zealand – *www.real-estate-nz.com*
  Portugal – *www.litagale.com/property.html*
  Spain – *www.spainexpat.com*
  USA – *www.realestateabc.com*

- Spain has consistently been the UK buyer's favourite location and continues to attract investors, despite rising prices. There is a useful free *Guide to Buying Spanish Property* that explains some of the main costs and legal issues involved. It is available from:
  www.moneynet.co.uk/borrowing/mortgages/overseas_ mortgage/spanish_property_guide.PDF

GETTING INDEPENDENT LEGAL ADVICE

Most foreign states require the legal procedure to be handled by a solicitor native to the country of purchase. This makes good sense, because they will be familiar with the legislative framework and language. It is also advisable and sometimes a requirement, to have a UK solicitor as well. Although this increases the legal expenses normally incurred, it acts as a safeguard against potentially unscrupulous representatives acting (so called) on your behalf and is thus a worthwhile outlay. Be aware that some developers may instruct the same solicitor *they* are using to act for you, resulting in a considerable conflict of interest – that is, the same solicitor acting for two parties involved in the same contract. Although this is forbidden in the UK, the laws and ethics of some other countries may not be quite so thorough.

Buying new development property as part of an all-inclusive package is particularly hazardous for UK citizens. Some real estate developers offer 'complete solutions' for foreign buyers, with everything included in a single payment: the property purchase, land registration fees, local taxes, legal expenses, insurance and management fees. Although such package deals may seem attractive on the surface, bear in mind that your legal representative will be chosen by the developer and they may not act entirely on your behalf or necessarily in your best interests. Employing an independent UK solicitor is the best way of obtaining impartial advice, even if you end up having to pay twice for receiving the same service.

Some UK legal firms also operate abroad or have working partnerships with legal practices overseas. This is an ideal solution to getting both a UK and 'country of purchase' legal representative. Unfortunately, there is no contact list available of conveyance solicitors who operate in this way, which means you will probably have to make extensive enquiries and approach numerous practices before you identify someone suitable.

PROPERTY WITH RENTING POTENTIAL

People go on vacation for many different reasons and it is important your holiday home satisfies at least some of them. Location isn't everything, but it *is* a very influential element. The accommodation should either be in a picturesque region or a position convenient for local attractions, such as a long sandy beach or a historic site popular with tourists.

Holidaymakers don't usually want to cook meals while they are away, even if there are facilities available, so a few good nearby restaurants and bars are desirable assets (as long as the establishments are not rowdy or rundown). Transportation is another important issue. People are sometimes prepared to hire a car so they can get out and about while on holiday, but it is an added expense and one that may deter some from renting your property, particularly if alternative public transport services are lacking. A pool is an alluring facility that will increase the volume of bookings and might be essential if the property is beyond easy reach of the coast, but maintenance will be a major expense at around £50 a week.

A crucial question is not whether the property is located in an area you would like to visit yourself, but whether a large enough number of other people will find it attractive? In other words, does comparable property nearby achieve continuous letting? Extensive research will be needed to assess and confirm the situation. Local estate agents usually offer good advice, particularly if they think you might employ them as managing or booking agents. Doing your homework thoroughly will herald success. It is absolutely vital to find out what people expect from a holiday – and then aim to supply it.

The price of property invariably reflects rising or falling popularity, which means the renting potential of a dwelling should never be considered in isolation from its capital value. If the appeal of a holiday home begins to wane or fails to meet earning expectations, it is important that you are able to sell it and still make a profit. This involves acquiring an asset at low value and keeping it long enough to realise capital growth, which is hard enough to achieve in the familiar UK market, but even more difficult in a distant country where the market might be far less predictable. Keeping an eye on the performance of popular holiday destinations may help, but you will also need professional advice from a respected, experienced and native estate agent at some stage.

A successful investor once told me that the single most important thing about buying a property is that it must have the right qualities to survive in a competitive market: 'A toothless tiger is no good to anyone,' he said.

The rate property prices' rise is a clear indicator of a location's 'boom time' – a window of opportunity for the would-be investor – as long as you can enter the market at the very start of this period, you are certain to gain in the long term. Although it is difficult to provide up-to-date statistics due to the rapid movement of property markets, Figure 15 shows the general growth in values during 2002. The data describes regions popular with holidaymakers. Just as in the UK, there are clear discrepancies between zones and even specific regions of some towns and villages, so current and dependable information should always be sought from those experienced in the market and familiar with the territory.

The world's economies are now so interlinked that the financial stability of a country is not only reliant on its geographic neighbour, but also on those who trade with it. If recession hits one it causes ripples with far-reaching consequences. These events are largely predictable or, at least, there is usually some advance warning of them occurring, giving owners enough time to sell the property and avoid disaster. However, some events are not so predictable. The terrorist attack of 9/11 on the USA and the subsequent war in Iraq had devastating consequences for the economic structure of each country, *and also* on those that were geographically and monetarily associated with them. As a direct result, property prices tumbled and tourism markets crashed. This proves that despite a holiday home investor taking every precaution before buying a property, events will still sometimes conspire against him. The intention should always be to minimise risk by accumulating knowledge about the country's political and fiscal circumstances. It is then important to keep up to date with how they develop by closely monitoring European and international news. Be aware that political and economic red flags are likely to be ignored at an investor's peril.

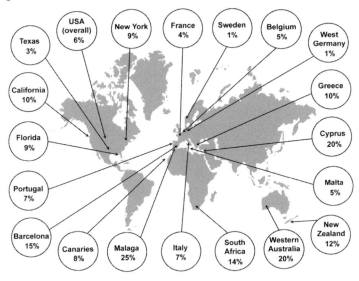

Figure 15. The increase in value of property in popular holiday destinations (2002)

RAISING FINANCE

Cash buyers are free to invest without geographic limitation, but first-time investors rarely have such convenient wealth at their fingertips. Most require a mortgage and, although there are plenty of products available, borrowing inflicts restrictions (particularly if you do not have a UK property to remortgage). In addition, each country has its own peculiar rules, procedures and idiosyncrasies when it comes to lending money – these not only add to the frustration by reducing the number of accessible countries, they can also cause you to stumble into a legal minefield.

The problem relates to a familiarity with UK mortgage practices and a reluctance to accept that other countries might do things differently. For example, when someone arranges a structural or home condition survey in the UK, they are usually entitled to receive details of its findings; but the same is not true in some places abroad where the lender will more commonly deny access to unfavourable results.

It is **essential** for purchasers to get professional advice and guidance at **every** stage of an overseas investment. Ignorance of foreign laws, procedures and practices can lead to expensive mistakes. Assume nothing and guard against everything – 'buyer beware' has never been more aptly stated.

There are two major obstacles for first-time buyers seeking a mortgage on a foreign property:

♦ The deposit required is usually greater than for UK property. Most lenders restrict borrowing to below 80% of the property value and some even less than this. In addition, the maximum term is usually 20 years and sometimes as low as 15. So, although you may be able to access funds up to three and a half times your annual income (two and half of a couple's joint income), there will still be a high deposit and monthly payment schedule to overcome. This might be bad news for many – but see 'good news' below.

◆ A decision must be taken at an early stage about whether to acquire funds in sterling or the country's own currency. There are considerable financial risks to either approach. UK lenders operating abroad often provide loans in sterling and if the value of the pound rises against the country's own currency, mortgage payments will be exorbitant compared with the value of the property. There are also costs incurred of about £25 for every monthly payment transferred abroad. Conversely, if the mortgage is received in the country of purchase (local currency) and it rises against the pound, instalments could become very difficult to manage compared against the value of a UK salary. Close observation and a careful assessment of currency performance, together with independent professional financial advice, should guide you into making the most appropriate decision.

The *good news* is that you are not looking to buy a foreign holiday home for your own exclusive use, but one that will be let for profit. This fact alone improves the opportunities to borrow across several countries. Some lenders operate according to 'buy-to-let' mortgage principles, as outlined in Chapter 6, where holiday let income is taken into consideration alongside an occupation salary.

Investors relying on this formula might find themselves in a quandary – do they first find a property in the country of choice and then apply for a mortgage? Or, do they identify a suitable mortgage lender and then explore the property market in that particular country? Circumstances will probably dictate which course you should follow. In any event, there are several mortgage sources worth looking at. These include:

Conti Financial Services. Tel: (01273) 772811.
Website: *www.mortgagesoverseas.com*

HSBC. Tel: (01534) 616000.
(*What Mortgage* 2003 award winner)
Website: *www.offshore.hsbc.com*

Intelligent Capital. Tel: (01622) 693713.
Website: *www.intelligentcapital.co.uk*

Propertyfinance4less. Tel: (020) 7924 7314.
Website: *www.propertyfinance4less.com*

TQ Mortgage Services. Tel: (01908) 547837.
Website: *www.tqms.co.uk*

MANAGEMENT AND SECURITY ISSUES

The day-to-day management and security of your property are fundamental matters that need attention at the point of purchase. For practical purposes, these services are likely to be supplied through an agent operating close to the location of the property. The advance identification of a suitable agent will help kick-start the earning capability of your holiday home (after the legal aspects of the purchase have been completed). From the moment ownership is established, time becomes a precious commodity and every additional day spent organising these matters will cost you money. Remember: having an empty property also involves having an empty pocket!

Finding a good managing agent is not easy and you may have to rely on the recommendations given by the selling agent. There is much more choice in popular tourist regions, such as those along the Costa Del Sol in Spain and the USA's Florida coast, but far less in some of the more remote regions of France and Italy. Costs also vary significantly. Fees of 20% to 50% of rental income are not unusual and depend on the country of purchase, the services provided and extent of local competition.

CAPITAL GAIN POTENTIAL

All property owned has the potential to generate a double pay-off, that is, regular rental income plus capital appreciation over time. Some investors try to balance the benefits, acquiring property with qualities that will encourage both rental income *and* capital appreciation. However, others concentrate on a single quality, accepting low rental income in favour of a greater pay-off when a property is sold.

Existing rental markets are the safest to invest in, because they have an established letting performance history. Large rental conurbations are relatively dependable – income is almost guaranteed – but capital appreciation is often less certain, because there are so many comparable properties and vast numbers may be advertised for sale all at the same time. Aggressive and abundant competition always deflates prices. There are exceptions to the rule, but (generally) the more properties there are for sale in an area, the lower their prices become. In popular tourist regions, where there are many similar properties available, rental income remains steady – but capital appreciation is predictably sluggish.

Forgoing rental income in favour of maximum capital growth involves considerable risk, but the rewards are so much greater when the gamble pays off. This strategy involves investing in a country or the region of a country where tourism is currently underdeveloped. Property is likely to be inexpensive, easy to acquire and available in great quantities – but signs of increasing popularity amongst holidaymakers *must* already have begun. The risk-assumption is that growth in the region's tourism will increase the demand for property, eventually generating higher prices. It is possible for an asset's capital value to double within two or three years, given favourable circumstances (buying just before prices start to escalate), but such a venture is not for the faint-hearted because losses can be substantial if things don't work out.

TAXATION AND INHERITANCE ISSUES

The economies of the world are becoming ever more interlinked, resulting in increased harmonisation of taxation and inheritance law. But there are still many exceptions and anomalies to trip you up and failing to become familiar with them *before* you invest can have catastrophic consequences. You can, for example, find yourself liable to pay income tax on rent received *both* in the country of purchase *and* in the UK; or discover that capital gains tax is so high it becomes impractical and unprofitable to dispose of a property.

Extensive research and further reading are essential. In addition, the Inland Revenue is a valuable source of advice. They have produced a free practitioner's booklet (IR150), *Taxation of Rents: A Guide to Property*

Income, which can be downloaded from the Internet at *www.inlandrevenue.gov.uk/pdfs/ir150.pdf* The Inland Revenue also have a page on their Website dedicated to links for most foreign tax offices and government sites. Go to: *www.inlandrevenue.gov.uk/menus/links.htm*

Recommended websites

www.livinginthesun.com
Expertise and local knowledge is available on Greece and the Greek Islands, Cyprus, Crete, Spain, Turkey and Florida. This site contains a wealth of information. It is a superb resource and an excellent vehicle for armchair exploration.

www.property-abroad-com
This website includes a property search facility for France, Italy, Spain, Portugal and Turkey. It also has links for agents dealing with just about every country of the world – as well as buying guides, solicitor lists, insurance details and mortgage contacts. This is a helpful and easy to navigate site with lots of useful information.

www.timesonline.co.uk
Choose 'property' from the menu bar and then click on 'overseas property' for an enormous range of articles on this subject. Topics covered include taxation, funding and hints and tips for buying property abroad.

9

Self-Build

Since ancient times, people have built their own homes when they couldn't afford to buy property already constructed. In Britain today, house prices have escalated beyond the reach of many and, by default, self-build is making a dramatic comeback. There are over 20,000 new homes a year created this way in the UK alone and the custom is even more widespread in other parts of the world, such as America and Australia.

Long-established traditions of buying new from developers or through the secondary market purposely discouraged self-build to the point of extinction, but it refused to die quietly and has risen again to challenge purely profit-driven building practices. It can be a first-time buyer's ultimate financial solution, because the costs of building your own home compared with buying one are significantly reduced. Savings of up to 70% can be achieved, if you are willing to undertake most of the work yourself, but the concept is flexible and even if you only fulfil the role of project manager, you can still save thousands of pounds.

The beauty of self-build is that you can do as much or as little as you are able or desire – and still earn more in profit than you might from a full-time job. Acquiring a home this way is not an instant fix, it takes time and effort, but the physical and financial rewards make it a worthwhile endeavour.

THE FINANCIAL INCENTIVE TO SELF-BUILD

There are many elements that determine the market value of property. These include:

♦ Local competition (the volume of similar property on the market).

♦ Popularity of the location (creating high or low demand).

♦ Interest rates (determining how much people can afford to borrow).

♦ Build costs (for new-build development housing).

A major influence is the market strength of comparable property. Newly built dwellings lead the way, usually being valued higher than established property. Because prices are pushed down on the secondary sales market, older homes can compete and attract investors. So, it is the price of newly built property that controls the value of all others on the residential sales market. Bear in mind that a commercial developer is not operating like an individual owner wanting to sell his house; the developer's intention is to sell a product and make a profit.

Most developers expect to make at least 25% profit on each house built, after deducting land acquisition and construction costs. It doesn't take a genius therefore to work out that this is the basic saving *all* self-builders can achieve, even if they employ an entire labour force to undertake the work for them (called a 'turnkey' operation). Significant additional savings can be made when a self-builder supplies himself with services normally bought in, such as general labour or a skilled trade. The cost of construction usually comprises 40% materials and 60% labour, which means there are huge financial advantages to having a personal involvement in the actual building process.

The financial incentive is a prime motivator for most self-builders. It creates an opportunity to acquire a home for less than half the cost of comparable property *and* create something that is not only unique, but also designed to satisfy all the needs and desires of contemporary living.

ASSESSING THE DEGREE OF INVOLVEMENT

When people think about self-build, they think of construction – bricklaying, concreting, joinery and roofing; but there are so many other skills involved and it is likely you already possess at least one transferable ability. Remember that every service you provide yourself will save you money and increase your profit.

Perhaps your forte is a trade, such as plastering or plumbing; or you might have an organisational aptitude and are best suited to planning timetables and dealing with the day-to-day schedule of work. Typically, architects supply themselves with drawing services and deal with planning consents, then buy in skilled manpower for the main labour-intensive aspects. An accountant might deal purely with the financial side of the venture – organising the mortgage, dealing with receipts, bookkeeping and the VAT element. Even if you have no transferable skills you can still act as a general labourer, fetching and carrying for a builder you employ.

The degree of involvement is not only determined by the skills you possess or can acquire, but also the the time you can devote to the project. Thorough, realistic assessment and advance planning are essential, as they will help reduce anxiety and ensure the work continues in a productive direction.

LOCATING SUITABLE LAND

This is the most difficult aspect of a self-build project. It is hard enough to find land for sale, but finding a suitably sized and economically viable development plot is much more challenging. The main problem is that good building plots are now scarce and landowners are becoming increasingly aware of ways they can increase their value. For example, most development land is now marketed for sale *with* outline planning consent (OPC), because this fact alone considerably enhances its value. The price of land is assessed according to:

◆ Its 'development potential' – that is, its most profitable function. For example, a plot with OPC for eight apartments will be valued much higher than the same land with OPC for just a single dwelling.

- The amount of preparation required before construction can begin. For example, undulating land may need levelling and mains utility services (water, gas and electricity) may have to be brought in from far away.

- Whether access routes are already established. A plot may need a new access to be created from a local highway and, depending on the distance and terrain involved, this can be expensive and problematic.

- Comparable land values and property prices in the neighbourhood.

How much you spend on land depends on whether your primary intention is to maximise 'profit' (gained by immediately selling the building at completion) or improve your 'quality of living' (gained by sacrificing some of the available plot space and using it as a garden or other non-development area). The best solution is to find land that partly satisfies both ideals, so that the profit potential is not totally compromised.

This raises a question of what should come first – the house design or the plot of land? Having an architect's plan means you could spend a long time trying to find a suitable plot for it, whereas finding a plot first might mean having to alter your original design concept to build within the available space or to meet planning consent restrictions. There is no right or wrong way of doing this, though experienced self-builders suggest finding a suitable plot is the easiest first step.

Land can be found through various means. These include:

- Estate agents who have contact with builders and developers and gain information about plots before they are advertised.

- Local newspapers, where owners and builders advertise land surplus to their needs.

- Personal enquiry. Talking to shopkeepers and local people can often pay dividends.

- Land auctions and agents. Estate agents and surveyors sometimes act as land agents. They may sell individual plots direct or organise the occasional auction. Consulting local firms in person is usually more productive than trying to get information by telephone or letter.

- The Internet is rapidly establishing itself as *the* place to find suitable building plots and the following are some of the best sites (an alternative postal address and/or telephone number are supplied, where available, for non-internet users):

  www.buildstore.co.uk
  Buildstore Ltd, Kingsthorne Park, Nettlehill Road, Houstoun Industrial Estate, Livingston EH54 5DB. Tel: 0870 870 9994.

  www.landsaleuk-profit.co.uk
  (no other contact details available)

  www.land-sales-uk.co.uk
  Land UK, 1 Glasshouse Lane, Kenilworth, Warwickshire CV8 2AH.

www.perfectplot.co.uk
Gladwish Land Sales Ltd. 47 London Road, Horsham, West Sussex RH12 1AW. Tel: (01403) 262523.

www.propertyspy.com
PropertySpy plc, Chaucer House, 4–6 Upper Marlborough Road, St Albans, Herts AL1 3UR. Tel: 0845 1244 277 or (01727) 817310.

www.selfbuildcentre.com
Landbank Services, PO Box 2035, Reading, Berks RG6 7FJ. Tel: (0118) 962 6022.

www.uklanddirectory.org.uk
(no other contact details available)

ASSESSING THE SUITABILITY OF PLOTS

A plot may seem ideal for building on at first sight, but you should never judge a book by its cover. The land may appear level, have clear panoramic views, be near to mains services and have an existing access point – but it is not so much what can be seen as the elements that might be concealed from view, that really matter. A thorough investigation of the sub-soil structure is *always* useful, before considering purchase.

For example, the soil could be contaminated if it has previously been used as an industrial site or for tipping. It may also be considered a 'cleared site', that is, one that has been used for a variety of purposes over many years, but which is now cleared for a new use. Alternatively, the site may appear good during the summer months, but could regularly flood in winter; established trees may have been felled, causing cavernous voids in the sub-soil where roots have been left to rot; there may be old concrete foundations still beneath the surface (from a structure long since demolished) and they will need removing before any new construction can begin. Before a final commitment is made to buy the plot, these potential complications need to be investigated and the full cost of rectifying them assessed.

The planning and building control department of the local authority is a good starting point, as they will have historical information and are certain to have details about any likely contamination. If there is any doubt about using the land for residential purposes, the local authority will demand a full site investigation. A professional report will have to be commissioned and submitted, before an application to build will be considered. It is worth noting that architects also sometimes require a soil sub-structure report, so they can choose the right type of foundation for the scheme.

BUYING LAND

The procedures involved in buying land are much the same as buying a house and most conveyance solicitors are very familiar with them. However, the onus to check facts and figures falls on the buyer. It is worth remembering that solicitors generally do not view the plot and may only have a plan to work from, so the shape and dimensions are best checked personally on site, before proceeding with the legal formalities. The main question to consider is whether the size of plot, boundary markers and geometric form are consistent with the plans.

Once all the relevant documents have been received and checked for accuracy, your solicitor should make enquiries about VAT charging. As long as the vendor is informed in advance that the site is to be used for residential purposes, no VAT should be applied to the purchase. It is important to note that if this information is not transferred and VAT is later charged in error, it *cannot* be reclaimed.

RAISING FINANCE

The good news is that self-build is treated in a completely different way to traditional house buying. With a standard mortgage, a property is purchased instantaneously with a single lump sum loan and, as a result, the borrower incurs interest charges on the entire amount. Despite the full advance amount being agreed at the outset, self-build loans are released in multiple stages, as and when required; repayment interest is applied only to each of the staged amounts, thus prolonging the liability onset period and reducing the overall financial burden. Typically, the loan is released in five stages:

Stage 1: Land purchase (usually about 80% of its value).
Stage 2: Foundation to damp proof course.
Stage 3: First floor level.
Stage 4: Highest wall plate level.
Stage 5: Roof and interior completion (plastering, electrics and plumbing).

The borrowing capability of a self-builder is not only assessed on the usual elements (existing assets, income level and credit rating), but also the eventual market value of the proposed scheme. This makes self-build an ideal opportunity for first-time investors with enough time, stamina and skill to go the extra mile. There are currently over 50 lenders offering specialised loans and they include:

Buildstore Limited, Lomond House, Beveridge Square, Livingston EH54 6QF. Tel: 0800 018 5740.

Claycross Building Society, Freepost, Claycross, Chesterfield, Derbyshire S45 9BR. Tel: 0800 834497.

Lloyds TSB Scotland, Henry Duncan House, 120 George Street, Edinburgh EH2 4LH. Tel: (0131) 225 4555.

Loughborough Building Society, 6 High Street, Loughborough LE11 2QB. Tel: (01509) 610707.

Norwich & Peterborough Building Society, Peterborough Business Park, Lynch Wood, Peterborough PE2 6WZ. Tel: 0845 300 6727.

Skipton Building Society, The Bailey, Skipton, North Yorkshire BD23 1DN. Tel: (01756) 705 030.

PROFESSIONAL INVOLVEMENT

Most self-builders require outside professional assistance for some part or for the entire project. At the very least, many need to employ an architect to:

◆ devise a construction style;
◆ design the main structural elements;
◆ deal with the planning application; and
◆ ensure compliance with building regulations.

Others may have certain skills, such as electrical expertise, but might need to employ a plumber, plasterer and joiner. The more wide-ranging your proficiency – the more profitable the venture will be, because you will not need to pay for too many imported trades and professions.

It is important to analyse the expense of professional involvement at the outset, as this will impact considerably on the final cost of construction. It is also crucial to ensure that chosen individuals will be available to work for you during the dates you have programmed otherwise delays will occur, spending will rise and the schedule of work will go catastrophically adrift.

Time is one of the most influential elements of a project such as this and, when spent unproductively, it can have alarming secondary financial effects. For example, delays may cause exterior work to continue into the cold, wet and windy months of winter, resulting in newly laid brickwork and site-stored materials becoming drenched or frost damaged. Equally, contractors inundated with work may be unable to absorb long delays into their schedule, resulting in you having to wait weeks or months before they are free again. In construction, there is a natural order and progression of work and anything that interferes with one aspect invariably affects another. Maintaining a smoothly running programme is a major managerial feat and those with an organisational aptitude could find their personal input is best employed attending to this aspect alone.

COMPLETION ISSUES

Whether the house is built entirely under your own steam or not, there are issues that should be addressed by you personally, once completion is achieved. One of the most significant and advantageous is the submission of a VAT (Value Added Tax) refund application. It may be surprising to learn that most of the materials purchased to construct your own home qualify for a VAT refund and this can amount to thousands of pounds. However, it is important to recognise that only one claim can be made and this must be done **within three months** of the formal completion date.

Completion is said to occur when the property has been built according to the original plans or, in cases of doubt, when the local planning authority issues a certificate of completion. Inspections are conducted regularly through-out the project and by arrangement with the local authority building control officer. This is to ensure that the methods of construction and the materials used, accord with the planning application and original drawings – and conform to building regulations. The final inspection brings to an end the local authority's supervision of the scheme. A certificate is issued to confirm this, at which point the property is officially considered safe to be sold on to third parties, if desired.

Most materials for which VAT can be reclaimed must be 'ordinarily' incorporated into the structure of a dwelling. These include logical elements such as bricks, timbers, cement, concrete, nails and roofing felt; but can also include less obvious supplies such as air conditioning units, heating and security systems, kitchen cupboards, turf, garden plants, light fittings, paint and wallpaper. To ensure you are able to claim everything you are entitled to, it is vital that all the *original* receipts and records of purchase are retained from commencement of the project. HM Customs and Excise provide full details of VAT refund in their 'Self-Build Claim Pack', obtained from the National Advice Service by telephoning 0845 010 9000. The VAT Refund Notice (No. 719) and other appropriate forms are included in the pack. A fictitious example page from a VAT claim is given in Figure 16.

CALCULATING THE COST

Other than the cost of materials and labour, it is the burden of loan repayments that threatens a self-builder's constrained financial plans. For this reason, it is always beneficial to have enough resources at the start to buy land, have plans drawn and complete preparatory work on the plot. Preparing the site, setting-up services, creating an access route and installing foundations, can take considerable time to achieve and sometimes longer than the actual construction work on the dwelling; resisting a loan advance until this point delays the start of repayments and thus reduces the pressure to work at breakneck speed from the outset.

The cost will reflect the size and quality of the project and the length of time it takes to complete. In addition, the self-builder's personal involvement in providing labour and trades will also affect how much is spent on importing services. There is therefore no such thing as an average cost. However, as a general rule of thumb, allow £30 (minimum quality build) to £60 (high quality build) for each square foot of construction on a flat plane, using your architect's plans or rough drawings as a guide. Figure 17 shows a useful table of the major expenses

VAT refunds for DIY builders and converters

2A

HM Customs and Excise

Part 2A: Description of building and quantities of goods and materials used

Please write in **black** ink.

If you make a mistake, cross it out and insert the correct details above it. The person making the claim must initial the alteration.

Description of building
Type (eg bungalow, village hall)

DETACHED HOUSE

*Detached/semi-detached/terraced

Number of storeys (Count ground floor as one storey)	TWO	
Number of bedrooms	FOUR	
Number of kitchens	ONE	

Number of reception rooms	FIVE
Number of bathrooms/ cloakrooms	THREE
Ground floor area	250 m²

Garages

Built-in | Number NO | Single/double | Total floor area ft²/m²

Detached | Number ONE | Single/double | Total floor area 36 m²

Number and description of other rooms

GAMES ROOM — 1.
SAUNA — 1.

Quantities of materials used. If your claim is only for goods used to 'fit-out' or 'finish off' the building, you need only list those goods you are claiming for. If not, you must list **all** materials used, even those you are not claiming for. Please fill in the quantities in the units specified. The conversion table on the folder will help you to do this.

Item	Quantity Amount	Unit
Cement	15	Tonnes
Sand	60	*Tonnes/m³
Aggregate	10	*Tonnes/m³
Lime	—	Tonnes
Facing Bricks	26,750	Number
Common Bricks	8,000	Number
Stocks/engineering etc bricks	—	Number
Windows	16	Number
Glazing	38	m²
Roofing tiles	3,000	Number
Roofing felt	28	Rolls
Floor tiles	260	Number
Copper tubing	200	Metres
Plaster	30	Tonnes
Partition blocks	800	Number
Plaster-board	1·7	m³
Timber-carcassing	29·5	m³
Timber-Joinery	18·7	m³
Timber-tongued and grooved flooring	42	m³
Staircase and handrail	2	Number
External doors	2	Number
Internal doors	16	Number

Item	Quantity Amount	Unit
Paint - undercoating	75	Litres
Paint - emulsion	75	Litres
Paint - woodprimer	10	Litres
Paint - finishing coat	20	Litres
Cold water storage tank	1	Number
Copper cylinder	1	Number
Ironmongery for doors	32	Number
Sink, drainer and taps	1 SET	Number
Washbasin and taps	3 SETS	Number
WC Suite	3	Number
Bath and taps	1 SET	Number

Heating
Brief description | WATER SYSTEM | Number of radiators
Type of heater unit | GAS FIRED BOILER | 19

Kitchen units (brought-in cupboards, worktops, etc)
Please give number, type and dimensions of each
FULLY FITTED KITCHEN — SCHEDULE ATTACHED

Electrical installation Amount and type of cable used
Number of power points | 40 | 350m 2·5 t+e
Number of lighting points | 20 | 200m 1·5 t+e
Number of switches | 26 | Number of fuse boxes ONE

*Delete as appropriate

If you have used items not listed in this part, please list them overleaf with the quantity of each. If you need more space please continue on a separate piece of paper.

VAT 431 (Pt 2) Page 1

PCU(April 1996)

Figure 16. Completed example of VAT refund form 2A

Expense element	Average	My build
Professional reports regarding ground conditions, land contamination, stability, foundation requirements, etc.	£500 to £1,500	
Outline planning application (per 0.1 hectare)	£220	
Detailed planning application (per dwelling)	£220	
Building regulation approval (plans, inspection and notice)	£350	
Architect (production of drawings and plans only – not acting as project manager)	£1,000 to £5,000	
Demolition of any existing derelict building and any associated site preparation and debris removal	£5,000 to £15,000	
Professional and legal costs (solicitor, interior design, quantity surveyor, structural engineer, etc.)	£1,000 to £5,000	
Creating suitable access on to the building site	£2,000 to £10,000	
Supply and connection on to the site of services for mains gas, electricity, drainage, water, sewerage and telephone	£1,000 to £5,000	
Construction of the dwelling with ___ sq ft of floor space (amend according to the quality of materials and the degree of personal involvement in the work)	£50 per sq ft	
Labour, sub-contractor(s) and tradesmen costs	£10,000 to £25,000	
Loan interest payable over the term (average is based on £100,000 borrowed with repayments over 25 years and with a static interest rate of 5.95%). *Note*: total interest falls dramatically with shorter loan terms, appropriate if the dwelling is to be sold on completion	£92,000	
Mortgage application and other loan associated fees (average is based on a £100,000 advance)	£300 to £800	
Site security (hire of fencing and lighting plus indemnity insurance for public liability)	£1,500 to £2,500	
Hire of tools and equipment during construction	£250 to £5,000	
Landscaping (hard and soft)	£5,000 to £15,000	
Total of estimated costs involved		

Figure 17. Typical self-build expense elements

involved and can be used to assess your own scheme's specific budget requirements.

ADDITIONAL INFORMATION

The Internet is a rich source of information and guidance on self-build. There are both independent and commercial sites covering all the economic and construction issues involved. A few recommended website addresses are provided below.

In addition, *The Daily Telegraph – Build Your Own Home* (ISBN: 1 85703 901 7), co-written by me and self-building architect Mike Dyson, is a valuable reference that will help you turn your dream into reality. It explains the entire process, step-by-step, and includes chapters on finding and buying suitable land, submission of a planning application, raising funds, house style and design, taxation, how to comply with building regulations, construction issues and completion. There is also a compilation of over 100 pertinent website addresses and contact details for all UK self-build mortgage lenders. This ultimate guide is published by How To Books and is available at all good bookshops.

Recommended Websites

www.buildstore.co.uk
Buildstore's site will help you to find a suitable plot of land, organise materials and assist with financing a self-build scheme.

www.ebuild.co.uk
Packed full of useful resources, this site also has a

discussion forum where novices can gain advice from more experienced self-builders.

www.self-build.co.uk
The *Build It* magazine website supplies information, features, practical advice and case studies on the subject.

$\left(10\right)$

A Business Enterprise

Some yearn to become self-employed and strive to pursue it until achieved. A few stumble into it following unexpected redundancy, while others realise a hobby has the potential of becoming an alternative job. Regardless of how people become self-employed, most recognise the advantages without truly considering the many disadvantages. The decision to go it alone should never be taken lightly, because there can be far-reaching financial, practical and emotional consequences.

As with all things in life, running your own business involves risk and it is the depth of risk that mostly influences the outcome – turning an opportunity sweet or sour – making the venture lucrative or perilous. The business you invest in will probably depend on your skills, knowledge and experience acquired from employment, training or an academic course. Alternatively, it could be something completely unfamiliar that will require additional knowledge and new skills.

It is impractical to explore all the potential avenues open to you in this short chapter. There are books covering every conceivable subject and you would be wise to read extensively about prospective career choices, self-employment, taxation and the rules and regulations that might affect you.

This chapter deals exclusively with **commercial property** and **business opportunity**. Most business owners require premises that are detached from their own home, so they can trade, work or create productively – therefore choosing suitable property is fundamental to the success of your venture. There are also non-involved opportunities to profit by providing premises to other self-employed individuals, for example, acting as a landlord supplying competitive retail or office space. Although only a few small-scale speculators consider these as viable alternatives to residential investment, they are easily managed lettings that can generate a secure, long-term income.

The information in this section is intended only as an introduction. If the subject is attractive to you, you should investigate it thoroughly and research your chosen field in much greater depth.

EXPLORING SELF-EMPLOYMENT OPPORTUNITIES

The advantages of self-employment are:

◆ **Autonomy** – you become your own boss, make your own decisions and steer your career in the direction you wish.

◆ **Financial** – you keep all of the profit.

◆ **Flexibility** – you decide the amount of time you devote to the business and the days you work.

◆ **Satisfaction** – you see the results of your effort and labour, reaping the rewards immediately and personally.

◆ **Certainty of completion** – long-term plans can be followed and fulfilled without interference from people in positions above you.

The disadvantages are:

◆ **Isolation** – a lack of colleagues may entail long working hours devoid of conversation or opportunities to socialise. Decisions will be without the breadth of opinion and knowledge normally made available through teamwork.

◆ **Financial** – inaccurate financial planning, poor performance and unforeseen events may produce a loss, rather than a profit – this will significantly affect your personal income and the business.

◆ **Self-reliance** – in the early years, you may need to become multi-tasked, undertaking all aspects of the business yourself. Apart from the main activities of the venture – this could include bookkeeping, administrative work, reception duties, training (keeping up with new techniques), posting letters and invoices, cleaning the office, even making your own coffee.

◆ **Timekeeping** – most self-employed people say they have never worked so hard in their life. There are no rules about the number of hours you work, so the amount of time you give is entirely up to you. In extreme circumstances, this can involve working every available hour at the expense of normal family life.

Conversely, the business may become neglected because other events and activities become more alluring.

♦ **Lack of holidays** – when employed by someone else, you are entitled to paid holiday leave; but this is not the case when you are self-employed. If you don't work, you don't earn! The pressure of work or a poor profit indicator can manifest as a reluctance to take holidays, which in turn can produce family conflict, stress and fatigue.

♦ **Taxation** – being self-employed means you are responsible for dealing directly with the Inland Revenue. You must calculate your liability for tax and pay it. Failure to meet payment deadlines incurs expensive penalties.

♦ **The weight of responsibility** – you cannot walk away from a situation at the end of the day or leave problems for someone else to resolve. The responsibility may be onerous for those lacking managerial and organisational skills, leading to conflict between work and family life.

Self-employment is not suitable for everyone, but the opportunities are endless for those with enough stamina and self-discipline. For trading, service provision and retail ideas, look through a *Yellow Pages* directory. There are hundreds of different established business ventures, but starting something innovative and new is often difficult and very risky. Successful entrepreneurs like fashion designer Jasper Conran and Easyjet founder Stelios Haji-Ioannou, admit to multiple early business failures and base part of their success on being in the right place at the right time. They also quote perseverance, gritty determination, the ability to think and act fast, good health and good fortune as the qualities that are needed, particularly in the early years.

It is often less precarious to tread a well-worn path. By participating in an enterprise known to work, success becomes more certain. The Internet is bursting with useful suggestions and advice for those intending to become self-employed: *www.businessbureau-uk.co.uk* and *www.smallbusiness.co.uk* are two particularly good web-sites. Barclays Bank plc also have a site at *www.clearlybusiness.com* where they promote and sell a PC programme, *Clearlystart-up*, endorsed by the Small Firms Enterprise Development Initiative. This aims to help novices understand key marketing, planning, operational and financial issues, using easy-to-follow tutorials and interactive presentations. More general contact details and resources are given at the end of this chapter.

BUYING A FRANCHISE

A **franchise** is a business idea or format created by someone else and supplied under a legal arrangement (usually through license) to another person. The franchisee gains the right to sell the franchisor's product or services and, in return, the franchisor usually receives payment by commission (a percentage of sales). It is a combination of two perfect partners: one supplies the 'product' (retaining legal title to it) while the other provides the means of selling it. When a franchise is granted, it is often limited to a predetermined geographic area – so a single business concept, brand name or product might have numerous independently-run franchise outlets operating at the same time throughout the country.

By buying a franchise you acquire a ready-made, tried and tested business that can be started very quickly. The usual arrangement involves paying an upfront fee for the right to provide the service or sell the product, then commission-based fees continue throughout the franchise period. Contractual arrangements also influence how the business will be managed and how products will be advertised. The franchisor does not take an active role in running the business, other than offering help and support when required.

A further advantage of franchising is that banks are usually more willing to offer loans if the franchise is a proved, reliable and steadfast scheme. However, they are still likely to demand a comprehensive business plan – see *www.bizplans.co.uk/plan.html* from the London Business School for more information and an interactive online programme to help you construct a professional presentation document.

The main disadvantages of franchising are an intrusion in your business by another party and the added expense of paying commission. Some franchise arrangements are very restrictive and can turn a business owner into little more than a sales representative. In addition, success of the venture depends largely on the success of the product and the management and marketing structure imposed by the franchisor. The loss of autonomy could be frustrating – particularly if you feel things could be done better or in a more productive or profitable way.

> **Warning**: some franchises are little more than shams – a fraudulent method of obtaining money from vulnerable and inexperienced investors. Always investigate thoroughly and seek hard evidence of 'success' or 'profit'. Beware of multi-level marketing schemes and check the franchise with the DTI's Trading Schemes Guide (*www.dti.gov.uk/ccp/topics1/guide/tradescheme/ pdf*) before committing yourself.

Buying a franchise involves signing an agreement – a licence to use the product and operate a business scheme. Never sign a franchise agreement without first consulting your solicitor, because contractual arrangements are legally binding and once committed you may not be able to back out, no matter how limited you later find the deal to be. Questions you should ask the franchisor include:

- How much influence will you demand to have in the day-to-day selling, marketing and management of the product or service?

- What support will you give and how will it be provided?

- What is the initial fee and when does this have to be paid?

- What is the level of commission and are any other fees involved?

- How are the costs and fees calculated and when do they become due?

- What period does the franchise cover?

- Can either party terminate the agreement at any time and, if so, are there additional fees (to the franchisor) or compensation (to the franchisee) involved?

- At the end of the franchise term, will I have an automatic right to renew the licence for another term?

- Are there any restrictions on how I run the business and the type of premises I decide to use?

- Do I have exclusive rights to use or sell the product/ services within a particular location?

- Can I sell the franchise to another party?

More information on franchising is available from *Whichfranchise.com*, whose address is: 78 Carlton Place, Glasgow. G5 9TH. Tel: (0141) 429 5900. Website: *www.Whichfranchise.com*

A guide to choosing a franchise and a range of franchise products, services, brand names and business concepts for sale are offered by the British Franchise Association, Thames View, Newtown Road, Henley-on-Thames, Oxon. RG9 1HG. Tel: (01491) 578050. Website: *www.british-franchise.org*

THE 'FLATS OVER SHOPS' INITIATIVE

Governments have recognised that throughout the UK there is a growing lack of suitable accommodation for single people, single-parent families and young couples with children. This is partly due to recent sociological changes and an aging housing stock that no longer meets the needs of the current generation. The bulk of existing dwellings were originally built for large families and are now simply too big and too expensive for the average household.

A number of innovative schemes were introduced to remedy the situation. Some helped bring vacant property back into use or encouraged the conversion of wasted space into residential use. Others encouraged investors to provide more appropriate housing through various tax breaks and allowances. The 'Flats Over Shops Initiative' (Flat Conversion Allowance) was created in 2001 and has been one of the more successful housing and regeneration proposals pioneered by government. It is also a very lucrative proposition for investors who want to buy a retail outlet.

The major benefit of the scheme is that a speculator can buy a shop with wasted space above it, convert the space into a letting unit (eventually receiving rental income from it) and have the entire cost of the conversion qualify as a 100% capital allowance. There are strict qualifying aspects to the regulations; for example, the property must have been built before 1980 and the upper floor must have been originally constructed for residential use; but when a property does qualify, the advantages are considerable and can extend to repairs incidental to the conversion, new bathrooms and kitchens, dividing walls, and so on.

More information is contained in the Inland Revenue leaflet *Capital Allowances for Flats Over Shops* (No. IR2007), which can be obtained by telephoning 0845 9000 404 or by e-mail: *saorderline.ir@gtnet.gov.uk* or it can be printed direct from *www.inlandrevenue.gov.uk*. More comprehensive guidance notes are also available: *www.inlandrevenue.gov.uk/specialist/flatsovershops.htm*

NON-INVOLVED OFFICE/RETAIL PREMISES

Buying a commercial property doesn't mean it has to become a hands-on business. You could, for example, purchase office or retail space and then let it to someone else to trade, manufacture or administrate their own venture. As the owner, you would become the landlord and receive rent in a similar way to a residential investment unit – though the procedures and regulations differ and there are also special financial elements you would need to consider.

The basic appraisal matters to contemplate when buying commercial investment property vary significantly from the residential buy-to-let assessment given in Chapter 6. Experienced chartered surveyor and specialist commercial property agent, Philip Gibbs of P R Gibbs & Co, tel: (01942) 844100, suggests the following seven-point strategy:

1. **Location**
    Make sure the location is compatible with the use of the property. For example, it would be inappropriate to provide a launderette in an area where most people are likely to have their own washing machine. It is also

important to establish that the immediate vicinity is at least stable, improving, or likely to improve. The council's planning department will have details about proposals for significant development, which might enhance, or conversely be detrimental to, the property value. Other indicators include the demand (or lack of demand) for similar properties in the area, rising or falling prices and premises that are vacant or boarded-up.

2. **Rental level**
   Establish a market rent for the property, that is, find out what rent a lessee would expect and be prepared to pay. Researching other existing rents in the area and consulting commercial agents can help to identify this. Once assessed, compare it with the rent currently being paid (if the property is already let to a business tenant). If the current rent is higher, bear in mind that the tenant may have long-term problems paying it and, if they vacate, a new tenant may not be prepared to pay the same high rent. Alternatively, if the rent is lower than a market rent, there is potential for rental growth, making the property purchase more lucrative.

3. **The tenant**
   If there is a lease running while the property is being considered for purchase, is the tenant financially sound? Buyers should obtain a rent payment history, find out how long the tenant has been trading and identify the period of occupation. In addition, it is imperative that potential buyers undertake their own credit checks and investigations. Though it may be

difficult, try to gain access to the tenant's trading figures for at least the last three years and their profit and loss accounts and balance sheets. These documents will help you assess profitability, liquidity, net assets and upward or downward trends – downward trends are bad news and suggest the tenant may be struggling to survive in business. Is there a guarantor to the lease? If so, conduct credit checks against them as if they were the tenant.

4. **The lease**

How long is the lease? When does it expire? When is the next rent review date and do provisions exist to increase the rent up to a market rent? The lease should also specify who is responsible for internal and external repairs and buildings insurance. If other tenants occupy the same building, who is responsible for common parts and structural maintenance? Net rent is often quoted in marketing brochures and comprises rent less landlord expenses; but if a service charge exists, the landlord's expenditure may not be recoverable and must therefore be deducted from rent received, before a true assessment can be considered.

Some leases include a 'break clause', which means the only certainty of tenancy duration will be the next date-tied break clause, rather than expiry of the term as may be quoted in an abridged description of the lease. Be wary of short leases, unless you can be certain a new tenant could easily be found at or above the current rent. Also check the lease for unbalanced or onerous covenants (contractual promises) on either the landlord or the tenant – those imposed on the tenant will reduce the rental value and any imposed on a landlord will decrease capital value.

5. **The property**
   There are obvious matters to consider in relation to the property itself, such as whether it is structurally sound and conforms to fire and other building regulations. Prospective buyers should also investigate whether it is easily accessible (according to the operation conducted or planned) and whether sufficient facilities exist for visitors. For example, are there adequate service provisions for deliveries and car parking? See also 'Access for the Disabled' below.

   If the property is old, has its design and functionality now become obsolete and inefficient? Would there be high demand for the property in the future? Has it been maintained in accordance with the lease obligations? If the property becomes vacant, would it need significant repair or alteration to make it viable and attractive to a new tenant or purchaser?

6. **Be aware**
   Be suspicious of properties offered with what may appear to be good rents or long leases let to newly formed limited companies or individuals with no track record or substance. These are all unknown quantities and potential problems.

7. **Alternative use**
   Should the current or proposed nature of business conducted at the property fall into decline or become

difficult to sustain in an area with high competition, it may be necessary to change the use. Research all possible alternative uses, particularly any with higher returns, such as site assembly with adjoining properties to form a new development. Marketing the property when empty and gaining good new tenants will be easier if you are forearmed with a list of alternative uses.

Details of retail investments, offices, catering units, guest houses and many other types of business premises for sale can be found in *Dalton's Weekly*. This publication is available at most good newsagents or it can be obtained by subscription from *Dalton's Weekly*, C.I. Tower, St George's Square, New Malden, Surrey KT3 4JA. Tel: (020) 8329 0100. They also offer an online database with thousands of businesses for sale at *www.daltonsbusiness.com*

Other useful websites for commercial property are:
www.agentalert.co.uk
www.allotherproperty.co.uk
www.businessesforsale.com
www.compropregister.co.uk

COMMERCIAL VERSUS RESIDENTIAL

Following the residential buy-to-let boom of recent years, you may be wondering why the same expansion has not occurred in the commercial sector. The truth is, it has always been quietly popular among experienced speculators. However, it hasn't received the same amount of publicity and consequently the general public are less aware of it. Residential letting quickly became a roller-coaster, gathering speed and momentum, but rapid growth in this sector is now causing problems of oversupply and in some regions aggressive competition has produced falling rents and profits.

Leasing commercial property has several advantages over residential property letting. These include:

- Terms are often longer – up to 25 years or more. The continuity provides much greater certainty of rental income and assists with long-term financial planning.

- Tenants can be made liable for *all* repairs, reducing long-term liability and expenses.

- The amount of time required for managing the property is significantly less.

- There is far less statutory and local authority inter-vention in the tenancy.

- Good business tenants can be more reliable and less risky than their residential counterparts. For example, leases can provide for forfeiture against contractual breaches and distraint of tenants' goods in the event of rent arrears.

ACCESS FOR THE DISABLED

In October 2004, new regulations become effective, which means anyone providing services and goods to the public must make alterations to their premises, if required, so that disabled people have equal access to them. This is a major legal obligation for commercial property owners, business people and employers – and for some, it will have far-reaching financial ramifications.

Some previously acceptable premises will no longer be able to operate as commercial property if necessary alterations cannot be made, either due to physical limitations or because the cost of doing them would be too expensive. For example, a shop with steps leading up into it is unlikely to satisfy the regulations; but it may not be possible to install a low-incline ramp, because the access is too near to a public footpath. This could significantly damage the value of the property and even make it unsaleable. The implications are worth considering if you are currently looking for suitable premises – be aware that the price of some commercial units may be drastically reduced, because they don't meet the regulations.

A property built after 1985 should conform to modern building requirements and the needs of disabled people will have been taken into account when it was designed and constructed. In theory, premises have a 10-year protection period from the date of construction, so something built in 2001 should not require any alterations to comply with the latest building regulations for disabled people, unless they become necessary by 2011 – for example, because a change of use is being considered or the property undergoes substantial design modification. However, a property built *before 1985* may require substantial work to provide disabled people access and so that they can use the services provided by it.

To view changes in the law, which will be introduced in October 2004, visit the Disability Rights Commission website at: *www.drc-gb.org*

A full version of the guide *Access and Facilities for Disabled People* can be downloaded from: *www.odpm. gov.uk/stellent/groups/odpm_buildreg/documents/page/ odpm_breg_600512.pdf*

The Disability Rights Commission (DRC) Code of Practice, which describes the new duties of business premises' owners and service providers from 2004 under the Disability Discrimination Act, is available from the TSO, tel: 0870 600 5522. The DRC also have a helpline for enquiries: 08457 622 633.

GRANTS AND INCENTIVES

There are a variety of grant and incentive schemes available to help both business and commercial property owners, particularly those just starting up. Most are funded by central government and administered by local authorities; others come from charitable organisations or private enterprise partnerships. Funding often depends on the operation or premises being located in a disadvantaged urban area, a region approved for regeneration or a business enterprise zone. Financial support may be available to assist with:

◆ Property repairs.
◆ Shop front improvements.
◆ Advertising and promotion.
◆ Education, training and development.

- Recycling of waste products.
- Increasing productivity.
- Access to technology.
- Employees' salaries.
- Expansion and growth.
- Energy conservation and efficiency.
- First year's business expenses.
- Banking expenses.
- Export development.

There are three main routes to finding out about and gaining grant assistance. Each should be exploited to the full. They are as follows.

1. **Consulting the local authority**

   Ask the planning or development officer about regions defined as (or proposed for) regeneration and improvement, because grants are likely to be targeted at these areas. Find out about any enterprise and partnership schemes, as funding may be available to help with new business start-up expenses or commercial property acquisition. Seek advice and information from the council's strategy and regeneration officer about any funding-assisted schemes they operate and contact the publications department for explanatory leaflets.

2. **Scouring the Internet**

   The Internet is a rich source of information. Comprehensive directories of UK government grants are available at:

   www.businesslink.co.uk

www.have.org.uk/assets
www.j4b.co.uk

There are also 'grant agents' promoting their services on the Internet. These are agents who collect information about your venture, then identify the grants accessible to you. Charges and services vary, but their assistance might be useful if you are baffled by the myriad of grant schemes and the often bureaucratic application process.

3. **Seeking expert help and advice**
   Business Link is an easy to use business support, advice and information service, managed by the Department of Trade and Industry. It is run by business people – for business people – and has a network of operators throughout England, with associated organisations in Wales, Scotland and Northern Ireland. They don't just advise on grant assistance, but on a range of subjects affecting and of interest to people in business.

   England: Business Link – tel: 0845 600 9006.
   Scotland: Business Gateway – tel: 0845 609 6611.
   Wales: Business Eye – tel: 0845 796 9798
   N. Ireland: Invest Northern Ireland – tel: 028 9023 9090.

RAISING FINANCE

Buying business premises is one thing, but buying a 'going concern' is quite another matter altogether and requires a cautious approach. The first question to ask is, 'Why is it being sold?' Lenders will want evidence of:

- the financial history of the business (three years' accounts);

- the current turnover, sales and profit performance;

- information about local competition and development proposals;

- the cash flow situation and running expenses; and

- details about personal assets, current income and liabilities.

Secondly, it is important to assess the market value of the assets and deduct an appropriate amount for depreciation. Assets might include:

- the premises;
- the 'goodwill' (the customer base);
- stock of goods;
- equipment;
- fixtures and fittings; and
- registered trademarks and company name.

Only after *every* aspect of the property and business has been checked and verified (including obtaining information from Companies House and having a solicitor substantiate legal claims and inspect relevant documents), can an offer be made based on the thorough market value assessment previously undertaken. After negotiation (*always* bargain to get a better deal), the matter of raising sufficient funds will need to be addressed. Finance is likely to combine two or three supply sources:

- personal savings
- grant assistance
- borrowed funds.

Borrowing money for commercial or business investment purposes differs from the more traditional and familiar home buying mortgage, although the lending principles are similar (that is, they depend on an acceptable market valuation, the amount of additional security available and the applicant passing a risk assessment). Above all, the lending institution must have confidence in the viability and profitability of the proposal. A watertight business plan is crucial and substantial time and effort spent on it will be well invested.

Most high street banks and building societies supply commercial mortgages and, if you have been a customer of one of them for some years, it is worth approaching *that* particular lender first, to find out if they offer preferential rates. The Internet is a rich source of commercial mortgage lenders and also a vehicle through which different products, rates and terms can be compared (see 'Recommended websites' at the end of this chapter).

The Department of Trade and Industry's (DTI) Small Firms Loan Guarantee Scheme (SFLG) might be useful to you, if an approved lender has refused to grant you a loan entirely due to a lack of personal security (rather than a lack of business viability). The SFLG guarantees loans from £5,000 to £100,000 up to 75% and for periods of between two and ten years (subject to terms and restrictions). In return, the borrower pays the DTI a premium of 2% per year of the outstanding amount. Full details are contained in the DTI's *SFLG Booklet* obtained by telephoning 0870 150 2500 or it can be printed out direct from the Internet at *www.dti.gov.uk/sflg*

FURTHER INFORMATION

The 100-page *No Nonsense Guide to Rules and Regulations* is a free booklet available from Business Link. It tells those considering self-employment or starting a new business what they need to know about tax, VAT, premises, health and safety, trading regulations and more. Telephone 0845 600 9006 or print it from the Internet at *www.businesslink.gov.uk*

How To Books publishes a range of valuable reference guides and tutorials for those who are considering investing in commercial property. These include:

- *Starting and Running a B&B*, Stewart Whyte (ISBN: 1 85703 883 5).

- *Starting Your Own Business*, Jim Green (ISBN: 1 85703 859 2).

- *Raising Start-Up Finance*, Phil Stone (ISBN: 1 85703 705 7).

- *Buying and Running a Guest House*, Dan Marshall (ISBN: 1 85703 898 3).

- *Starting and Running a Sandwich-Coffee Bar*, Stephen Miller (ISBN: 1 85703 805 3).

◆ *Preparing a Winning Business Plan*, Matthew Record (ISBN: 1 85703 881 9).

A full catalogue of current publications can be viewed at *www.howtobooks.co.uk*

Recommended websites

www.business.barclays.co.uk
Everything about starting, running and financing a new business from Barclays Bank, including access to an extensive range of easy-to-read fact sheets.

www.comproperty.com
Locate thousands of commercial properties for sale throughout the UK.

www.quote.easy-quote.co.uk/CommercialP
Access the Business Mortgage Guide and compare commercial mortgage products to find the best lender for your venture.

(11)

Borrowed Funds

This section of the book returns to the primary subject of first-time home buying, although the information given continues to have some relevance to other types of property investment referred to in the previous six chapters. Here we begin exploring the process of borrowing and the elements that either restrict or enhance it.

WHAT CAN I AFFORD?

It is interesting to note that most first time buyers begin this procedure with an inappropriate question – 'What can I borrow?' – which is a little like putting the cart before the horse. Being able to borrow an amount doesn't mean you will necessarily be able to afford it. Getting on the wrong track at this early stage could set you along an inflexible and perilous course. The difficulty is, once you know how much you can borrow, you may be tempted to accept it to buy the home of your dreams, regardless of how disproportionate or impractical the loan might be when set against *future* income and expenses (that is, after the property has been bought). Commonsense dictates the first question to answer should be: 'What can I afford?'

To identify this, you must be ruthlessly honest about your spending habits and current outgoings (adding forecasted estimates from Figure 2 in Chapter 1) – and then be *realistic* about your income and savings. By conducting this exercise and deducting expenses from income, you will calculate three 'affordability' figures:

◆ The excess monthly amount you **have available** to spend, save or invest today (prior to buying a property).

◆ The excess monthly amount you **will have available** after buying an affordable property (this being your surplus or 'buffer' amount).

◆ The funds you **have already saved** or need to save for the deposit and purchase expenses (legal, administrative, relocation, loan application and set-up costs).

Armed with this data you can begin exploring property, restricting your search to appropriately sized and suitably priced dwellings. You can also now confirm the cost of borrowing by approaching various mortgage lenders for information.

WHAT CAN I BORROW?

These are the standard calculations, offering general guidance about the amount you can borrow. They are termed 'lending multiples':

◆ Single person applicants are usually able to borrow three and a half times their *gross* annual income (that is, before tax and other deductions).

◆ Partnered applicants seeking a joint mortgage are usually able to borrow either:

1. Three and a half times the gross annual income of the higher earner **plus** one year's gross income of the lower earner;
    or
2. Two and three quarter times the **combined** gross annual income of both partners.

Proof of earnings is required and this is usually satisfied by the production of wage-slips for the previous 12 months. These are *not* strict maximum or minimum borrowing formulas adopted by all lenders – some lenders are prepared to offer single applicants up to four times their income, plus up to two and a half times the annual salary of a joint applicant. However, the highest rates of income-related borrowing often require larger deposit sums. These fluctuations are defined by what is termed the 'Loan To Value' (LTV) rate.

LTV is the amount (expressed as a percentage) of mortgage funds advanced, set against the formal valuation (not necessarily the purchase price) of the property. So, a 95% mortgage on a property valued at £100,000 would involve the applicant receiving £95,000 in borrowed funds and paying a £5,000 deposit. The valuation is a crucial element in this calculation and often the focus of contention between lenders and their clients. The valuation is usually arranged by the lender and conducted by a surveyor, but *not any* surveyor; it usually has to be one authorised by the lender. Thus, borrowers rarely consider the valuation to be independent, despite having to pay for the service.

A typical scenario is a house put on the market for £115,000. Potential buyers view the property, like what they see and negotiate the price down to £110,000. The buyers submit their mortgage application and the lender arranges for a surveyor to assess the condition of the property and value it. The value is determined at £95,000. Despite attempts at renegotiation by the buyers, the owners refuse to reduce the property price any more than they already have. The buyers originally sought a 95% mortgage and expected to receive £104,500, paying only £5,500 deposit. The valuation changes things considerably. Now they can only borrow £90,250 and will have to find £19,750 for a deposit, if they want to proceed.

There are lessons to be learned from the example above: it emphasises the importance of checking the accuracy of a property's market value and its condition. If there are defects in the structure or fabric of the building, the cost of correcting them must be considered prior to agreeing a purchase price, because it *will* affect the amount you can borrow. Sometimes it is also important to recognise that it makes more sense to walk away from something unaffordable, rather than pursue it regardless of cost. We will cover these matters more fully later. Given the frustration and complexities involved (just to borrow enough money) it is perhaps little wonder that buying, selling and moving home are widely recognised as some of the most stressful events in life. And the problems don't stop there ...

Banks and building societies won't even consider applying their calculation until they have received full details about your current financial commitments. If you have read and acted on the information so far contained in this book, you will be fully prepared to present this data; but there is one element you **must** give full attention to, because it is highly influential to mortgage lenders:

Credit cards can be benefical as long as they are used responsibly, but if you are an impulsive spender and rarely or never pay the full balance off each month, the resulting credit payment history can be extremely damaging to your mortgage application.

If in doubt…be drastic…ditch the plastic!

Lenders consider credit cards in the same way as loan commitments but, unfortunately, they are one of the most expensive forms of loan on the market. The mortgage company will determine minimum monthly repayments and deduct the annual sum from your salary, before the 'lending multiple' calculation above is applied. So, act now by reducing or eliminating your repayment obligations to enhance your mortgage borrowing capacity.

HOW SELF-EMPLOYMENT AFFECTS LENDING

If you are self-employed and are able to provide a lender with your last three years' audited accounts, you will be treated in much the same way as someone in full-time employment. The lender will assess your income (pre-tax profit) and apply the figures to the standard 'lending multiple'. Some lenders will also require details of your accountant, so they can contact them for confirmation about consistency and accuracy, and may ask for bank statements over the prior six-month period. If one year's accounts are awaiting completion, lenders will usually accept a written statement from your accountant describing the estimated profit.

There are a few lenders who will accept just two years' audited accounts and these include:

- Bank of Ireland – tel: 0800 0850 444.
- Bank of Scotland – tel: 08457 273747.
- Birmingham Midshires – tel: 0500 228822.
- Nationwide's UCB Home Loans – tel: 0845 950 1500.
- Portman Building Society – tel: 0800 548548.
- Teachers Building Society – tel: (01202) 843500.

Self-employed people, who have just begun trading and do not have a minimum of two years' audited accounts, can still obtain a loan by applying for a 'self-certification' mortgage (see the last section of this chapter).

AN ADVERSE CREDIT HISTORY

A history of underpaying, late paying or defaulting on payments for hire purchase goods and other loan and credit agreements, will probably have produced an adverse personal credit record (see 'Creating a Golden Profile' in Chapter 2). If unfavourable data cannot be removed or 'satisfied' from your personal record, you may find it difficult to borrow funds from high street lenders. There are three remedies to this situation:

- Wait until the bad data has been resolved or marked as satisfied (this can take anything up to six years), before applying for a mortgage.

- Apply to a specialised 'adverse credit mortgage lender' for a loan, but be aware their products generally have the highest interest rate charges. You may also have to pay for a 'mortgage payment protection' insurance policy to shield the lender against you defaulting on instalments. Mandatory MIGs (mortgage indemnity guarantees) or MIPs (mortgage indemnity premiums) can add thousands of pounds to the standard cost of a mortgage over the term of the product.

- Apply for a 'guarantor mortgage', which involves finding someone who is prepared to accept the legal responsibility of your mortgage schedule, should you be unable pay the instalments yourself. To access the best rate deals, the 'guarantor' needs to be an owner-occupier or have other assets they can use as security; they must also have a clean credit history and a regular income. Parents or other relatives are an obvious first choice and the oldest building society in the world, the Chesham (tel: 0800 684 784), accepts guarantors for the entire mortgage sum; while the Newcastle Building Society (tel: 0845 606 4488) accepts guarantors for any shortfall between income and the cost of the property being purchased.

COUNTY COURT JUDGEMENTS

County Court Judgements (CCJs) are among the more serious adverse credit markers and they deny access to best-value mortgage products. The remedy is to satisfy the debt that caused them as soon as possible, then apply for a Certificate of Satisfaction (see Chapter 2). This should help provide access to some products from some lenders, but lenders may still discriminate by raising interest rates or by insisting on a mortgage indemnity guarantee. The best solution, in the short term, is likely to be a self-certification mortgage.

ARE YOU A FREQUENT MOVER?

People who relocate frequently are viewed with suspicion by lenders. The reason could be legitimate, for example, because your career demands it; but equally it might be to avoid debts, service bills or credit arrangements. To access the best mortgage products, try to remain at one address for at least three years and pay bills (gas, electric, council tax, and so on) on time. This provides evidence of stability and reliability – mortgage companies give high regard to these qualities when considering an application.

CONSIDERING SHARED BORROWING

One answer to low income or a bad credit history is to share your borrowing with other people. This provides many advantages and a few disadvantages, but essentially it enables you to get your first foot on the housing ladder and acquire an asset you might otherwise be unable to obtain. The advantages include:

♦ A single mortgage product can usually be shared with up to four people. There is (strictly) no limit to the number who can be involved, though the space available on legal documents and the complexities of administering multiple titleholders can be prohibitive beyond four.

◆ The lending multiple adopted is usually three times the annual income of the highest paid earner plus one times the annual salary of each sharer. This considerably raises borrowing ability without excluding those on low incomes. At the time of writing, the Skipton Building Society (tel: 0800 446776) were offering a singularly generous choice of multiples, which could be advantageous depending on the range of incomes involved:

Up to 75% loan to value –
Two buyers: 4 × main salary + 2nd salary or
   3.25 × joint
Three buyers: 3 × all salaries
Four buyers: 2.75 × all salaries

Over 75% Loan to value –
Two buyers: 3.5 × main salary + 2nd salary or
   2.75 × joint
Three buyers: 2.5 × all salaries
Four buyers: 2.25 × all salaries

◆ Properties that were previously unaffordable, due to size and location, can become affordable.

◆ Mortgage payments can be formally organised so that liability is proportionate to each sharer's legal interest in the property. For the lowest paid sharer, this might involve him or her making the lowest monthly repayment (though it would also involve them receiving the least amount of profit when the property is sold).

The disadvantages include:

◆ It may be difficult to reach amicable decisions on everything the group choose to do with the property.

◆ There will be a need for a formal, legally binding agreement, which will protect each party's rights (such as what will happen to the asset should one sharer die). This form of contract is called a 'tenants-in-common agreement' and should be created by a solicitor. In addition, a 'declaration of trust' (sometimes referred to as a 'trust deed' or 'deed of trust') should be devised, which deals with day-to-day living arrangements and consensual agreements for disposing of the asset.

◆ If one or more of the group decide to vacate, the remaining sharers may be forced into meeting the full mortgage payment schedule *and* raising enough funds to compensate those who leave. If a unanimous and congruous agreement cannot be achieved, the only option remaining may be to sell the property. This is a matter the group should explore in advance of any commitment and agree what will happen if the worst-case scenario occurs.

A PENSION MORTGAGE

This product is mentioned simply because some people may be tempted to consider it as an option to under-funding, particularly if retirement seems a long way off and therefore something of little significance. Most financial experts agree that the risks of this type of mortgage outweigh any potential benefit.

A 'pension mortgage' operates in a similar way to an 'endowment mortgage', except that contributions are made into a pension scheme rather than a life assurance policy. Interest on the loan is paid each month, together with separate payments into a personal pension scheme. The theory is that the lump sum (generated when your pension is collected) pays the outstanding mortgage. Perhaps the only advantage is that all three payments are tax-free. The problems that can ensue include:

◆ You might be left with inadequate income at retirement.

◆ Since the lump sum is only payable at retirement, the term of your loan could extend beyond the standard 25 years (depending on commencement age and the planned date of retirement).

◆ If the pension scheme performs poorly, there may be insufficient funds generated to pay the outstanding mortgage.

◆ Paying for an adequate life-assurance policy is usually mandatory.

At the time of writing, the industry's Mortgage Code prevents lenders from advertising these schemes – and *that* should tell you a great deal about their value to borrowers!

OVERTIME AND BONUSES

Some lenders will include **regular** bonuses, commissions and overtime payments as part of the income element of a mortgage consideration – though most will only accept half the value in their calculations. Other lenders will only include supplemental income if the employer guarantees it. A bonus, commission or overtime is guaranteed if it is recorded in writing and clearly appreciated by both parties as an employee's right. If in doubt, consult your employment contract and any subsequent agreements, or ask your employer direct.

SPLIT EQUITY PURCHASES

These are unusual but ideal arrangements for buyers who are unable to raise sufficient funds through traditional mortgage products. However, they require the vendor's full agreement and participation, which may not always be forthcoming. A split equity deal is only viable when a seller's attempts at selling a property have been prolonged, frustrating and unproductive, because it is only in these circumstances they may contemplate such a proposal.

Essentially, the keen buyer offers to raise funds on a percentage of the value of the property, say 80%, with full title being obtained under the sale contract. The vendor retains a second legal charge over the remaining portion (the lender keeps the first legal charge), until the outstanding balance is paid at an agreed future date. The buyer arranges sufficient alternative funding (an insurance policy, a remortgage or a saving scheme) to mature by the future date or the property could be sold, if its value has increased by the required margin.

The buyer gains by acquiring a property – but only pays for part of it until an agreed future date; the vendor gains by selling the property – but retains a share in it, which will probably increase in value.

These schemes need a great deal of legal work and the cost of arrangement can be prohibitive, particularly if the two parties are unable to reach a swift and amicable agreement. In addition, high street mortgage lenders are not generally equipped to consider loans outside the standard format and even if you find a lender prepared to offer a suitable product, the interest rates may be discouragingly high.

A SELF-CERTIFICATION MORTGAGE

The 'self-certification' or 'non-status' mortgage is a product primarily designed for the self-employed; it is also widely used by others who have difficulty proving their income, but have enough savings to pay a substantial deposit. Although some brokers and intermediaries claim they can arrange this type of mortgage with a 15% deposit (85% LTV), most products stipulate 25% (75% LTV) or more.

With self-certification, you declare your income and provide other pertinent financial information – but the lender doesn't seek confirmation of the data from third parties, such as your employer or accountant. That is the theory; in reality, they reserve the right to consult them or make any checks deemed necessary. These products can provide a fast-track route to borrowed funds, without the usual bureaucracy and complications. However, interest rates are usually higher than standard products, so repayment levels could be burdensome if they have to be sustained over a prolonged period.

Most borrowers see self-certification as a short-term remedy and switch products by remortgaging after a few years. This is possible because their credit rating improves, authorised accounts become available or equity is realised from an increase in property value. The change in circumstances allows access to better mortgage products and thus more favourable interest rates.

Recommended websites

www.1st4ukmortgage.co.uk
Find the best deal from 7,000 products with specific sections dealing with the self-employed, first-time buyers and adverse credit mortgages.

www.1stmortgageline.co.uk
A mortgage bureau that specialises in lending to people with adverse credit and County Court Judgements.

www.acmortgages.co.uk
'Alpha One' claims to find better deals than are offered by high street lenders, for people with an adverse credit history.

(12)

The Mortgage Maze

Even a seasoned investor can fail to comprehend the terms and expressions professionals use to describe mortgages. Banks, building societies, intermediaries and brokers all suffer from the same infuriating habit of talking gobbledegook! First-time homebuyers have little hope of understanding anything but the bare essentials and certainly not enough to make an informed decision on how they should go about borrowing thousands of pounds.

Borrowing money is a straightforward process with a comparatively predictable outcome, providing you appreciate the terms and conditions relative to the kind of loan being offered. This chapter describes the different types of mortgage in a clear and concise way, so you can then choose the one appropriate to your needs and circumstances.

In previous chapters I have illustrated and summarised such topics as loan to value (LTV), self certification, split equity, CCJs, guarantor mortgages, adverse credit and buy-to-let; the rest of this section introduces financial terminology and explains the fundamental difference between mortgage products. To all intents and purposes, this chapter is a glossary and one you may need to refer to several times before completing a mortgage application.

Once you have decided the kind of mortgage you would prefer, you can then arrange a 'mortgage in principle' and begin the search for your new home.

WHAT IS A MORTGAGE?

A mortgage is not just a financial loan repaid over an agreed period of time and where fixed or variable rates of interest add further debt to the outstanding balance; it is also a legal transfer of property, where the lender holds the property as security for the debt. The familiar term, 'your home is at risk if you do not keep up the repayments', applies to all mortgages, because the lender retains a legal right to repossess the dwelling and sell it if substantial arrears occur or there are other breaches of the mortgage conditions. All mortgages are based on the same principles – but there is a range of options within these principles and different mortgage products are created to satisfy the different needs of borrowers.

At the end of some of the descriptions of mortgage types that follow, there is a summary of five important elements of 'good value' products currently available ('good value' is a subjective term and assessed for these purposes using average personal criteria regarding employment status, income and credit details). The elements are:

- The fixed, variable or discounted period interest rate.
- The monthly repayment amount of an £80,000 loan over a 25-year term.
- The total amount payable over the term of the mortgage.

◆ Fees and charges payable (other than early redemption).
◆ The early redemption penalties (payable if the mortgage is changed to another lender during the term or if the loan is paid up prior to completion of the full term).

This will help you compare different mortgage types, because the data was collected at the same point in time; but bear in mind that interest rates and product details change frequently, so the data is unlikely to be accurate at the time of reading.

THE ANNUAL PERCENTAGE RATE (APR)

By law, lenders have to quote a mortgage product's APR, even though few people know what it represents. An APR is an attempt at quantifying the *real cost* of borrowing. It not only takes interest payments into account, but also the other charges and fees associated with the loan. This might include arrangement and administration fees, the lender's legal costs, valuation fees and mortgage indemnity premiums. Borrowers should identify the APR of all mortgage products they consider, because it provides a more accurate comparison of cost. Remember that although the rates of interest promoted by different lenders may be very similar, the APR (true cost) of each product can be very different.

One problem is that a mortgage APR is based on a minimum 25-year term, but many borrowers remortgage or switch products every four or five years, counteracting the value of an APR figure as a comparison tool. In these circumstances, it makes sense to identify and add together all the expenses associated with a product over varying time periods, then compare like with like.

REPAYMENT MORTGAGE

This is the most basic form of mortgage available. There are numerous products of this type including fixed, standard variable and capped rate alternatives (see below). Monthly payments comprise an amount of interest plus an amount of capital (borrowed funds). If payments are maintained, the loan will be fully paid within the term of the mortgage, though instalments in the early years consist more of interest than of capital. The simplicity and relative security of this type of mortgage make it an ideal choice for many first-time buyers.

One of the main advantages is there is a very low risk of suffering negative equity (having a bigger outstanding mortgage debt than the current value of your property), because a small amount of capital is always being paid off as the term progresses. However, moving home in the early years, when very little of the capital will have been paid, may involve taking out another 25-year mortgage for the new property.

INTEREST-ONLY MORTGAGE

The sole advantage of an 'interest-only' mortgage is that monthly payments tend to be lower than most other types, because only the interest on the amount borrowed is being paid and none of the capital. Payment of the full amount borrowed becomes due at the end of the term. These products are mainly of value to professional investors, as they can claim the interest element of mortgage payments as an allowable expense against tax. The intention is often to sell the property before or at the end of the term, thus raising enough equity to pay the borrowed sum *and* make a profit (assuming the property value has increased sufficiently). There are two main complications:

- Most interest-only mortgages have mandatory and exorbitant early redemption fees, which prohibit changing the mortgage lender to get a better rate in the early to mid-term years.

- The entire capital amount borrowed becomes payable at the end of the term, so an alternative savings plan or investment scheme is sometimes demanded by the lender to meet the debt at the appropriate time. The risk with an investment scheme is that it may not build up enough in funds to pay the end-of-term debt.

Good value 'interest-only' mortgage example (£80,000) APR = 4.6%
Source (2003): Abbey National. Your home is at risk if you do not keep up repayments on a mortgage or other loans secured on it. Be sure you can afford the repayments before entering into a credit agreement. Loan examples given are subject to status. A life policy or other insurance may be required.

Interest rate	Monthly payment	Total payable	Fees and charges	Early redemption fee
4.5% Bank of England rate + 0.75% over the mortgage term	£300	£169,824	£320 on application (£1,250 total completion, land registry and stamp duty expenses)	Benefits must be repaid plus a penalty applies for the first two years

CAT MORTGAGE

A CAT mortgage is not really a product in its own right, but a range of mortgages that meet certain standards – a little like the way that British Standards apply to some household goods. CAT stands for low Charges, easy Access and fair Terms. The government introduced the standards to help borrowers and savers identify reputable lenders and products of a certain quality. A CAT awarded mortgage may not necessarily be the most suitable loan for your needs and circumstances, but does ensure a reasonably priced and fairly termed financial package.

Good value 'CAT standard variable repayment' mortgage example (£80,000) APR = 4.8% Source (2003): Abbey National. Your home is at risk if you do not keep up repayments on a mortgage or other loans secured on it. Be sure you can afford the repayments before entering into a credit agreement. Loan examples given are subject to status. A life policy or other insurance may be required.				
Interest rate	**Monthly payment**	**Total payable**	**Fees and charges**	**Early redemption fee**
4.75% Bank of England rate plus 1% over the mortgage term	£454	£136,410	£170 on application (£1,100 total completion, land registry and stamp duty expenses)	None

CAPPED MORTGAGE

This is a variation on a 'fixed rate mortgage' (see below) and its title is descriptive of how it works. The monthly payments of a standard mortgage fluctuate up and down, influenced by changes in interest rates. A fixed interest rate product prevents the rise in payments for a predetermined period of time, 'fixing' the rate at a preset level from commencement of the loan.

Capped mortgages stop the effect of rising interest rates at a certain point – usually called the 'upper limit' – which means you benefit by knowing the maximum amount you will have to pay if interest rates escalate upwards. Capped mortgages rarely have a lower limit, so you still benefit from falling interest rates (capped lower limit products are called 'collared rate' loans). Unfortunately, these types of mortgages frequently suffer from high initial charges and restrictive terms, which usually make them a little too expensive at the outset and sometimes too inflexible during the mortgage term for first-time buyers.

Good value 'capped rate' mortgage example (£80,000) APR = 5.7%
Source (2003): Bristol & West. Your home is at risk if you do not keep up repayments on a mortgage or other loans secured on it. Be sure you can afford the repayments before entering into a credit agreement. Loan examples given are subject to status. A life policy or other insurance may be required.

Interest rate	Monthly payment	Total payable	Fees and charges	Early redemption fee
4.74% rate capped at 5.65% for five years	£461 for five years then variable (£505 at current rates)	£149,241	£210 on application (£1,399 total completion, land registry and stamp duty expenses)	Plus £100 (5% of loan payable within two years or 4% payable within five years)

FIXED-RATE MORTGAGE

Fixed-rate mortgages are probably most suited to first-time buyers, because they offer both certainty and consistency of payments during the first few years. Budgeting is made easier by knowing in advance exactly how much will be required for the monthly mortgage expense. The fixed period varies between one and ten years according to the particular product. However, early redemption fee periods can sometimes be longer than the fixed period, causing problems if interest rates rise excessively – at the end of the guaranteed interest rate term, the mortgage often reverts to the lender's standard variable rate. In addition, should interest rates fall during the fixed period, there is usually no benefit bestowed on fixed-rate borrowers.

Good value '5-year fixed-rate' mortgage example (£80,000) APR = 5.3%
Source (2003): Standard Life. Your home is at risk if you do not keep up repayments on a mortgage or other loans secured on it. Be sure you can afford the repayments before entering into a credit agreement. Loan examples given are subject to status. A life policy or other insurance may be required.

Interest rate	Monthly payment	Total payable	Fees and charges	Early redemption fee
5.39% fixed for 5 years then variable	£490 (then £473 at current rate)	£142,890	£414 on application (£1,100 total completion, land registry and stamp duty expenses)	2 years = 8 months' interest 3 years = 7 months' interest 4 years = 6 months' interest 5 years = 5 months' interest

CASH-BACK MORTGAGE

Remember – there is no such thing as a free lunch! Receiving a lump sum at the beginning or end of a mortgage term is an attractive proposition, but the incentive may be withdrawn or become repayable if the mortgage is switched to another lender prior to completion. It is also worth inspecting interest levels closely, because the inducement could simply be financed through higher rates early on or at the end of any discounted period. Many cash-back products offer up to 6% of the loan back. Just make sure you understand the terms and conditions.

Good value 'cash-back variable repayment' mortgage example (£80,000 with £4,000 cash-back at completion of the loan) APR = 6%

Source (2003): Leeds & Holbeck. Your home is at risk if you do not keep up repayments on a mortgage or other loans secured on it. Be sure you can afford the repayments before entering into a credit agreement. Loan examples given are subject to status. A life policy or other insurance may be required.

Interest rate	Monthly payment	Total payable	Fees and charges	Early redemption fee
5.74% variable	£508	£152,610	£480 on application (£1,100 total completion, land registry and stamp duty expenses)	Year 1 = 5% of £4000 Year 2 = 4% of £4000 Year 3 = 3% of £4000 Year 4 = 2% of £4000 Year 5 = 1% of £4000

DISCOUNT MORTGAGE

These are just what they say they are – an early knockdown interest incentive – but they usually only apply to 'variable rate' mortgages and offer first-time buyers no real help with budgeting. Similar to fixed-rate mortgages, they reduce the lender's standard rate for a limited period – but unlike a 'fixed-rate' product, interest levels still fluctuate up and down – it simply means the rate will remain below the lender's usual standard rate for the 'discounted' period.

The main advantage is that you get a bargain rate when interest rates drop and continue to benefit over and above the standard rate when they rise. However, initial charges and early redemption fees are typically high. There can also be a sudden and high increase in payments at the end of the discounted period, which may be difficult to absorb into an established or strained budget regime.

Good value 'discount variable rate' mortgage example (£80,000) APR = 5.3%

Source (2003): Northern Rock. Your home is at risk if you do not keep up repayments on a mortgage or other loans secured on it. Be sure you can afford the repayments before entering into a credit agreement. Loan examples given are subject to status. A life policy or other insurance may be required.

Interest rate	Monthly payment	Total payable	Fees and charges	Early redemption fee
1.99% discount for six months then 4.99% for 78 months	£338 for six months then £463 for 78 months (then £490 at current rate)	£144,027	£435 on application (£1,595 total completion, land registry and stamp duty expenses)	'Help With Costs' incentive repayable if mortgage is redeemed within three years. 1% of loan to be paid for up to three years.

FLEXIBLE MORTGAGE

Borrowers who consider this type of mortgage often misinterpret the word 'flexible'. It doesn't mean you can stop paying instalments at any time, for example, because income has been unexpectedly reduced; nor does it mean you can borrow more when an unforeseen need arises. Flexible mortgages were designed primarily for the self-employed and those who expect their income to rise considerably over the medium term.

Most of these products allow you to pay more than the minimum instalment **without being penalised** by early redemption fees; they also allow you to take a payment holiday **once a sufficient reserve of funds has been built up**. By paying more of the loan off early, you benefit by reducing the length of the term. In addition, interest is usually lower than some lenders' standard rates and, as it is generally charged on a daily basis, you benefit from making an overpayment straight away (by incurring less interest).

Good value 'flexible' mortgage example (£80,000) APR = 5.1% Source (2003): Royal Bank of Scotland. Your home is at risk if you do not keep up repayments on a mortgage or other loans secured on it. Be sure you can afford the repayments before entering into a credit agreement. Loan examples given are subject to status. A life policy or other insurance may be required.				
Interest rates	**Monthly payment**	**Total payable**	**Fees and charges**	**Early redemption fee**
2.84% discount rate for three months then variable rate	£372 for three months then variable (£470 at current rates)	£140,548	£550 on application (£1,100 total completion, land registry and stamp duty expenses)	None

100% MORTGAGE

If you have followed the advice contained in earlier chapters you will have no need to contemplate a 100% mortgage, despite the fact they may appear attractive to first-time buyers. There are several lenders providing this kind of loan – but be aware – most 100% products are expensive.

The reason why they are expensive can be more fully appreciated by analysing the loan-to-value (LTV) risk element. Lenders evaluate risk through several mechanisms, but primarily they think about worst-case scenarios, for example, if the borrower defaults on payments, would repossessing and selling the property raise enough to pay off the loan? The lower the LTV the more likely it is that sufficient funds would be realised, because even if the property value stagnated or fell slightly, it could still be sold for more than the amount borrowed. A 100% mortgage assumes property value will rise – and therein lies the problem – the lender simply trades greater risk for higher upfront charges and interest rates.

The Yorkshire Building Society, Sainsbury's Bank and NatWest are among those prepared to lend 100% LTV to first-time buyers. Some 'Graduate Mortgage' scheme providers (see Chapter 13) will even consider loans beyond this threshold. Scottish Widows offers 102%, covering legal expenses and stamp duty, and will go up to 110% for a select number of professions. Mortgage Express offers 105% to employed borrowers and Northern Rock goes the extra mile by offering 125% to customers who combine their mortgage with an unsecured loan.

Good value '100% fixed-rate' mortgage example (£80,000) APR = 6%

Source (2003): Royal Bank of Scotland. Your home is at risk if you do not keep up repayments on a mortgage or other loans secured on it. Be sure you can afford the repayments before entering into a credit agreement. Loan examples given are subject to status. A life policy or other insurance may be required.

Interest rate	Monthly payment	Total payable	Fees and charges	Early redemption fee
5.25% fixed for three years then variable rate	£511 for three years (then £506 at current rate)	£151,963	£495 on application (£3,300 total completion, land registry and stamp duty expenses)	2% of loan amount redeemed to be paid for two years, then 1% for a further year

ENDOWMENT MORTGAGE

There is really no such product, though many believe or imply they exist. Endowment schemes are combined savings and investment policies, sometimes sold as a vehicle to repay a mortgage. The theory is that during the term of the mortgage the interest element will be paid and, at the end of it, there will be enough realised profit from investing in stocks and shares to pay off the capital borrowed. The problem is that investments may not live up to expectations, resulting in an outstanding deficit.

Endowment mortgage schemes operate by having an investment policy *linked* to an interest-only mortgage. If there are not enough funds to repay the borrowed amount at the end of the term, policyholders may need to extend the mortgage term, switch the shortfall to a repayment mortgage or convert the existing mortgage into a repayment mortgage. All this assumes these arrangements are possible within the terms and conditions of the present loan.

During the 1980s and 1990s, some endowment products were sold inappropriately to homebuyers. Government intervention encouraged the Association of British Insurers (ABI) to introduce a new code of practice. Products sold since September 1999 have required the provider to undertake regular performance reviews, the objective being to analyse whether the policy is *likely* to be worth enough to pay the loan in full by the end of the mortgage term. Although this has improved the earlier situation, there is still no guarantee of satisfying the entire debt. Unless a safe and adequate alternative funding system is put in place at the outset, endowment products are probably still too great a risk for most first-time buyers.

ISA MORTGAGE

This is another version of the 'endowment mortgage'. ISA stands for Individual Savings Account and is a tax-free method of buying shares or unit trusts, life assurance and keeping a savings account. Although it can be used to repay an interest only mortgage, there are risks involved and first-time buyers might be wise to explore alternative products.

REMORTGAGE

A remortgage is not available to first-time buyers because lenders require an existing property (an asset) as security for the loan. It is mentioned here simply to explain the term. Remortgaging is becoming an increasingly popular way of raising finance to acquire a second home in the UK or abroad and to make improvements or extensions or to secure a better mortgage deal on an existing property.

TRACKER MORTGAGE

These mortgages 'track' interest rates in a similar way to variable rate loans. The difference is they follow the actual market, rather than depending on when and by how much the lender decides to alter interest levels. The two main types are 'Base Rate Trackers' and 'LIBOR Trackers'.

- ◆ **Base rate tracker mortgages** have an interest rate set at an amount above or below the Bank of England (BoE) base rate. Changes in monthly payments then automatically mirror the BoE rate.

- ◆ **LIBOR tracker mortgages** operate in the same way, but follow the 'London Inter-Bank Offered Rate', which means interest rates are determined by money market rates set at intervals between different banks (rather than a single lender). Payments usually change less frequently using the LIBOR method, but sharp and unpredictable increases can also occur.

Whether these products are beneficial or not depends on your knowledge of and confidence in the financial markets. Some banks, building societies and other lenders help spread the onset of interest rate changes over a period, thereby cushioning the effect on borrowers –

whereas tracker mortgage rates change with market performance, which can be erratic. Be aware that volatile changes in payment schedules can make budgeting difficult.

Good value 'base rate tracker' repayment mortgage example (£80,000) APR = 4.5%

Source (2003): Abbey National. Your home is at risk if you do not keep up repayments on a mortgage or other loans secured on it. Be sure you can afford the repayments before entering into a credit agreement. Loan examples given are subject to status. A life policy or other insurance may be required.

Interest rate	Monthly payment	Total payable	Fees and charges	Early redemption fee
2.99% discount at BoE −0.75% for three months then at BoE +0.75% for remaining term	£378 for three months (then £443 at current rates)	£132,642	£250 on application (£1,499 total completion, land registry and stamp duty expenses)	None

---

BUY-TO-LET VARIANT MORTGAGES

The introduction of the popular buy-to-let mortgage (described fully in Chapter 6) has spawned many variations, all of which have evolved from the same basic concept. Some of them are a great help to struggling first-time buyers. Specific schemes, such as 'let to buy' and 'rent to buy', are described fully in the next chapter.

FIRST-TIME BUYER MORTGAGES

Many lenders have devised mortgage products specifically for first-time buyers. These are always worth looking at because they usually offer considerable advantages, discounts and incentives. But beware – incentives sometimes only exist as an initial enticement – a means of converting you into a long-standing customer.

Typically, lenders will combine various existing products into one package with a few sweeteners added. These might include fixed-rate and discount deals with up to 100% LTV; plus a free valuation, a rebate, cash-back, free accident or sickness and unemployment protection insurance and all-inclusive legal and administration expenses. Some of the best discounted packages on offer at the time of writing were available from the following lenders:

◆ Staffordshire Building Society – tel: 0800 216121.

◆ Yorkshire Building Society – tel: 0845 120 0899.

◆ Alliance & Leicester – tel: 0845 300 2569.

◆ Cheshire Building Society – tel: 0845 755 0555.

◆ Britannia Building Society – tel: 0845 120 7063.

ARRANGING A 'MORTGAGE IN PRINCIPLE'
Once you have decided the type of mortgage you would prefer and the lender you intend getting it from, it is a good idea to apply for a 'mortgage in principle'. This should not cost, or commit you to, anything, but will provide you with several advantages:

◆ Estate agents will take you more seriously and will be more keen to help.

◆ Once you have found a suitable property, you will be able to act faster than competing buyers (who don't have a mortgage in principle).

◆ There is much more certainty of getting the mortgage you want and the usual last-minute rush to complete forms will be largely avoided.

A 'mortgage in principle' can be obtained by approaching appropriate lenders and completing the necessary application forms (the same as if actually taking out a mortgage). The lender will assess the information you provide and make a decision based on it, without you having to provide evidence of income at this stage. The lender will assume the information you have given is correct and, providing it is, the conditional offer they make will eventually be realised. In the meantime, they provide you with a written certificate or statement confirming the offer. Although most high street lenders have systems in place to consider a 'mortgage in principle', others may not – a quick telephone call to your preferred lender should be enough to verify the situation.

Recommended websites

www.mortgages.charcolonline.co.uk
This is a valuable all-round resource for information about borrowing money and has an impressive range of mortgage calculators.

www.mortgages.co.uk
This is a great site for exploring best-buy mortgages and to acquire full product information.

www.mortgagesorter.co.uk
Apart from supplying informative mortgage and home-buyer guides, there is also an excellent resource identifying the top first-time buyer mortgage lenders.

(13)

Ten Alternative First-Time Investor Solutions

This section covers a number of established schemes, special mortgage arrangements and government-led incentives intended for those who find more traditional forms of borrowing inaccessible. If all other attempts at raising finance have so far failed, one of these alternatives may help.

ALTERNATIVE 1: EXTENDED TERM FIXED-RATE MORTGAGES

At present, most mortgages have a repayment term of 25 years, but this is all set to change and it could have considerable advantages for young first-time borrowers. People are not only living longer, they are working longer too, which has resulted in UK financial institutions taking a more pragmatic approach to extended lending.

Thirty-year mortgages are not uncommon in the USA and Europe. In Japan, where exorbitant property prices excluded most of its population from buying a home, the markets developed loans as long as 100 years. With such long terms, borrowers never succeed in owning the property and only ever pay the interest on the loan (not any of the capital) – offspring then normally inherit the dwelling along with the mortgage. Although this may be completely alien to our way of thinking, it has helped the Japanese obtain homes they could not otherwise have afforded.

Despite more being paid in interest over the duration of the loan, extending the term of a mortgage reduces the amount of monthly repayments and is one answer to ever-rising and ever-more unaffordable housing. For example, a £100,000 repayment mortgage over 25 years at 5% interest would cost around £585 a month. Extending the term to 30 years would reduce the monthly expense by almost £50 (see Figure 18).

An even more startling development is that a group of leading European banks recently joined forces to launch the European Mortgage Finance Agency, which hopes to introduce a standard Europe-wide mortgage market. This agency could initiate the first **full-term fixed-rate** mortgage product – a 25 year fixed rate could be the final solution for struggling first-time buyers, many of whom are fearful of how changeable interest rates might affect them in the future. UK lenders have so far been very cynical about demand for this kind of product but, as they say, watch this space.

In the meantime, many high street lenders and familiar names will consider mortgage applications for longer than the standard 25 years, even though few advertise the fact. Make an appointment with your preferred lender's mortgage advisor to identify any suitable products that may be available. Of particular interest is the recent best-buy mortgage award winner, The One Account, which considers terms up to 50 years and has a maximum applicant age of 70. The One Account can be contacted on 08456 000 001.

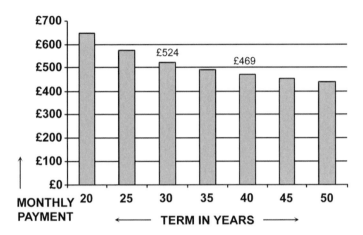

Based on a £100,000 mortgage at a consistent 5% interest (in reality, interest rates will vary throughout the term, unless 'fixed' for the full duration).

Figure 18. How extending the term affects mortgage payments

ALTERNATIVE 2: THE CASH INCENTIVE SCHEME

An existing council tenant or the spouse of a council tenant may be able to get a grant from the 'cash incentive scheme' to help buy a private property anywhere in the UK, providing they have been a council tenant for at least two years and the local authority where they live is engaged in the scheme. The grant comes under the 'right to buy' initiative and part of the process involves giving up all rights to the council home.

There is an application process and the award is means tested, so even those who qualify may not get the maximum amount possible under the scheme. The grant is usually paid direct to a client account held by a solicitor and discharged at the point of property purchase. Any new property bought must be owned for at least three years; otherwise part of or the entire grant has to be repaid. For further information and an application form, contact the housing department of your local authority. General advice and information on the 'right to buy' initiative can be obtained by contacting the Office of the Deputy Prime Minister:

♦ Tel: (020) 7944 3423.
  E-mail: rtb@odpm.gsi.gov.uk.
  Website: *www.odpm.gov.uk*

ALTERNATIVE 3: LODGERS

If you have enough space, you could consider taking in lodgers to help boost your monthly income. Done properly, this is a safe and straightforward way of sharing accommodation without suffering the potential complications from granting exclusive possession. Lodgers are distinguished from tenants by being classed as *licensees*; this restricts their rights to occupation and prevents security of tenure becoming an issue. In effect, if a lodger fails to vacate at the end of the agreed period and after being given due notice (usually four weeks), they become a trespasser and can be easily and quickly removed from the premises with a court order.

However, to prevent potential misunderstandings and legal misinterpretation, it is **essential** to have a written agreement that states the terms of the arrangement in a clear and unambiguous way:

◆ *www.landlordzone.co.uk* provides a free Lodger Application Form, which can be printed out and used to screen potential candidates.

◆ *www.legalhelpers.co.uk* provides a reasonably priced House and Flat Share Agreement, which is suitable for lodgers.

The Inland Revenue currently allows you to earn up to £4,250 a year *tax-free* under the Rent A Room scheme. Contact your local tax office for further information or telephone the Inland Revenue on 08459 000404 for explanatory leaflet *IR87 – Letting And Your Home.*

ALTERNATIVE 4: RENT-TO-BUY

Rent-to-buy is one of a rare brand of new investment concepts promoting a mutually beneficial relationship between landlords and their tenants. More importantly, tenants at last have a means of gaining a tangible financial interest in the rented property they are living in. It is the first-time buyer's ideal solution to under-funding. The scheme's success is likely to be based on the fact that it delivers reciprocal rewards to all involved. Rent-to-buy works as follows.

The tenant commits to a seven-year lease and is granted a right to buy the property after three years. The rent payable is set at the market value. Over the term of the agreement, the tenant acquires a 6% per year share in the rising value of the dwelling – possibly realising up to 40% of the price of the property at the end of the seven-year period, which should be more than enough to pay for a decent deposit. In return, the tenant agrees to pay for all maintenance required to the property. Any rent arrears of more than two months' duration is a breach of the agreement and causes a loss of the right to buy – the landlord can also terminate the entire deal under such an infringement.

Landlords benefit by having no voids, a secure income and a property maintained at nil cost. Although they may begrudge parting with 6% of rising value per year, landlords retain the largest share of capital appreciation and can dispose of the asset to the tenant without incurring estate agency and other marketing costs.

'Homelet' pioneered the 'rent-to-buy' concept and they welcome enquiries from interested would-be tenant-investors or the owners of suitable property (dwellings must be under 25 years old to qualify). Telephone 0845 117 6045 for an information pack or get more details online at *www.rent-2-buy.co.uk*

ALTERNATIVE 5: LET-TO-BUY

This scheme is so new that most borrowers and even some lenders have yet to discover it. 'Let-to-buy' is a variant of the 'buy-to-let' product described in Chapter 6 and could be better value for some investor landlords. The fundamental idea is to buy a new home while letting your old one and use the rental income to pay the existing mortgage. The concept provides several advantages:

- ◆ As long as the rent on the old property is enough to pay the old mortgage, lenders will usually offer a new mortgage for the new property based on standard income multiples. Result: two mortgages at normal owner-occupier rates, rather than one at the usually higher buy-to-let rate.

◆ Compulsory deposits are usually 10% to 15% lower than many buy-to-let products.

◆ Rental yield (profit) on the old property will probably be better than that of one newly bought because, assuming the property was acquired some years ago when values were lower, mortgage payments will be substantially less.

These schemes also offer the opportunity to retain and exploit a home that is temporarily too big or too small. It is also a potential solution for inherited properties still mortgaged, whose location or size makes them unsuitable for use as a personal home – 'let-to-buy' allows them to produce an income (or pay the outstanding loan) *and* allows the owner to borrow more capital for an alternative investment.

Anyone considering 'let-to-buy' should first discuss the situation with their existing mortgage lender, because they might legitimately object to the idea. Failing to inform them is inadvisable – you would probably be in breach of the mortgage agreement and the consequences can be dire. It is also important to inform contents and buildings insurers, because letting may invalidate your cover. Contact the following for more information on let-to-buy schemes and products:

The Mortgage Business Direct is part of the Bank of Scotland and offers let-to-buy mortgages. Tel: 0845 300 1604.

Your Move is a letting agency associated with the insurance company Norwich Union and offers free let-to-buy mortgage advice. Write to them at Your Move Head Office, Talbot House, 83 High Street, Winchester, Hants SO23 9AP. Website: *www.your-move.co.uk*

Finance For Living is a mortgage broker dealing with let-to-buy products. Tel: (020) 7023 7928. Website: *www.let-to-buy-mortgage.co.uk*

The Mortgage Option is a broker with access to let-to-buy loans up to 95% LTV. Tel: 0800 731 9408. Website: *www.themortgageoption.co.uk*

Flagstone Finance is another mortgage broker dealing with let-to-buy lenders. Tel: (01923) 840995. Website: *www.flagstonefinance.co.uk*

ALTERNATIVE 6: SPECIALISED MORTGAGES

The problem is not always an inability to raise sufficient funds, but more an incompatibility that arises with the borrowing system itself. For example, there are approximately two million Muslims in Britain and many are discouraged from opening a bank account or taking a mortgage, because receiving and paying interest is forbidden under Islamic Sharia law. This predicament forces those who can afford it to pay cash when buying property – but young first-time buyers stand little hope of raising enough funds and either turn to relatives for help or forego the opportunity altogether.

The Muslim Council of Great Britain has welcomed a new initiative by the HSBC, which it is hoped will address the problem. This involves the bank buying a property and leasing it back to the customer over an agreed period. The customer makes monthly payments consisting of rent and contributions towards the purchase price. The bank continues to own the property until the customer makes their final payment. This arrangement avoids *interest* payments by introducing a carefully calculated *rent* element and, although some have criticised it as a sham, others are satisfied it is a viable alternative to conventional borrowing. There are two variations of the so-called *'Islamic Mortgage'*:

◆ The *Murabaha* (deferred sale) mortgage involves paying about 20% of the property value upfront and then a fixed regular payment to the end of the agreed term. This version works because the bank buys the property and then sells it to the customer at an inflated price, thus avoiding interest.

◆ The *Ijara* (lease to own) mortgage is as described above and is significantly more popular, because it has more flexible options and a lower deposit.

These mortgages are gradually becoming available through established lenders. Application forms and more information about how they operate can be obtained from:

Manzil Home Purchase Plans. The Ahli United Bank (UK) PLC, 7 Baker Street, London W1U 8EG. Tel: 0800 783 3323. Website: *www.iibu.com*

The Ahli United Bank (UK) PLC. Tel: (020) 7487 6500.
Website: *www.ahliunited.com*
HSBC Amanah Finance. PO Box 59, Bond Court, Leeds
LS1 1LL. Tel: 0800 5877 786.
Website: *www.amanahfinance.hsbc.co.uk*

Another specialised product has grown out of our more ecologically aware society. The 'green mortgage' aims to reduce negative impact on the environment and some lenders offer contributions to appropriate charities or have strict rules about the kind of properties acquired. Most lenders also exclude any involvement with businesses that are known to pollute or harm the environment. This product appeals to conscientious borrowers who are concerned about these issues.

There are currently only three providers of a 'green mortgage' (all support restoration schemes):

The Co-operative Bank. Tel: 08457 212212. Website:
www.co-operativebank.co.uk
The Ecology Building Society. Tel: 0845 674 5566.
Website: *www.ecology.co.uk*
The Norwich & Peterborough Building Society. Tel: 0845
300 6727. Website: *www.npbs.co.uk*

ALTERNATIVE 7: HOUSING ASSOCIATION SCHEMES

Housing associations are the main providers of new social housing and they currently manage around one and a half million homes in England alone. 'Right to acquire' is the housing association equivalent of the local authority 'right to buy' scheme for council tenants. Housing associations seek to provide homes for the most disadvantaged or those in most need, such as young single people and the elderly. Some also build homes specifically with 'low cost home ownership' in mind.

The 'Right to acquire' scheme gives eligible tenants of registered social landlords (RSLs) the legal right to buy the home they currently rent. RSLs are registered with the Housing Corporation – they are mainly housing associations, but can also be trusts, co-operatives or companies, which are run as a business but do not trade for profit. Surplus funds are ploughed back into the organisation to maintain existing homes and to help finance new ones.

The public register of social landlords provides local contact details of housing associations registered with the Housing Corporation. You can access this online at *www.housingcorp.gov.uk/resources/register/select.htm* or telephone the Housing Corporation on (020) 7393 2000.

There are various qualifying elements to the scheme. For example, you must have spent at least two years as a public sector tenant or in accommodation provided by the armed forces; live in a self-contained house or flat that is your only or main home; and the property must have been built or purchased by a registered social landlord, funded on or after 1 April 1997 through a social housing grant provided by the Housing Corporation or a local authority. As long as you and the property meet the criteria, grants of between £9,000 and £16,000 may be available to help you buy your home.

ALTERNATIVE 8: HOMEBUY SCHEME

'Homebuy' is the equivalent of the council tenant 'cash incentive scheme'. It is funded and supervised by the Housing Corporation and backed by government to help release suitable homes back to those in housing need. The scheme is operated by a select number of registered social landlords (RSLs), which are mostly housing associations in England. To qualify for participation in 'Homebuy' you must be an existing tenant of an RSL or local council *or* be on a housing waiting list *and* be nominated by the local authority as being in need of housing.

Those who qualify can acquire 25% of the purchase price of a property through a loan supplied by their RSL. The remainder must be found through personal savings or an approved mortgage lender. Unlike a standard mortgage, the RSL loan does not have to be repaid until the property is sold, at which point the percentage will be calculated according to the value at that time. There is an option to repay it earlier, in which case the amount will be based on the property value at that stage. Some properties do not qualify for 'Homebuy' and these include:

- Caravans, houseboats and mobile homes.

- Dwellings sold at auction.

- Discounted properties or properties bought through a RSL shared ownership scheme, a local council or other public body.

- Self-build schemes.

- Property owned or part-owned by a partner, family member or business associate.

- Property in a poor condition.

- Certain types of rented accommodation or properties with sitting tenants.

Full details of the scheme can be obtained from the Housing Corporation, Maple House, 149 Tottenham Court Road, London W1T 7BN. Tel: (020) 7393 2000.

ALTERNATIVE 9: GRADUATE MORTGAGE SCHEMES

If you have graduated within the last seven years from a recognised UK university and have been employed on a permanent basis for at least twelve months, a 'graduate mortgage' may be the best means of raising finance for a new home. The main advantage is that this product doesn't usually take student loans into account when the lender considers suitability, unlike other standard products, and there are 'base rate tracker', 'fixed-rate' and '100% LTV' product options. In addition, some lenders will accept a parent as guarantor to extend the LTV to 102% to cover expenses (subject to application and terms). There are also various incentives often associated with these mortgages, such as an offer to pay valuation and legal fees.

General salary multipliers usually apply – three and a half times basic annual salary for single applicants and the same plus a second applicant's salary for joint applicants. The term of the mortgage is usually from five to forty years or up to retirement age (whichever is earlier) and there are both capital repayment and interest only options as well. The following two lenders provide specific 'graduate mortgage' packages, rather than just variations of 100% and discount products:

♦ Scottish Widows takes a realistic view of graduate finances. For example, they are unusual insofar as they don't credit-score their applicants, although they do take other loans and credit card debits into account when working out how much an applicant can afford to repay. This lender also offers loans up to 110% for certain professionals, such as vets, doctors and lawyers (but bear in mind, anything over 100% effectively puts you in a negative equity situation at the outset). Tel: 0845 608 0371. Website: *www.scottishwidows.co.uk*

♦ HSBC have a graduate mortgage available for up to five years following graduation. The product has variable options, up to 100% LTV and a borrowing multiple up to four times salary. Tel: 0800 494 999. Website: *www.ukpersonal.hsbc.com*

ALTERNATIVE 10: STARTER HOME INITIATIVE

The Starter Home Initiative (SHI) is sponsored by the government and aims to help certain professionals buy a home (if they can't otherwise afford to live near to where they work). The scheme is primarily restricted to various National Health Service workers, teachers and members of the police force living or working mainly in London and parts of the south and southwest of England, where property prices are prohibitively expensive. There are a number of individual schemes operating for fire fighters, social workers, prison officers, probation officers, transport workers and occupational therapists. Some of these are located outside the main regions mentioned and include Bedfordshire, Cambridgeshire, Essex, Hertfordshire and the West Midlands.

The initiative provides financial assistance through equity loans, interest free loans and shared ownership schemes. The type of scheme and benefits afforded depend on the area. More information is available from the Housing Corporation (see page 225 for contact details). A comprehensive 14-page brochure can also be obtained from *www.housingcorp.gov.uk*

Recommended websites

www.mortgageland.uk.com
This broker site claims to provide independent advice on the best mortgage from every product currently available in the UK.

www.nationwide.co.uk
If time is short, the Nationwide Building Society claim to give a lending decision within one minute. I tested this; they responded in less than 50 seconds.

www.whatmortgageonline.co.uk
This is a superb resource for first-time buyers and provides free guides and page after page of valuable up-to-date information on new products and schemes.

(14)

Choosing a Lender

The choice of lender is no longer limited to familiar names seen in the high street. The world's entire mortgage market is now accessible through the Internet and borrowers can select the most suitable loan from a vast and diverse range of products. Sheer lender numbers have also created intense competition, producing some excellent discounted and fixed rate deals for first-time buyers.

But spotting these bargains can be a difficult task because products are presented in the best possible light, with features highlighted and weaknesses concealed. Borrowers have to be ever more vigilant in their assessment of mortgage packages, before making a decision about which to apply for.

TRUE APR VERSUS HEADLINE RATES

As explained in Chapter 12, the APR of a mortgage is a better indication of good value than the headline interest rate advertised, because it combines all the costs involved over the full term of the loan.

But this assumes you are going to stay with the same lender throughout the term whereas, in reality, borrowers tend to change lender every five years or so to get better rates of interest and more flexible terms. If switching your mortgage is the long-term plan, an assessment of the first five years' costs (typically the fixed-rate period), plus any redemption fee, is likely to be a more accurate method of comparing products.

LOOKING FOR FLEXIBILITY

Anything can happen in the future – you could be earning more, in which case you might want to pay off your mortgage earlier, saving thousands of pounds in interest charges; or financial difficulty may call for a reduction in monthly payment instalments (known as a payment holiday). The degree of flexibility built into your mortgage should be confirmed at the outset, as it will determine whether changes can be made to the schedule, if and when needed.

ASSESSING REDEMPTION FEES

Early redemption fees are a crucial element affecting flexibility. If they are set too high, they can prevent you from moving from one lender to another and cause you to miss out on reduced interest rates in the future. Most fixed-rate mortgages have some form of penalty built into the terms. This is designed to discourage you from switching lender during the fixed-rate period and the practice might be considered fair enough, since they are giving you a guaranteed discount and are perhaps justified in expecting something in return. But you should examine products and assess what the financial consequences are for moving lender *after* the fixed term, as this will determine whether the redemption fee is a reasonable or punitive measure.

It is important to add early redemption fees to the overall cost of the mortgage, because the calculation will provide a more accurate assessment of the product value. This is a time when switching mortgage is considered customary, so lenders should not impose heavy-handed restrictions or exorbitant costs and any products that have them are probably best avoided.

OTHER COMMON CHARGES

Because the mortgage market is so competitive, lenders reduce interest rates to the lowest possible level to attract customers – but some also attempt to increase profit by expanding the margins of other charges. It is interesting to note that borrowers rarely challenge these supplementary restrictions and fees, despite the fact that many are negotiable. Bear in mind lenders are keen (and occasionally desperate) to sign you up – so always ask whether any of the following can be removed or reduced:

◆ **Administration fee**
This term can cover a multitude of miscellaneous costs. You should always ask for a complete breakdown of them, so you know what you are paying for. Many lenders add a small charge of about £50 when borrowers decline buildings and contents insurance. The amount of extra administration incurred by the lender in such circumstances is dubious at best. Let's face it, it probably takes little more than a mouse click and is almost certainly just an excuse to claw back some lost revenue.

◆ **Application fee**
Application fees are invariably paid in advance and

before the lender makes any decision about granting a mortgage. The motive for charging customers is therefore questionable, since the product being sought might never be provided. The justification usually given is that it encourages only serious borrowers to submit an application, thus reducing non-productive time and administration. With fees averaging between £100 and £300, it may also persuade some customers to look elsewhere.

◆ **Arrangement fee**
This charge is often associated with fixed rate and other special deal mortgages. Although usually described as being paid on completion, lenders commonly ask for a 'non-refundable payment' of between £100 and £300 to be made on application.

◆ **Booking fee**
A booking fee usually only applies to very special mortgage deals or limited supply offers where a minimum amount of funds is available. The charge is made to reserve the amount requested until the application procedure has been completed. Booking fees are not usually refundable.

◆ **Life insurance**
Life insurance is not always a requirement of mortgage acceptance, except where the borrower has a history of poor health or is likely to reach retirement age prior to the end of the term. Even under such circumstances, borrowers should make sure they are not tied to the lender's product, because there may be cheaper and equally agreeable alternatives available from other providers.

- **Mortgage Indemnity Guarantee (MIG)**
  The higher your mortgage LTV (typically 90% or more), the more likely it is you will be asked to pay an MIG by the lender. This is an insurance policy that protects the lender (**not** the borrower) against losses. For example, in cases of serious mortgage payment default, the lender may repossess the property and subsequently sell it – but not raise enough to cover the outstanding loan. The lender can claim against this policy to recoup the loss.

  Some set the threshold for paying an MIG as low as 75% LTV, while others don't require one at all (regardless of how high the LTV might be). The cost of an MIG can be anything from one hundred to several thousand pounds, so shopping around for the lowest rate or a lender who doesn't demand one is always worthwhile.

- **Retention**
  A retention is not a fee as such, but a measure undertaken by the lender to withhold an amount of the mortgage until certain work is completed on the property. This is common practice following the valuation process and can take new borrowers by surprise. The work required doesn't usually have to be undertaken as soon as the dwelling is purchased, though there is always a time limit and delaying it merely postpones receiving the rest of the loan. The problem for borrowers is that the shortfall (the amount retained by the lender) has to be raised from personal funds so that the purchase can proceed.

♦ **Valuation fee**
Regardless of what you might have agreed to pay for a property, the lender will have it professionally valued so they can assess their risk and calculate the LTV. Building societies *must* undertake a valuation to comply with the Building Societies Act 1986.

The lender will usually employ a local surveyor to undertake this task (sometimes referred to as the 'valuation officer') and you will be required to contribute towards the cost or pay for it in full. Standard valuation fees vary – typically they are £100 to £200 – and they can sometimes be combined with survey (property condition) reports, costing anything from £350 to £600. If properties have serious defects, a full structural survey will be required and these cost considerably more (see Chapter 19).

It is also worth remembering that some of the above charges and fees *can* be added to the total sum borrowed (thereby reducing the amount of upfront personal funds required), but taking this option will raise the level of monthly repayments. In addition, because interest will be added to the fee over the term of the mortgage, the combined amount you ultimately pay could be more than double the original sum.

TIED INSURANCE POLICIES
Lenders sometimes have *tied* buildings (and very occasionally contents) insurance policies associated with a mortgage. This practice is less common now, but an adequate buildings policy will nonetheless be required to

protect the dwelling against destruction and it will need to be in place prior to the mortgage release. If the lender's own insurance or one recommended by them is not used, they will want to see a copy of the alternative policy to establish suitability. They may also charge a 'checking fee' for the additional time required for this task.

MORTGAGE BROKERS

The service given by good and independent mortgage brokers are worth their weight in gold – the only problem is finding one that is *good* and *independent*! Brokers usually have access to mortgage products not generally advertised on the high street and they can scour thousands of loans to help you find the best and most suitable product. Unfortunately, some are mere mortgage introducers (termed 'intermediaries'), offering products from a select few lenders who pay them a commission. The only way of assessing a broker's quality of service is to ask questions. For example:

◆ Are you associated with any particular lender or insurance company?

◆ Do you receive regular commission from particular lenders?

◆ How many *different* lenders did you deal with last year?

◆ How many *different* mortgages did you arrange last year?

◆ How many mortgage products do you have access to?

◆ What are your qualifications?

- How long have you been operating as a broker?

- Is arranging mortgages your principal business activity?

- Are you a member of a professional organisation?

- Are you familiar with the problems faced by first-time buyers?

- What are your charges? (Many brokers are paid commission by the mortgage lender once a loan has been approved, but some charge the applicant to help assure impartiality.)

Even if you have identified a mortgage yourself by consulting a bank or building society, or have found a suitable product via the Internet, it may still be worth engaging a broker to see if they can find you a better deal. Sometimes they can get you the *same* product from the *same* lender – but with lower interest rates or fewer charges.

All brokers are licensed, otherwise mortgage lenders will refuse to deal with them; it is always useful to obtain the licence number in case you have cause to complain at a later date. The Consumer Credit Act regulates the industry and if a broker fails to address a complaint or acts in any way unprofessionally, you should inform the Office of Fair Trading who will investigate the matter and take appropriate action.

INDEPENDENT FINANCIAL ADVISORS (IFAs)

IFAs tend to offer a better service than brokers, because they are legally required to provide you with the best advice according to your circumstances. Moreover, they can sell products from *any* lender – not just those they are associated with. It is important to identify IFAs who are members of a self-regulating or recognised professional body, such as the Law Society or Institute of Chartered Accountants, because these organisations regulate their members and guarantee a higher level of professional competence.

The important ingredient here is the term 'independent', because a straightforward financial advisor can also be an agent of a particular lender or financial institution (a tied agent) and, if so, may not offer advice or information about the widest range of products. The charges made by IFAs vary greatly and it is essential you find out what these are before you consider taking their advice. Some are commission-based, that is, the lender pays them when a client is granted a particular mortgage, while others have a variable fee structure.

Recommended websites

www.360-mortgage-broker.co.uk
An independent brokerage portal that offers free quotes from 7,500 products.

www.mortgagecode.org.uk
The site of the Mortgage Code Compliance Board, where you can verify that a particular lender is registered

(registration provides the consumer with a greater degree of protection).

www.unbiased.co.uk
This is a recommended link by *What Mortgage* that will help you find a local IFA.

(15)

Assessing the True Cost of Buying

Experienced property buyers are usually familiar with the numerous expenses involved in acquiring and maintaining a home, but novice investors can find the volume of bills suddenly landing on their doorstep onerous and bewildering. It is only by being aware of these costs in advance that you can adequately prepare and budget for them. This chapter consolidates what has been described so far and provides a few simple analysis tables you can complete with relevant data, according to circumstances. This is essentially a 'checking' phase – a stage when you confirm that current income and proposed outgoings are adequately balanced.

PROPERTY PRICE (THE FINAL ELEMENT)

When you begin looking for a suitable new home, try to keep at the forefront of your mind that it isn't only the price of property that denotes affordability – it is also the array of **running costs** *and* the **stability of mortgage repayments**.

Running costs can be reduced considerably by buying new. Despite the fact that newly built homes cost more than comparably sized older properties, there are some advantages to buying from a builder:

- ◆ Reputable builders usually cover minor repairs to the fabric of the building for two years and, providing the dwelling has a NHBC certificate, structural parts are indemnified for 10 years. This considerably reduces the likelihood of experiencing unanticipated maintenance costs over the first few years of ownership.

- ◆ Many builders operate an incentive scheme whereby carpets, fitted kitchens and some kitchen appliances may be included in the price of the property.

- ◆ Newly built homes have to comply with the latest building regulations and this means they must meet minimum energy efficiency standards. Up-to-date heating systems, double-glazed windows and loft insulation also help minimise heat loss and reduce energy bills.

The stability of mortgage repayments depends on the fluctuation of interest rates. Although we are unlikely to witness the huge peaks and troughs experienced by homeowners of decades ago, an incremental rise of 2% over a year is still possible and would have enormous financial consequences for many.

For example, if interest rates rose by just 1%, the repayments on a 25-year £80,000 mortgage at today's average interest rate (5%) would increase from £473 per month to £521. This added financial burden could overwhelm struggling first-time buyers, particularly if they originally borrowed the maximum their earnings would allow. Fixed-rate mortgage deals are undoubtedly an advantageous solution to this predicament because, despite marginally higher monthly repayments, they offer short to mid-term stability and certainty. However, if the economic trend suggests falling interest rates, a fixed-rate deal is probably best avoided (otherwise there will be no gain from reduced monthly payments).

CAN I AFFORD WHAT I CAN BORROW?

This subject has already been dealt with in Chapter 11, but it is worth reiterating that if you intend taking a straightforward repayment mortgage with fluctuating interest rates, it is highly recommended that you incorporate a financial safety buffer into your calculations. Bear in mind that if interest rates rise by just 1% a year for the first three consecutive years of ownership, it could affect you to such a degree that your home becomes unaffordable. Unfortunately, rising interest rates sometimes coincide with falling property prices and this disastrous combination *can* cause negative equity.

There is little point in being overcautious because buying property will *always* involve risk – however, it is vital the risk is reduced to a safe and acceptable level. Once you have identified the monthly repayment (calculated from the maximum amount of a mortgage you intend taking), consider the affect of rising interest rates by using an Internet calculator. Figure 19 is a useful quick reference guide and shows how rates influence varying loan amounts.

Loan amount (£)	Monthly repayment			
	Year 0 = 5% (£)	Year 1 = 6% (£)	Year 2 = 7% (£)	Year 3 = 8% (£)
70,000	413.88	456.32	500.56	546.45
80,000	473.01	521.51	572.07	624.52
90,000	532.14	586.70	643.57	702.59
100,000	591.27	651.88	715.08	780.55
110,000	650.39	717.07	786.59	858.72
120,000	709.52	782.26	858.10	936.78
130,000	768.65	847.45	929.61	1014.85

Based on an initial interest rate of 5% and annual interest rising at a steady 1% per year.

Figure 19. The effect of rising interest rates on mortgage payments

The objective of this exercise is to gauge your own personal 'affordability margin' for the first three critical years of ownership, then amend your prior calculations accordingly and identify a new *maximum* monthly repayment expense. This may seem a bizarre route to assessing affordable properties but, because it absorbs the potential hazard of higher costs, it is much more accurate and promises better sustainability than traditional methods (such as a 'borrow to the hilt' philosophy).

PRE-PURCHASE COSTS
Figure 20 represents the conventional range of pre-purchase cost headings. The elements contained within it are not exhaustive – there may be others pertinent to your own situation that will need adding in the blank spaces provided. Some of the charges may be estimated at this

early stage and will need to be more accurately assessed later.

Description	Cost (£)
Mortgage application fee	
Mortgage administration fee	
Mortgage arrangement fee	
Booking fee	
Mortgage indemnity guarantee (MIG)	
Valuation fee	
Broker/financial advisor charge	
Tied buildings insurance (initial premium)	
Tied life insurance (initial premium)	
Property registration fee or holding deposit (usually only applicable for 'new build' dwellings)	
Property survey	
Total	£

Figure 20. Pre-purchase costs

PURCHASE (TRANSACTION) COSTS

Figure 21 lists costs that become due at the point of purchase (known as 'completion'), which is when legal title transfers to the new owner. We will explore these charges and expenses more fully in Chapter 21.

Description	Cost (£)
Property deposit (the balance remaining beyond the mortgage amount, which is usually lodged with the solicitor when contracts are signed)	
Solicitor's fees and disbursements (which usually include the following elements):	
• basic conveyance charge (solicitor's time and expertise)	
• local authority search	
• stamp duty	
• land registration fee	
• leasehold agreement (registration of new owner)	
• other searches according to locality (e.g. mining search)	
• extra letters, telephone calls or supplementary administration	
• VAT on solicitor's charges (not disbursements)	
Moving possessions (self-drive van hire or removal firm)	
Landline telephone installation charge (commonly payable when buying a newly built property)	
Retention shortfall (if survey proves detrimental)	
TV licence	
Essential furnishings (carpets, bed, seating, hob, oven, etc.)	
Total	£

Figure 21. Point-of-purchase costs

REGULAR ONGOING COSTS

Figure 22 consists of the regular monthly costs that will be involved in running your new home (excluding personal expenses). Armed with several blank copies, the table can be completed as you explore different properties and ask for information about gas and electricity bills, council tax, etc.

Description	Cost (£)
Mortgage payment (add 2% for safety, unless the rate is fixed)	
Council tax (beware the highest charging local authorities)	
Gas (ask to see bills over 12 months to get a true estimate)	
Electricity (ask to see bills over 12 months to get a true estimate)	
Buildings insurance	
Contents insurance	
Service or management charge (for managed leasehold estates)	
Water (rated or metered)	
Ground rent (charged annually, if appropriate)	
TV rental	
Satellite subscription	
Tied life insurance or a mortgage protection payment insurance	
Telephone (land line)	
Second telephone line for the Internet (if appropriate)	
Maintenance and repairs (calculate at least 5% of income)	
Total	£

Figure 22. Regular monthly costs of the new property

PERSONAL EXPENSES

If you made the lifestyle changes suggested in the early chapters, you should by now have a more streamlined group of personal expenses. These are often costs over which you can have the greatest influence. Figure 23 is a useful reminder of what you are spending money on now and what you will need to allow for, once you begin living independently (away from the parental home):

Description	Cost (£)
Food	
Mobile phone	
Car (road tax, petrol, insurance, servicing) or public transport	
Social events (e.g. weekends out or attending football matches)	
Cigarettes (perhaps now is a good time to quit)	
Magazines/subscriptions	
Club or organisation memberships (including fitness centres)	
Clothes	
Existing loans and credit card payments	
Regular saving schemes and investments	
Health and beauty costs (e.g. regular hair or dental appointments)	
Holidays	
Annual costs (e.g. extra spending at Christmas on food and gifts)	
Total	£

Figure 23. Personal expenses

CREATING A BUDGET ANALYSIS TABLE

You should now have gathered together enough information to fine-tune your budget and be able to assess with much greater accuracy a range of affordable properties. Despite the fact that many of the elements in the aforementioned figures will be estimations (by necessity), you are in a stronger position to make calculated judgements and enduring decisions. By factoring in your income, you can create a budget analysis table to disclose surpluses and deficits. There will be many opportunities to alter the figures over the coming weeks and months, according to changing circumstances and the different property data collected. In the meantime, it is important to recognise that the maximum amount you have available to spend on a new home is determined by a **realistic assessment** of:

◆ existing savings *less* purchase costs; and
◆ income *less* general living and monthly property expenses.

Remember that it is also important to provide yourself with a financial safety net to cushion any unforeseen events or interest rate rises that occur during the first few years of ownership. This will help prevent difficulties and turn independent living into a more rewarding experience.

Recommended websites

www.free-financial-advice.net/create-budget.html
This useful all-round budgeting resource is an American site, but UK visitors can easily adapt the information.

www.halifax.co.uk/mortgages/budget.shtml
The Halifax Building Society provides a quick and easy interactive budget analysis calculator.

www.moneymatterstome.co.uk
A fun and practical guide to personal finance from the National Institute of Adults Continuing Education (NIACE), which is ideal for students and all novice homeowners.

(16)

Finding Suitable Property

With thousands of properties on the market at any one time, it can be an overwhelming task to find something that is a suitable size, in a preferred location *and* affordable. There are two measures that can help:

1. Only obtain details of properties *within your criteria* (price range, size, age and location).

2. Once in receipt of property brochures, apply a *strict pre-selection* (short-listing) of dwellings you intend to view.

The level of borrowed funds (decided by personal assessment and a 'mortgage in principle' certificate) determines the upper price limit of dwellings that are worthy of consideration; a list of key features will further help streamline this selection process. It saves time and aggravation to restrict viewings to suitable homes rather than desirable ones, which may be unreasonably expensive or impractical.

ASSESSING KEY FEATURES AND ESSENTIALS

The secret here is to be realistic and think primarily about basic requirements. We would all like four en-suite bedrooms, a sweeping conservatory and heated swimming pool, but perhaps a home with a garage is more of a priority at this stage.

Choose six prime elements from the list below (Figure 24) as the **key-features** of a home you would like to live in. Mark three of the six as **essentials** the elements that *must* exist in properties identified for viewing. The list is comprehensive, but not exhaustive, so there may be other pertinent criteria you would like to add.

Number and type of bedrooms		
☐ 1 bedroom	☐ 2 bedrooms	☐ 3 bedrooms
☐ En-suite shower	☐ En-suite bathroom	☐ Fitted wardrobes
Type of property		
☐ Ground floor flat	☐ Upper floor flat	☐ End-terraced house
☐ Mid-terraced house	☐ New-build flat	☐ New-build house
☐ Semi-detached	☐ Bungalow	☐ Modern town house
Condition of property		
☐ No work required	☐ Minor works required	☐ Full renovation needed
Other elements		
☐ Car parking space	☐ Secure garage	☐ Small garden area
☐ Large garden area	☐ Open fireplace	☐ Modern kitchen
☐ Gas central heating	☐ Second bathroom	☐ Double glazing
☐ Original features	☐ Dining room	☐ Shower cubicle
☐ Burglar alarm system	☐ Lift access (flats)	☐ Balcony or terrace
☐ Fenced/walled garden	☐ Timber floors	☐ Open aspect
☐ Exploitable loft space	☐ Dry and lined cellar	☐ Exterior lighting/power

Figure 24. Property key features

CHOOSING A GEOGRAPHICAL AREA

The site of your new home is perhaps *the* most value-orientated influential element of all. For generations, estate agents have shouted 'location, location, location' to both buyers and sellers and with very good reason - it has more bearing on the price than any other individual property characteristic. There will always be practical matters to consider, such as the range of local facilities, public transport or motorway links and the travelling distance to work, family and friends; but there is also the potential your home might have to increase its value, which should be explored and quantified (see 'Up-and-coming or down-and-out' below).

One of the simplest and most useful tasks to perform is a 'neighbourhood Internet search'. There is a wealth of valuable data available on matters such as local crime rates, public and private school performance tables, the proximity to health centres and leisure facilities, pollution, traffic congestion, council service rating, the likelihood of flooding or subsidence, housing types, property prices and lifestyle information – and it's all freely accessible. If you submit a postcode reference to any of the following sites you will receive a comprehensive report within minutes:

www.checkmyfile.com
www.homecheck.co.uk
www.upmystreet.com

ASSESSING UP-AND-COMING AND DOWN-AND-OUT AREAS

Assessing the prospective value of property is not always easy. A good estate agent will offer advice and guidance, but bear in mind their first and foremost objective will be to sell you one of their clients' properties, regardless of its location. Intuition alone will also not be enough to guarantee success – but there are a number of observations that might help identify whether an area is popular with buyers and whether values are increasing. The process involves spending a few hours walking around neighbourhoods that interest you and taking note of the following indicators:

◆ **Scaffolding and skips.** The sight of these suggests owners are busy making repairs and improvements to their property. This is a good sign that an area is improving.

◆ **Neat and well maintained gardens.** This implies that owners are the occupiers, rather than short-term tenants who often have little interest in the area outside their accommodation.

◆ **Functioning streetlights.** Local authorities have a tendency to repair lights once informed that spent bulbs need attention. If people don't complain, it suggests a lack of community spirit and general lack of interest in the surroundings.

◆ **Graffiti and vandalism.** Although this is rife throughout many communities, damaged bus-shelters and smashed telephone kiosks should be repaired and graffiti removed within days of their occurrence – but this only happens when occupiers have some sense of pride and demand restoration.

◆ **The quality of local shops.** The types of shops evident in neighbourhoods usually reflect the kind of communities they serve. Boarded-up fronts or poorly maintained displays indicate shopkeepers are struggling to survive; while popular shops conducting brisk business signifies a flourishing local economy.

In addition to these straightforward observations, it is vital you visit the local council office and speak to a planning officer who will advise about any new developments intended for the area. Major demolition or construction proposals can have a severe impact on a community's economic structure, particularly if it involves the loss or introduction of a significant local employer. Such changes might lead to an area rising or falling rapidly in popularity.

Speaking to local people in a shop or at a bus stop is probably the easiest and quickest method of gaining valuable 'insider' information. Locals are usually aware about what is happening to their neighbourhood and are often more than willing to divulge the details to a friendly and inquisitive visitor.

USING HIGH STREET ESTATE AGENTS

Despite being much maligned, estate agents remain the customary route to extensive information about local properties. Make sure you visit each one in person and ask to be placed on their mailing lists. The key features you previously identified will decide the type of brochures sent out and will help restrict details received to significant properties. Most estate agents' mailing lists are updated every two or three months, so if nothing suitable is found within the initial registration period, be certain to re-establish your details with them.

It is worth remembering that residential property is a fluid and constantly changing market. Just because you have been unsuccessful in finding your ideal new home today doesn't mean you won't find it tomorrow – the 'for sale' board could have been erected in the front garden while you were reading this paragraph, so don't stop looking!

ACCESSING INTERNET PROPERTY SITES

The Internet continues to build into a formidable source of properties for sale, but it is becoming so vast that searching for a suitable home can be a little like trying to find a needle in a haystack. Mountains of property details churn from the printer – hours disappear – while fatigue, frustration and confusion mount. To remedy this situation, it may be advisable to limit your search to a few carefully chosen sites you can visit on a regular basis. In addition to local estate agents, who will have a website address of their own (check their advertisements or letterheads), try a few of the following:

www.assertahome.com	*www.housenet.co.uk*
www.easier.co.uk	*www.housewb.co.uk*
www.finadaproperty.com	*www.numberone4property.co.uk*
www.fish4homes.co.uk	*www.primelocation.com*
www.home.co.uk	*www.privatehousesale.co.uk*
www.homepages.co.uk	*www.propertyfinder.co.uk*
www.home-sale.co.uk	*www.rightmove.co.uk*
www.house-moving.co.uk	*www.ukpropertyshop.co.uk*

CHECKING OUT NEW-BUILD DEVELOPMENTS

If a newly built home is desirable and financially feasible, you should have no difficulties finding something to tempt you in your chosen area. There are thousands of new housing estates and apartment blocks springing up throughout the country, partly due to the fact that government is encouraging the construction of new stock to help fill the shortfall anticipated over the coming decade.

However, not all developers are equal and some take undesirable risks with land they buy and build on, despite completing legally required ground checks and site surveys. We have all heard the horror stories of historic flood planes and landfill sites being redeveloped, sometimes causing dreadful problems in later years, and these simply reaffirm the importance of researching prior land use *before* buying property built on it. Seek information from the builder *and* from the local planning authority, as well as from local people who may remember what existed on the site prior to development. Regardless of whether doubts exist about the suitability or stability of the land, ask the builders what underwritten structural guarantees will be provided (such as an NHCB certificate – see below).

There are several key matters first-time buyers should consider when viewing or deliberating the purchase of a newly built property:

1. Be certain to examine all phases of the builder's development plan before choosing a particular plot or property. What may at first sight appear an ideal south-facing home with panoramic views could eventually be surrounded and obscured by other

buildings that have yet to be built. Make sure you are fully aware of how the estate will appear upon completion.

2. Buying new property is subject to the same rights of price negotiation as older and more established homes on the secondary market, particularly as the construction phase reaches completion or during the lean winter months, when traditionally there are fewer people willing to buy. Builders will also often consider reducing the price by 5% to 10% if you are in a position to act quickly.

3. Many newly built leasehold properties are subject to a mandatory management or service charge covering the cost of, for example, communal garden upkeep and exterior painting. The initial charge levied while the development is under construction is usually subsidised by the builder to encourage sales. Bear in mind that the cost could increase considerably once the builder has vacated the site and services have to be provided at a standard charge by alternative contractors.

4. Try to look beyond the façade of a show-house. Remember that professional interior designers have been employed to 'dress' the accommodation and make it appear enticing. Furnishings, decoration and added features are unlikely to be provided in the home you actually buy, so avert your eyes from these trappings and look more closely at the build quality and space provided. If alternative units are under construction or have been completed, ask to view these rather than the show house itself.

5. Visit other developments by the same builder to assess how properties have weathered and matured. Don't be afraid to knock on doors to procure owners' opinions about the builder's quality of construction and after-sales service.

WHAT IS AN NHBC WARRANTY?

The vast majority of new properties are protected by an NHBC (National House Building Council) warranty or equivalent and any that are not are probably best avoided. This type of insurance safeguards the building against **major** structural defects for a period of 10 years from construction. It is important to recognise that an NHBC certificate is not a substitute for comprehensive building insurance, which will still be required to guard against malicious, accidental or weather-related damage.

UNDERSTANDING PROPERTY AUCTIONS

Auctions are wonderful events for cautious and experienced bargain-hunters – but novice first-time buyers can find themselves treading blindly through a minefield of potential problems.

The advantages include:

◆ The buying process is fast and, once the auctioneer's hammer falls and your bid is accepted, you immediately become the legal owner. The selling system is so swift it prevents any opportunity to be gazumped.

◆ Auctions usually contain properties that never reach the traditional market, so you may encounter dwellings that you would not otherwise get the opportunity to buy.

- Although most properties at auction have a reserve value (that is, a minimum selling price), these are usually well below market value, which means there are almost always plenty of bargains available.

The disadvantages include:

- Getting carried away with the heat of the moment and bidding too much for a property.

- Paying for a survey prior to auction (surveys are compulsory if a mortgage is involved in the proposed purchase), but then unsuccessfully bidding for the dwelling, once the auction gets underway. The survey becomes an unproductive expense as a result.

- The temptation to 'buy blind' (that is, without viewing the property or procuring a professional survey), so as not to miss out on what might seem on paper to be a potential bargain.

Property auctions are usually advertised in local news-papers and estate agents are often aware of forthcoming events. Notices are also displayed on specific properties announcing the date and venue of proceedings. If you are considering attending an auction and plan to bid at it, make certain you:

- View the dwelling beforehand and scrutinise its condition.

- Assess carefully the estimated cost of repair.

- Study the market value by comparing it with similar property in the area.

- Set a strict limit on how much you would be prepared to pay for the dwelling.

- Have a comprehensive survey undertaken.

- Make all necessary financial arrangements for the purchase prior to the auction (including a 'mortgage in principle').

- Obtain the auctioneer's catalogue or brochure in advance and read the small print *very carefully*. There will be clues given about the property's condition and any planning restrictions affecting it.

- Instruct your conveyancing solicitor in advance of the auction and get them to undertake local searches and check the property title.

If your bid is successful, you will be asked to pay a non-refundable deposit of 10% and receive a countersigned Memorandum of Agreement from the auctioneer or seller's agent before leaving the venue. The purchase then continues in the traditional manner. The fundamental difference between buying at auction and buying from the conventional residential sales market is that, if you decide to back out of the purchase, you lose your deposit.

CONSIDERING REPOSSESSED PROPERTY

Repossessed homes often end up on auction lists because the creditors (usually a bank or building society) want to dispose of them quickly. A repossessed property is one reclaimed by a lender following severe mortgage payment default and, as a direct consequence of the occupier being grudgingly forced out of their home, there can be a multitude of problems evident at the property.

Some take clandestine revenge on the lender by removing anything that hasn't been nailed down or they may cause extensive damage to fittings and fixtures. In severe cases, underfloor water pipes have been found punctured and holes punched into roofing felt. Although the actions of bitter prior occupiers might be considered understandable, given the circumstances, this degree of vandalism can be expensive to new owners who later discover it.

A repossessed property can be bought at a bargain price – but be aware that it may have concealed problems. Undertake an extensive survey and assess the full cost of appliance, system, fixture and fitting reinstatement.

THE ADVANTAGES OF FREEHOLD PROPERTY

There are considerable advantages to buying freehold property, because it provides you with the right to live in it in perpetuity (forever). In addition, there are no leasehold restrictions, terms or conditions to observe (see below). The 'freehold' element of residential property is quantifiable, that is, it has value. Many buyers are prepared to pay slightly more for the added security and flexibility a freehold dwelling provides, particularly in areas where short leasehold terms (99 years or less) are common.

CONSIDERING LEASEHOLD PROPERTY

A leasehold property is strictly owned by other people or a company (the freeholder) who grant the lessee the right to live in it for a predetermined period of time. Many properties are leasehold for 999 years (or the remainder of) but others are for much more restricted periods. It is now common to see lease terms of 99 years or less within large city boundaries, where planners expect the future application and value of land to change dramatically.

Short leasehold periods can seriously affect value and saleability. For example, new buyers may find it very difficult to acquire a mortgage when a property has just 40 years' lease term remaining and parents may worry about the residual value of a home bought primarily as an inheritance for their children. These concerns discourage people from buying short-term leasehold property, particularly where the value has been seen to fall in line with the small amount of term remaining. It has to be remembered that, at the end of the leasehold term, property ownership will revert to the freeholder.

A leasehold dwelling is also subject to a written 'lease', which is a legal document comprising terms and conditions associated with the property. It is essential that buyers discuss the lease with their solicitor **before** buying, because some are very restrictive. Many prohibit letting, keeping pets, altering the exterior structure, hanging washing out to dry and erecting satellite dishes. The document also records the arrangements for paying service charges and ground rent and explains who is responsible for maintaining the building.

Recommended websites
www.firstrungnow.com
This site deals entirely with co-ownership – a process of

sharing the expense of property investment with other like-minded people. It claims to be able to link those who are looking for other co-owners across the UK and provides advice, information and assistance.

www.propertyauctions.com
Everything you ever wanted to know about auctions, including details of forthcoming events throughout the UK.

www.smartnewhomes.com
This site is a showcase for all the major builders and developers. Find what is being built and where, throughout the country.

17

Viewing Property

Apart from completion day, when the keys of a new home are handed over, the viewing process has to be one of the most enjoyable stages of investing in property. It offers a chance to study the way other people live their lives. You can learn about their idiosyncrasies, their tastes and aspirations. You can also acquire knowledge about the dwelling they call home and try to find out why they want to leave it. A viewing appointment is much more than a property inspection – it is an opportunity to gain information, which you can later exploit when negotiating the price.

BOOKING AN APPOINTMENT

Once you have decided to view one or more properties from the details agents have sent you, it is important to book a convenient appointment as soon as possible. Some homes placed on the open market are termed 'hot properties' by estate agents – which means they have highly desirable qualities and are situated in popular areas of town. These dwellings usually sell very quickly, so any delay in viewing may provide an opportunity for others to make offers ahead of you.

GOING ACCOMPANIED TO VIEW A PROPERTY

It is never a good idea to undertake viewings on your own,

unless this would otherwise entail the appointment having to be postponed for another day. A second opinion and another pair of eyes are always advantageous. A partner, friend or colleague may register things you miss and they can also help distract a particularly talkative agent or owner, allowing you to concentrate fully on the matter in hand. If there is no option but to go unaccompanied, carry a mobile phone with you and make sure you let a trusted friend know where you have gone and when you are due back.

GOING PREPARED

The viewing will probably take between 30 and 45 minutes, so make sure you give yourself enough time to complete it without rushing. It is also important you write down all the questions you want to ask either the agent or the owner (if available), because crucial issues can easily be overlooked at a nervous first viewing.

Since the introduction of the Property Misdescriptions Act, estate agents have had to be very careful about the nature of text entered into a property detail sheet. Descriptions must be accurate and nothing is allowed that might mislead or misinform. This has caused brochures to become all too brief – they are not just concise, but often over-condensed and inadequate. Viewers therefore generally have scant initial information to go on and will need to confirm room dimensions, inclusive fixtures and fittings and all other relevant data on the day of the property inspection.

The owner might already have vacated a property being viewed and in such circumstances the electricity will probably be disconnected. It is always worth taking a wide-beam torch on appointments, just in case internal lighting is unavailable. It is also useful to have a camera handy, because photographs can be an invaluable memory aid, particularly when viewing lots of different properties over a short period of time. Always forewarn agents and owners before taking photographs, otherwise you run the risk of offending them and this could cause problems later.

THE AGENT'S INTENTION

It will come as no surprise to learn that the agent's sole intention is to sell you a property. However, what you may not know is that estate agents are passionate about selling to first-time buyers, mainly because they see them as malleable and gullible. They believe first-time buyers:

- are less likely to negotiate on price;

- lack property viewing experience;

- will believe almost anything the agent tells them;

- can be manipulated into buying almost any property; and

- do not have a property to sell and therefore are ready, willing and able buyers.

In short, first-time buyers are an estate agent's ideal investor and they will usually go the extra mile, chauffeur them to properties and spend more time with them than with other potential buyers, simply because they believe there is a greater likelihood of gaining commission. That 'something' won't necessarily be a dwelling that is suitable or affordable – some agents are very good at talking-up the positives and concealing the negatives – and your task will be to uncover *all* the negatives that might exist. Remember, agents are not your friends and are unlikely to consider your circumstances when promoting a purchase. Their main intention is to prise money from your pocket to benefit themselves and their client-owners.

THE OWNER'S INTENTION

One might imagine the owner's intention is the same as the agent's, that is, to sell their home to the first person that makes an acceptable offer. But this oversimplifies what can be a more intricate state of affairs. Some vendors are in complicated financial or emotional situations, such as divorce proceedings, redundancy or are grieving the recent death of a partner. These circumstances may have forced them into selling the home when, in reality, it may be the very last thing they want to do. Selling could symbolise the end of a chapter in their lives and they may be leaving cherished or painful memories behind. Either way, the process is likely to be traumatic.

While this may have little significance to viewers, it goes a long way to explaining what some will interpret as bizarre and contradictory behaviour. You will probably be fortunate enough not to meet many such owners during your search for a suitable new home, but if you do, bear in mind they could be going through a difficult, worrying or distressing period.

Then there are the proud owners – the ones who will explain their history of occupying the property in fine detail. They will relish describing how they knocked through to the kitchen, giving the house a modern open-plan feel; or how the creation of a downstairs cloakroom is a boon when old Aunt Glad comes to stay; or that they have the biggest collection of garden gnomes in the town and, if you decide to buy the house, they might even leave a few as permanent fixtures. Regardless of whether you find their 20-year-old alterations, eighties decorating flair or ornamental garden obsession an advantage or a disaster, you should always try to be polite – no matter how difficult it might be.

Having contact with property owners is sometimes unavoidable and it is worth noting that being courteous and complimentary can pay dividends. Owners find it difficult to rebuke cut-price offers made by people they are sympathetic towards and fond of. It's easy to say 'no' to the enemy – but much harder when the foe is a friend!

TAKING YOUR TIME

Some agents will try to rush your viewing appointment but you mustn't allow this to happen. You are inspecting what could become the largest and most significant expense of your life and a decision cannot be taken on a transitory visit. The agent's duty is to provide you with access to and information about the dwelling. Do not be intimidated by their concern about another appointment or, more likely, an overdue lunch break.

If they continually press you to move to other rooms or (worse) vacate the premises contact the agency office at the earliest opportunity and ask to speak with a senior partner or manager. Make it clear that you need a new appointment with a more understanding and competent representative.

KEEPING YOUR EYES WIDE OPEN

When viewing a property, it is very easy to be distracted by inconsequential things such as interior decoration, inclusive fittings and general cleanliness. Remember that these elements can be easily and inexpensively changed – but the location and design of the building cannot. View and inspect all internal and external aspects of the structure. Judge it according to the space it provides and positional merits, including the amount and quality of natural light and geographic situation. Carefully scrutinise the condition of the property and be aware that minor defects might point to bigger problems. For example, stains on a ceiling could be the result of a slowly leaking water pipe or a loose sub-floor beam could be the first sign of rotting timbers. Keeping your eyes wide open at this stage is vital – it could also prevent you getting emotionally attached to what might ultimately be a futile and expensive property.

TAKING NOTES

The more properties you view the more you will wish you had taken notes, because confusion between one house and another is inevitable. There is no reason why you shouldn't take notes while you are viewing though, if preferred, you could make them immediately afterwards, while the features and room shapes are still fresh in your mind. It is a good idea to pin notes to the property brochure together with any additional photographs, so they don't become lost or misplaced alongside other details. Remarks that describe internal features, the garden or perhaps just the shape and 'feel' of a dwelling can be invaluable reminders later, when you have several properties under serious consideration and need a clear way of differentiating one from another.

LISTENING, LEARNING AND QUESTIONING

It is easy to mention something to an owner that may seem quite innocuous at the time, but which could wreck later negotiations. For example, saying you have already seen several properties, but theirs is by far the best, tells the owner you are keen and probably prepared to pay the asking price to acquire it. The best approach is to say nothing or as little as you can get away with to maintain accord.

Try to redirect conversations about you into discussions about them and their property. Ask pertinent questions and listen carefully to what the owners 'give away' about their circumstances. Above all else, try to find out why they have chosen this point in time to move. Is there a problem with the property or the neighbourhood? Or is it just that their needs have changed and a different property would suit their situation better? Perhaps their children have left home, work is taking them to another part of the country or ill-health demands they move closer to their family located elsewhere.

You can also use this opportunity to find out how enthusiastic and prepared they are to move, because these matters will influence their attitude to offers, which could be useful later. Owners and their representatives must reply to enquiries openly and truthfully, but if you don't ask for information they are not obliged to offer it. One useful tip is to ask a deliberately blunt question, such as 'What are the neighbours like?' and then observe the interaction between the estate agent and his client. A nervous interjection by the agent suggests he is worried what the owner might say, whereas an offer to arrange a meeting at some future date is more reassuring.

A viewing should be thought of as a chance to employ skills, senses and instinct to the full. You will need to:

♦ Communicate effectively.
♦ Listen carefully.
♦ Look into every nook and cranny and create a visual reference of each room.
♦ Touch walls, doors and other surfaces to identify defects.
♦ Sniff out damp and mould.
♦ Recognise the truth behind gut feelings, hunches and first impressions.

NEVER FALL IN LOVE

It is a sad fact of property investment but there is no place for romance in the house buying process! First-time buyers instantly 'fall in love' with some dwellings, describing with careless abandon how they can turn them into a dreamy and idyllic home. This is irresistible encouragement to estate agents who will later use this knowledge against them. All agents know that an emotionally attached buyer is the easiest to sell to, so if you *do* fall in love with a property, try not to show it or be prepared to pay the price – quite literally.

EXPLORE THE AREA ON FOOT

Using a magnified copy of a local map, draw a half-mile circle around the property you have viewed and explore the entire area on foot. This will give you more insight into the neighbourhood than touring in a car could provide. There is also the opportunity to identify the nearest shop, bus routes, recreational land, train station, bank and so on. Repeat the process at different times of the day and in different weather conditions to assess other concerns, such as a busy local highway or school route.

UNDERTAKING SECOND AND THIRD VISITS

As an estate agent, it always amazes me that some people make their decision to buy based on a single half-hour viewing. Yet it is only on the second and third visits those previously unfamiliar components of a property become familiar, allowing the important aspects to be truly scrutinised and considered. Subsequent viewings are essential to gather facts and figures for a rational and calculated appraisal.

It is so easy for viewers to imagine things exist when they don't or overlook something that is staring them in the face. Try the following calculation as an example (do it in your head rather than using a calculator or pen and paper):

> Take 1,000 and add 40 to it. Now add another 1,000. Now add 30. Add another 1,000. Now add 20. Now add another 1,000. Now add 10. What is the total?

The answer is 4,100 – not 5,000. Use a calculator to check it, if you don't believe me. We can all misinterpret information and see something we want to see, rather than what may in fact be there. Second and third property visits can be used to confirm details, ask additional questions, firm-up plans or proposals and check the condition of the building with greater care. Never trust visual and factual information acquired at the first viewing because, just like the arithmetic above, nothing is ever quite as it first appears.

Recommended websites

www.burtonmail.co.uk/property/propertysearch2.asp
This is a great little property site from Staffordshire Newspapers. It includes a very handy checklist you can print out and use when you next attend a view appointment.

www.houseweb.co/uk/house/buy/hh/view.html
A short but useful guide to viewing.

www.ordnancesurvey.co.uk
Get a free map of any postcode region and print it out for your walkabout.

18

Making an Offer

Many commentators suggest it is good practice for a professional survey to be undertaken *before* an offer is submitted. A survey will disclose defects and, once estimates are received, an offer can be calculated inclusive of repairs. This is said to be a swifter and more equitable way of agreeing a price with the seller. However, while this approach may be good practice, it is not the best method for buyers who want to achieve a good deal.

Furthermore, the delay caused in arranging a survey and receiving the results might provide an opportunity for others to beat you to the winning post – this is an example of being gazumped before you even have chance to make an offer! It is therefore advisable to submit a preliminary offer and commence negotiations, getting the price as low as you can and then renegotiate again if there is a detrimental survey. This tactic is routinely employed by experienced investors and has proved to be consistently effective.

GAINING THE HIGH GROUND
Getting a head start will help you win the 'negotiation race' and this involves getting your hands on useful information. It's as simple as that. The process should begin at your first point of contact with the selling agent or with the owner and it should be further cultivated every time you view the property. Information accumulated will help you to:

+ set the level of the starting offer price;

+ decide a maximum purchase price; and

+ establish how far and how hard you can push the vendor while negotiating.

The kinds of information you need to acquire through inspection or extract from conversation include the following (all of which have the potential to be converted into bargaining elements):

+ The **condition** of the property (see Chapter 19). In addition to conducting your own 'visual' survey, you should also ask whether there are any property defects known by either the owner or estate agent. Bear in mind that the law expects both to answer honestly – but in reality, only a few do.

+ The **inclusive** fixtures, fittings, appliances and furnishings (for example, carpets, curtains, blinds, oven, hob, washing machine, dishwasher, fridge/freezer, satellite system, light fittings). The more you can establish at the point of viewing, the easier it will be to confirm them (rather than discuss them) when negotiations begin.

+ The **time** the property has been on the market. Estate agents will invariably be vague about this, unless it is genuinely a recent instruction, so ask the owner if you get the opportunity. The longer a property has been on the market, the more desperate the owner will be to sell – but be careful, because it may also indicate the property has a structural problem and is overpriced.

- The **reason** why the owner is relocating. Acquiring information about this will help you determine how motivated the owner is to sell.

- Whether the owner has found a **new home** to move to and, if so, the stage they are at with the purchase. If their own plans are advanced, they may settle for much less than the asking price just to be certain of achieving their own purchase.

USING THE FIRST-TIME BUYER ADVANTAGE

First-time buyers are the fuel that drives the housing market and most estate agents are keen to encourage and assist them with their purchases. Owners will also show a preference to sell to you, because they know you are not involved in a chain and are therefore likely to proceed smoothly to completion. You are, to all intents and purposes, a cash buyer, despite not yet having the money in your bank account. With both the vendor *and* their agent already on your side, you are in a unique and lucrative position. This is augmented by having a 'mortgage in principle' arranged, which will help speed up the whole process and further reassure all those involved.

The fact that you are a first-time buyer means you can negotiate that much harder, potentially bringing the price down further. Most don't even try, simply because they are inexperienced and nervous, but those brave enough to use their intrinsic value as a bartering element usually receive a substantial reward. Think of yourself as the person *everyone* wants to sell to – then assess what you think that quality might be worth to your particular seller.

STARTING WITH A LOW OFFER

Unless properties in a specific area are in exceptionally high demand, with buyers queuing up at the door, there are three golden rules about advertised brochure prices you need to be aware of:

1. Vendors **never** expect to receive the full asking price.

2. Agents **always** try increasing property values beyond actual market values, because by doing so they attract more clients than their competitors and boost their commission.

3. Agents' valuations are **sometimes** unreliable or inaccurate. An appropriate valuation relies on the number, size and condition of other comparable property recently sold in the neighbourhood. If there are insufficient 'comparables', agents will use prior experience or figures from other areas to gauge the price – and this is likely to be exaggerated to minimise the risk of undervaluing the client's property.

Long before a high and low margin can be considered, your task will be to assess how accurate the property price is (the agent's valuation). The method you should use is the same as used by the agent, that is, a study of local 'comparables'. Unfortunately, you will not have access to the true value of property, because you won't be able to find out how much houses or apartments have actually sold for; so you will need to collect pertinent advertised price data and use this to identify an appropriate brochure price.

When gathering comparable data, it is *extremely* important the following influential elements are as similar as possible to the property under scrutiny:

◆ Age.
◆ Condition.
◆ Number of bedrooms.
◆ Location.
◆ Type of property.
◆ Views from the property.
◆ Orientation to the sun.
◆ Features of the property (e.g. conservatory, large garden, en-suite shower).

The more properties in your survey, the more accurate the average comparable price will be. Measure your result alongside the actual brochure price, assessing whether they converge or contrast. If they contrast, you may want to reconsider the quality of your data and decide whether it can be relied upon for this exercise. If you conclude it *is* dependable, you can use it as a true valuation and calculate both high (minus 5%) and low (minus 10%) offers from it. As a general rule of thumb, submit a low offer first and see what reaction you get from the seller.

Offers should always be submitted to the estate agent as a hand-delivered letter, e-mail or fax, because these methods ensure a record will exist of the offer being made and reduces the likelihood of any misunderstanding between the parties. A typical example of a written offer is given in Figure 25.

Mr John Smith
307 Offer Road
Great Hopeful
Manchester
M77 9WL

E-mail: jsmith@john.smith.inf
Telephone or Fax: 0161 123 6789

To: AA Estates
     2 Many Homes Road
     Manchester
     M92 1FP

20 October 200X

Dear Sir/Madam,

I viewed the house you have for sale at:

14 New Home Road, Manchester

for the second time earlier today with your sales representative, Michael Helpful. I would like to submit an offer to purchase the property (subject to survey and contract) for **£175,000** inclusive of all carpets, all curtains, all light fittings, fitted 'Zenonay' electric hob and oven.

Please would you bring to your client's attention the fact that I am a first-time buyer and have no property to sell. I have already arranged a mortgage in principle covering the amount of my offer and could organise a survey and begin purchase formalities immediately. My offer (if accepted) is made subject to the property being removed from sale for a reasonable period and is dependent upon there being no other interested party involved at the current time.

Your early reply by e-mail, fax or telephone would be much appreciated.

Yours faithfully,

John Smith

Figure 25. Example of a written offer

The vast majority of first offers are refused. Some are refused instantly and without comment, while others may be declined after a few days. The time it takes an owner to respond is usually an indication of how seriously they have contemplated the offer – the longer they take, the more thought they have usually given to it and this should be considered positive and encouraging. Eager first-time buyers are likely to find the interval frustrating and there may be a temptation to contact the agent for an early answer – but don't, because it exposes your enthusiasm for the property, which in turn will adversely affect your negotiating position.

There could, of course, be other reasons why the owners have not responded. These include:

♦ Another potential buyer might have made an offer and the owners could be comparing the merits of both together.

♦ The owners could be away on holiday.

♦ The owners could be purposely delaying matters, because they are awaiting confirmation about an offer *they* have made on *their* next property.

♦ The agent might have been slow in communicating the offer to their clients (for example, sending information by post rather than by telephone). This could cause a response to take a week or more.

The best solution for buyers is to continue searching for alternative property, as if a negative reply had already been received. This will employ your time productively and it will help prevent you forming an emotional commitment to the dwelling under consideration. Once a reply is received you can deal with it accordingly and, if it is a negative response, you may have already found an alternative property to pursue.

NEGOTIATING

It is prudent to mention at this point that, even if the owner declines your offer, stating they will accept nothing less than the asking price – you *can* afford to buy it at that price, if you wish. Throughout this book I have advised that you should only explore property and mortgages within your means, rather than looking at inappropriate dwellings or seek to borrow beyond your budgeting capacity. So, although buying the property may not be the wisest investment (the asking price may be more than its comparable market value), it should nonetheless be affordable. Such matters aside, the more sensible decision might be to continue negotiating and get the price reduced.

Most property negotiations are antagonistic and foster embitterment and stubbornness among buyers and sellers. This approach depends on one or both parties giving way, losing face and backing down. Negotiating can reach absurd levels where the issues at stake are a 10-year-old washing machine or an amount of money many might spend going on a weekend break. Regardless of how you negotiate, it is essential you keep matters in perspective and remain calm. The goal should always be to reach an amicable solution, rather than follow an aggressive strategy that backs participants into a corner.

One way of responding to an owner is to justify how you arrived at the offer you made and why you believe it is a fair and reasonable sum for the property. If you have managed to find reliable data on comparable dwellings recently sold in the neighbourhood, quote addresses and selling prices in your letter to the agent. If you have reduced the offer based on the condition of the property, give specific details and supply estimated repair or reinstatement costs. This reply should encourage a review of the owner's original rebuff and create a situation ripe for concession and compromise. The owner could:

◆ ignore your response completely;

◆ justify his or his agent's initial valuation and maintain his position; or

◆ accede to your offer or go some way to meeting it.

Another method is to reply in a clear and resolute manner, stating that the offer is non-negotiable (it is the most you are prepared to pay) and time limited (available for say seven days, after which you will be submitting offers on other properties). The success of this forceful technique depends on how fraught you believe the owner's situation has become. The questions to consider are:

◆ Has the property failed to sell over a prolonged period at the price advertised?

◆ Has the owner recently reduced the asking price or changed agent?

- Is the owner now in circumstances where he must sell quickly?

- Is the owner committed to another property, which he may lose if he cannot dispose of this one?

- Are you primed and ready to walk away from this purchase, if the owner declines this offer?

KNOWING WHEN TO BACK DOWN

Until such time as a 'desperatometer' is invented, a buyer needs to use their own good judgement to assess how anxious vendors are to sell. At the same time, it has to be remembered that a seller and their agent will also be applying acumen to assess how eager a buyer is. Property investment should not be viewed as a game of winners and losers, because the most successful and least problematic deals are made between two equally satisfied parties. So, small financial gains might be considered a reward for undertaking comprehensive research; but the pursuit of huge profit often involves the heightened risk of losing the property altogether.

Negotiations always reach a stage where they can proceed no further and a potential buyer must then make a key decision – am I prepared to pay the amount being demanded for the property? It is impractical to give advice on this dilemma, because each individual case is different and the desires, needs and circumstances of the people involved are too wide and varied.

KNOWING WHEN TO WALK AWAY

Having set the maximum you would be prepared to pay

before negotiations began, you should already know when to cease pursuit of a property. It is effectively when an owner steadfastly refuses to give way and the price remains significantly higher than your predefined limit. Curiously, walking away can be the most positive action you could take, because it makes an unambiguous statement to the owner that you are no longer prepared to negotiate and this can push them into swiftly accepting your offer, albeit reluctantly.

CONFIRMING AN ACCEPTED OFFER IN WRITING

Confirm an accepted offer in writing to prevent any chance of the agent or owner misunderstanding the agreement. Include the phrase 'subject to survey and contract' in your letter, as this makes it clear that any serious defects, legal complications or adverse property issues could invalidate the offer. Finally, make the agreement conditional on the property being removed from sale, as this will protect you against being gazumped.

MAKING OFFERS IN SCOTLAND

The buying procedure in Scotland is fundamentally different to England and Wales. Owners sell property by inviting offers from interested parties and, once an offer has been accepted, a legally binding contract is created between the owner and the winning bidder. This removes the opportunity for negotiation, because the first offer must be genuine and accurate if it is to have any chance of success. It is also necessary to have a professional survey undertaken *before* submitting an offer, as to do otherwise involves running the risk of committing to a property without truly knowing how much repair costs might be. If offers made on different properties are consistently inaccurate and subsequently unsuccessful, buyers can face huge survey expenses before they secure a suitable home.

Recommended websites

www.housepricescotland.co.uk
Buyers of property in Scotland can access information about actual selling prices (not just the advertised price) of individual dwellings or data on multiple sales restricted by area. This can help bidders determine a more accurate figure for offer submissions.

www.landreg.gov.uk/propertyprice/interactive
Find the average prices of property sold within any postcode area together with other house price information direct from the Land Registry.

www.themovechannel.com/howto/buy/scottish-overview.asp
Learn more about the Scottish property-buying procedure.

(19)

Surveying the Property

Many first-time buyers are so concerned about saving money they fail to recognise the importance of an independent survey. It tends to become just another expense they will trim down or cut out completely, if they can. This is a serious and potentially expensive error. Complacency occurs because most buyers don't understand the real purpose of 'lender-tied' valuations and surveys. They assume these mandatory mortgage tasks are undertaken to safeguard both lender *and* buyer when in reality they *only* protect the lender. This chapter sets out to unveil the truth about surveys and why 'getting a good one' should be at the very top of every property investor's priority list.

CONDUCTING AN INFORMAL SURVEY

An informal survey should be conducted when you view a property for the second time. It is much easier to perform when the owners are not present; but even when they are, a simple explanation of what you intend doing is usually enough to complete it without a hitch. Inspecting someone else's home can be a daunting prospect, because you both know you are looking for faults. It is often helpful to keep uppermost in your mind that if you proceed with buying this property, you will be handing thousands of your hard-earned pounds over to the owners and taking on a debt for years to come. This thought should help you to complete the task, regardless of watchful eyes following your every move.

A survey of this nature is purely a matter of good observation and extensive exploration. Getting someone to accompany you on the second and third viewings might be useful, particularly if they have some experience of maintaining and repairing a property of their own. A favourite uncle who just happens to be a master builder would be even more useful, but in his absence a parent, friend or work colleague would suffice. The following is a summary of significant observations you should make:

Internal aspects

Doors and windows
Testing that all doors and windows open and close properly is the simplest of tasks, yet so few viewers do it. They then discover after buying the property that some doorframes have twisted out of true and some windows have been fixed shut with paint for years. Systematically test *all* windows and doors as you enter each room of the property and, at the same time, check for signs of rot by pressing hard against the timbers. Spongy, splintered or cracked surfaces should be considered suspect.

Dry rot
Dry rot is a very serious and invasive defect, which can affect both timbers and brickwork and is extremely costly to repair. It is a fungal growth created by damp timbers that have rested on or have been in contact with wet masonry, usually over a long period of time. Damaged timbers have a dull brown colour and cracks form along

and across the grain. Strands of fungus grow from a central fruiting body and travel outward through timber and brickwork. Spores of the fungus appear as a *fine orange powder* beneath affected materials – *this* is a sign to look for as you inspect property, as it is easy to recognise on windowsills and cupboard shelves. Unfortunately, dry rot often affects concealed areas, such as sub-floor beams and joists, making it essential that a professional surveyor checks these areas.

Blown plaster
Plaster lifting away from the brickwork is a problem that commonly occurs in older properties with central heating. The heat dries out the plaster and causes it to break free from the masonry. In extreme cases, the wallpaper is the only thing keeping the plaster from falling away. Blown plaster is easy to identify – tap the surface of internal walls with your knuckle. A dull thud indicates adhesion of the two surfaces, whereas a louder resonating sound suggests there is a hollow gap. To verify the extent of the problem, press the surface hard with an open palm – the more movement there is, the worse it is.

Damaged double glazing seals
If owners have prepared their property adequately for presentation to viewers, windows should be clean and free of net-curtains. This makes inspection very straightforward. Double glazed windows consist of sealed units, each having an inner and outer glass pane with an air gap in between. If the seal is damaged, moisture gets trapped inside the gap and condensation forms on the *interior* glass surface. Check each window for signs of condensation or any streaky deposits left by moisture droplets that

have dried. Units affected will need replacing.

Ceilings

Small hairline cracks are of no significance, as they are usually caused by plaster drying out or slight natural movement of the building. However, cracks big enough to slip a pound coin into are of greater concern and a professional should be employed to diagnose the cause. Slight bowing or discolouration (yellow stains) of a ceiling could be a sign of a new or old water leak from above. More significant bowing suggests the plaster has broken free from the joists or that the joists themselves have moved from their fixings. Wallpaper or (worse) polystyrene tiles on ceilings may have been used to cover a long-standing problem – any polystyrene tiles will have to be removed, as they are a fire hazard, while other coverings should be considered suspicious.

Roof space

Some owners may discourage you from inspecting the roof space, but by carrying a pair of kitchen steps in the car when viewing a property, it will thwart the excuse of 'we have no ladders', which is commonly used by those with something to hide. Check water tanks are properly lagged, roof felt is intact, timbers are dry and there is an adequate depth of insulation material.

Sub-floor void

Most properties with suspended timber floors at ground level have a sub-floor void. This is usually deep enough to crawl into but, in some cases, access can be very difficult. Your surveyor will need to examine the sub-floor void to check flooring joists and brickwork, so find out from the owners where the entrance hatch is located and forewarn them that carpets or furniture will need to be moved on the day of the survey.

Minor defects
Dripping taps, leaking overflows, peeling wallpaper, cracked windowpanes and loose switches or broken sockets might all be considered insignificant defects, but they also display a carefree attitude towards routine maintenance. The question to ask yourself is this: *Have the owners employed a similar casual approach to major defects and structural repairs during their occupation of the property?*

Dampness and mould growth
Moisture in a property is not usually a critical defect, as long as there is enough natural or mechanical ventilation to provide air replacement and circulation. Problems are however caused by the obsession of some people to eliminate *all* draughts, creating an airtight home in which moisture cannot escape. The average family breathes out several litres of humidity every day. Add a build-up of moisture into the atmosphere from clothes drying on radiators, steam from cooking and the daily use of showers and baths – and problems of excessive dampness and mould growth quickly present themselves. These can be a serious health hazard and, over time, they can also attack the fabric of the dwelling.

Dampness can also be caused by structural defects, such as a breached cavity wall or a failed damp-proof course. Signs of dampness are more likely to be seen on the ground floor and within the vicinity of exterior drains, chimney breasts and above or beneath windows. On upper floors, look in bathrooms and near ceilings (exterior roof guttering may be blocked or broken, causing rainwater to saturate the walls). Structural causes of dampness are more difficult and much more costly to rectify. They should be fully investigated by a specialist and any proposed remedies quantified.

Appliances and systems

As an estate agent, I can't count the number of owners that have telephoned me on the first day of occupation to complain about non-functioning boilers, ovens, washers, alarms and hot-water systems. Miraculously, the prior owners always report 'they operated perfectly well the day before.' Result: a stalemate where the new owners are forced into picking up the cost of repair or replacement. The answer is to test every appliance and system at the point of viewing. A plumber, gas engineer or electrician should be requested to examine anything that doesn't work or appears damaged. It is also a good idea to ask in advance whether manuals or instruction booklets are available.

Exterior aspects

The roof

If you own a pair of binoculars, take them with you when you undertake an informal survey of the exterior. Check for missing, broken or slipped tiles, as these can cause rain penetration into the roof space and allow the weather to rip felt or damage timbers. Also examine the flashing around chimney stacks and mortar at the eaves. Finally, look at the ridge tiles at the top of the roof and confirm they are all intact and secure.

Guttering

Confirm that guttering does the job it was designed to do, that is, transfer rainwater away from the building. It goes without saying that it would be best to visit the property on a rainy day and look for gaps, cracks and broken joints. Check that downspouts are properly secured to the walls and guttering is free of weeds. This is also a good opportunity to assess whether rain is being discharged properly into and through downspout drains. Water gushing out of them and onto paths is an indication the drains may be blocked.

Walls

Look closely at all exterior walls and check for any mortar line cracks, that is, cracks running under, above or between bricks. These are the weakest points in a wall and are more likely to show stress damage before other parts. Small fractures are likely to be insignificant, but gaps wide enough to put a coin into or any that cross through bricks may be an indication of something more serious. Mortar that has corroded or receded will need replacing (remortaring is an expensive job). Walls that have been rendered should be given special attention – check the render remains intact and is fixed firmly to the brickwork beneath. Any walls that appear to lean, bow or slope inappropriately indicate a major problem may exist with wall-ties or foundations.

Lintels

Lintels span over doors and windows and support the structure above them. The lintels of older properties were made from timber beams and these can rot if exposed to rainwater. Lintels can get dislodged when windows are replaced and viewers should check the brickwork above for signs of downward movement.

Garden boundaries

Are the boundaries clearly identified by fencing, walls or shrubs? If so, who is responsible for their maintenance or replacement? Undulating garden walls can be a sign of local subsidence – check neighbouring properties to see whether they are suffering similar symptoms.

TV aerials and associated cables

Aerials and cables should be firmly and neatly fixed. Any that are loose will require attention before they irrevocably disturb brickwork or timbers.

Garages and outbuildings

Make certain you inspect both the exterior and the interior of all other buildings on the site, including garages, greenhouses, garden sheds and conservatories. Check that doors open and close properly and that they can be locked. This is also a good opportunity to inspect the exterior areas for security. Put yourself in a burglar's shoes and assess the weakest access points – then consider what might be done to improve them.

Airbricks

Most properties have a cavity between the inner and outer shell and, unless they have been professionally filled with insulating material, they need to be ventilated. Check that airbricks are undamaged and free of debris.

Damp-proof course (DPC)

A DPC is installed into brickwork to prevent moisture rising up walls and causing dampness inside the dwelling.

The DPC should be visible as a thin black membrane in the mortar line about 150mm above ground level. Unfortunately, DPCs are frequently compromised by owners who install new paths on top of old ones, thereby effectively raising the ground level above the DPC. In such cases, paths must be removed and reinstalled at the appropriate height, otherwise damp problems will be inevitable. Inspect all around the property and assess whether the DPC is appropriately positioned.

Painting

All exterior timbers should be painted or stained at least once every three to five years, depending on paint quality and the manufacturer's recommendations. The sight of peeling or blistered paint on window frames and barge-boards suggests this task may be long overdue.

Trees

The proximity of established trees to dwellings can be a major concern. The *minimum* distance should equal the height of the tree at maturity, otherwise roots could potentially damage the foundations (see Figure 26). Tree stumps close to a building are also of concern because roots will gradually rot, leaving a cavernous void underground. The soil above the void will eventually collapse into it, which could cause the building itself to become unstable. Felled trees and their roots should be completely removed and the hole then filled and compacted with soil.

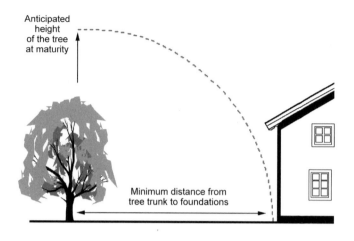

Figure 26. The proximity of trees to buildings

LENDER-TIED SURVEYS

Lenders typically require a valuation and survey to be undertaken before they will consider lending funds for a particular property. Most will also select the valuer and surveyor themselves, rather than offer the borrower a choice. The lender needs these assessments to confirm whether a property could be repossessed and sold for *at least* the sum of the loan, as this prevents financial loss being incurred by the lender should the borrower default on mortgage repayments. The lender also uses the survey report to identify defects subject to 'retention' (a withholding of part of the loan until the defects are rectified).

The purpose of a lender-tied survey cannot be understated: *it is a service **you pay for** to acquire information that is mainly of **relevance to the lender***. Buyers must not assume that a lender-tied survey report will be an accurate, comprehensive, reliable or independent description of the property's condition. They should instead procure their own independent survey at their own cost.

EMPLOYING AN INDEPENDENT SURVEYOR

Personal recommendation is usually the best way of finding a good surveyor, so ask friends, colleagues and family about any they may have used when buying their own property. It is also advisable to consider the following points:

♦ Surveyors operating in the same zone as the property will be more aware of local market forces, property values and common building faults (such as subsidence from redundant mining).

♦ Check the surveyor is not associated with or works for your mortgage lender, otherwise a conflict of interest may arise.

♦ Surveyors should always be prepared to check the roof space (providing access to it is no more than 3m from floor level), but they do not routinely inspect sub-floor voids, particularly if it involves moving furniture or pulling back carpets to gain access. It is a good idea to make suitable arrangements for access with the owners in advance and instruct the surveyor that you require a sub-floor inspection.

♦ The Royal Institute of Chartered Surveyors (RICS) is the governing body that regulates chartered surveyors. Members have to be qualified and experienced. The RICS operates a code of conduct and its members are obliged to update and enhance skills, knowledge and competence throughout their working lives. A RICS surveyor is more likely to offer you a professional standard of service and independent advice. You can check a surveyor's credentials by telephoning the RICS on (020) 7222 7000 or find a local member by telephoning the contact centre on 0870 333 1600.

♦ Speed is usually crucial when buying a property, so check how quickly the surveyor is able to conduct a survey and produce a report. Also find out whether the cost includes an option to clarify any uncertain aspects of the report.

♦ If concerns were identified from your informal survey, let the surveyor know so he can pay more attention to these defects.

If the surveyor has been instructed to provide a valuation, supply him with your 'comparable property' market research, as this will help him make a more accurate determination.

UNDERSTANDING THE TYPES OF SURVEY

There are basically two types of survey:

♦ the **least comprehensive** 'Homebuyer Survey and Valuation' (also commonly referred to as HSV, HBSV or a Homebuyer Report); and

♦ the **more comprehensive** 'Building Survey'.

A Homebuyer Survey is performed according to a standard format devised by the RICS and is appropriate for most conventionally designed properties built within the last 150 years. It does not provide a detailed report, because it only focusses on the major aspects of property construction and stability. A Homebuyer Survey will include:

- A valuation of the property.

- A description of any major structural faults to visible or accessible parts.

- Comments about faults, damage or defects that affect the market value.

- A description of the property's general condition.

- Comments about damaged or defective timbers (beams, joists, etc.).

- The results of damp-testing of walls.

- A recommendation for further tests and investigations by other professionals.

- Comments on the extent and condition of insulation and drainage.

- Guidance on the estimated rebuilding cost (useful for insurance purposes).

A Building Survey is useful for all properties, but particularly those that need extensive renovation, are more than 150 years old, are of an unusual design or have known defects. A Building Survey will include all the above (except a current market valuation and rebuild estimate) and reports will be in more detail. It will also include details of:

- Minor faults.

- Comments on the materials used in construction.
- Technical property and structural information.
- Supplementary information about the property location.

A Building Survey **does not** include a market valuation of the property as standard, though it *can* usually be included if requested at the outset.

A surveyor may recommend further tests or inspections are conducted by other professionals specialised in particular fields. This advice is usually given when a defect has been identified and more exhaustive investigations are required to establish the full extent of a problem. A mortgage lender is also likely to stipulate that specialist surveys are undertaken, when required. Reports could be required from:

- A structural engineer.
- A damp specialist.
- A timber specialist.
- A plumber.
- A gas engineer.
- An electrician.
- A drainage engineer.
- An arboriculturist (tree expert).
- A solicitor specialising in land law.
- A soil analyst.
- An architect.

Despite the type and extent of a problem, a specialist should undertake **the 6 Ps**:

✓ **Perform** a full site inspection of the problem.

✓ **Probe** and identify *all* possible causes.

✓ **Project** what might happen if the problem is not dealt with.

✓ **Propose** solutions to the problem.

✓ **Provide** estimates of repair, reinstatement or further investigation costs.

✓ **Produce** a clear and comprehensive report and summary of recommendations.

WHAT IS AN 'OWNER'S SURVEY REPORT?'

In 2006, owners will be required to provide interested buyers with a 'Home Condition Report' (HCR) as part of the Home Information Pack (see a summary of new legislation described in Chapter 21). The report will take the form of a very basic survey, arranged and paid for by the seller or their estate agent. The value and validity of information contained in an HCR is questionable at best and is certainly no substitute for a comprehensive independent survey arranged by the buyer.

IMPLICATIONS OF VALUATION AND SURVEY RESULTS

A detrimental survey report or valuation needs to be studied thoroughly. Serious defects are likely to result in a lender retaining part of the mortgage advance. A valuation below the asking price (or mortgage amount) is also likely to restrict an advance. The difference will have to be found either from personal funds or through further price negotiations with the seller.

Deciding to accept personal liability for the shortfall will involve you paying more than a current market value for the property and, should you decide to or have to sell the property in the short-term, it can have serious negative equity implications. So, the first question you must ask yourself is whether it is worth undertaking the repairs, given there may be other similar properties in a better condition available on the market? If the answer is 'yes' then start negotiating the price with the seller to offset some or all of the costs involved.

USING THE SURVEY TO RENEGOTIATE

The best way of renegotiating is to do it face to face with the owners. Arrange a meeting and present the findings of your survey and valuation. Explain that, according to the experts, the property is not worth the previously agreed price while in its current state of disrepair (or the price was initially inflated beyond a true market value). Provide the owners with a copy of the report, so they can read and absorb the evidence at their leisure. This also helps prove sincerity and openness on your part. The owners have four possible options to consider (these are presented in order of 'buyer preference'):

1. They could reduce the price to the valuation or by the amount of retention, so allowing the sale to proceed.

2. You could arrange for local builders to provide three estimates of repair costs. The owners could agree to reduce the property price by the lowest (or the average) estimate received, thereby allowing the sale to proceed.

3. They could undertake the repairs themselves at their own cost, but this would involve a considerable delay and you would also need to arrange a new survey and valuation with the mortgage lender.

4. They could deny the findings of the survey and valuation and refuse any further negotiations on price.

After being informed about the poor state or true value of their property, owners might make a rash initial decision to withdraw from selling it to you. If this happens, try not to react negatively or emotionally – many people change their minds and acquiesce after a few days' contemplation.

Recommended websites

www.rics.org
Find a local RICS surveyor and get advice about services and fees.

www.surveyorsreports.co.uk
Find contact details for all kinds of professionals, including structural surveyors and engineers.

ww.timberwise.co.uk
Learn more about identifying and treating dampness, mould, wet and dry rot in timbers.

(20)

Employing a Solicitor

The primary role of a solicitor in the house-buying process is to protect clients against purchasing a property under dubious or adverse legal conditions. They undertake this by investigating title ownership, checking official documents and arranging for and interpreting local search results. Their secondary role is to explain complex documents, such as deeds and leases, so buyers know what ownership is likely to involve. They also offer professional advice when appropriate and act as an intermediary between seller and buyer, until the transfer of property ownership is achieved.

USING A SOLICITOR OR LICENSED CONVEYANCER

Conveyancing is the legal process involved when transferring ownership of land or a building from one person to another. Historically, only solicitors were allowed to perform this task, but the Administration of Justice Act 1985 enabled licensed conveyancers to offer the same service. This broke up the prior monopoly held by solicitors and, as competition in the market increased, the amount charged for conveyancing gradually reduced.

A solicitor is a general legal practitioner, while a licensed conveyancer is a specialist dealing exclusively with property. Both are recognised by financial institutions, such as banks and building societies, and are equally able to perform the standard legal duties required by buyers and sellers. Just to confuse matters, solicitors' practices often also have licensed conveyancers on their staff.

CHOOSING A LOCAL SOLICITOR

By choosing a local solicitor:

◆ It will be easier to call in a person when you need to discuss, inspect or sign documents.

◆ You can hand-deliver copies of important letters and receipts, rather than having to rely on the postal system.

◆ In an emergency, you can arrange to see the solicitor at short notice (useful if telephone calls are not returned promptly).

The value of a local solicitor usually becomes more apparent as the purchase progresses and nerves get ever more fraught. Many buyers find it reassuring to have their legal advisor's office close enough to call in person, but beware – *convenience* should not be considered a higher priority than *quality of service*. If they are lax in attending to your purchase, it really doesn't matter whether they are local or not.

CONSULTING FRIENDS AND FAMILY

Some family members or friends may have recently bought or sold property and, consequently, they will have employed a solicitor. Ask whether they were satisfied by the service they received and have enough confidence to recommend them.

SHOPPING AROUND FOR THE BEST BARGAIN . . .

The fees charged by solicitors and licensed conveyancers vary enormously. Some have set charge rates, while others calculate fees according to the property price and complexity of the purchase. It is always worth getting at least three quotes from preferred conveyancers and gauging fees against the quality of service each has to offer.

Ten solicitors were asked to quote for a £150,000 leasehold property purchase. The least expensive was £275 + VAT – and the most was £625 + VAT. Though none of the professionals contacted were given an opportunity to justify their fees, it is hard to imagine the latter would provide £350 worth of extra service over the former.

It is also important to ask whether solicitors use the NLIS system (see 'Local Searches' in Chapter 21), because this can significantly reduce the length of time conveyancing will take.

. . . BUT BE AWARE THAT 'LOW PRICE' COULD MEAN 'LOW QUALITY'

There may be a temptation to go for what seems to be a 'bargain' solicitor quote – one that is significantly lower than others obtained. Bear in mind that such quotes may indicate an office junior or administrator will undertake most of the work, rather than a solicitor, thus reducing the cost. In theory, this shouldn't reduce the overall quality of service, because the solicitor should supervise the unqualified junior and check all work is completed to a professional standard. However, in reality, things might be *very* different!

INSTRUCTING AT THE EARLIEST OPPORTUNITY

You don't have to wait until a suitable property is found to instruct a solicitor. In fact, it is advantageous to sort this out beforehand, because there will be many other things making demands on your time once the purchase gets under way.

CONSIDERING HIRING THE LENDER'S SOLICITOR

Mortgage lenders sometimes recommend a solicitor or offer free legal services and, in such cases, the same solicitor will usually act for both buyer and lender. This can prove financially beneficial and help speed up the entire purchase procedure. It may also encourage a solicitor to act with greater care and attention, because he must protect both the purchaser *and* the lender against adverse legal situations that could arise (otherwise the lender will almost certainly sue him).

UNDERSTANDING 'DISBURSEMENTS'

Buyers are often confused over disbursement elements on a solicitor's bill. 'Disbursements' are the **expenses** incurred by a buyer or seller. Some are incurred whilst the solicitor undertakes pre-purchase property investigations and others at the point of completion (transfer of title). The solicitor usually pays these charges *on your behalf* and lists them on the bill together with his own professional service fees. Disbursements affecting purchasers are likely to include:

◆ **Telegraphic transfers**
Even with the advent of direct electronic banking, banks still charge for the *fast* transfer of funds from one person's account to another. The sum is usually about £25 and the amount could be incurred several times, depending on when the deposit, mortgage element and any other outstanding balances are transferred.

◆ **Stamp duty**
Property purchases are liable for 'stamp duty land tax'. The liability currently begins with any property bought for more than £60,000 (except for dwellings in certain designated zones) and rates increase depending on price:

Property price	Stamp duty liability
Up to and including £60,000, provided a certificate of value for £60,000 is included	Nil
Over £60,000 but not more than £250,000, provided a certificate of value for £250,000 is included	1% of property price
Over £250,000 but not more than £500,000, provided a certificate of value for £500,000 is included	3% of property price
Over £500,000	4% of property price
Data correct at March 2004	

◆ **Local authority searches**
Local searches are an essential part of buying property.

They confirm, for example, whether the highways authority intend to create a busy new byway along the bottom of the garden or whether there has been a history of mining in the region. Fees vary from council to council, but on average they are about £100.

◆ **HM Land Registry fees**
All land and property must be registered. The fees start at £40 and increase to a maximum of £750 according to property value. Additional fees may be incurred if pre-registration and land charge searches are undertaken.

◆ **Leasehold fees**
The new owners of leasehold properties need to have their details (and usually those of the mortgage provider) registered with the freeholder. An administrative fee is often made by the managing agent to provide copies of service-charge account details. Sums vary between agents and according to the amount of work involved.

◆ **Bankruptcy search**
Lenders will often insist on a bankruptcy search against the borrower, prior to the release of funds, to ensure the funds do not go direct to the borrower's creditors. The fee is negligible (usually less than £1).

◆ **Water authority search fees**
A few of the water utility companies charge separately for checking information about mains water, sewerage and drainage. When applied, fees are usually less than £40.

Recommended websites

www.conveyancer.org.uk
Obtain details of local conveyancers from the site of the Council for Licensed Conveyancers.

www.conveyancingsolicitors.biz
Conveyancing-Solicitors.biz professes to be the leading online legal services company in the UK. Their website offers instant quotes with a 'no completion – no fee' option.

www.reallymoving.com
Get instant multiple conveyancing quotes from a variety of local solicitors and conveyancers, based on information you submit (property price, location, leasehold or freehold, and so on).

21

The Legal Process

It takes an average of eight weeks to complete the legal process from pre-contract enquiries to completion. Even with an extraordinarily efficient and proactive solicitor, it will *still* take at least four weeks to complete local searches and another couple of weeks to administer the purchase contract. This can be a very frustrating time for impatient buyers who are eager to move into their new home. Matters are often made worse when solicitors fail to let them know how things are proceeding. This chapter explains what the legal process involves and might go some way to reassure anxious first-time buyers.

OFFER ACCEPTED AND SOLICITOR INSTRUCTED

Once your offer on a property has been accepted and a solicitor or licensed conveyancer has been instructed to act for you, the next step is to complete general enquiry forms from the vendor's estate agent and your solicitor. Much of the information required by them at this stage in the proceedings will be straightforward and could just as easily be collected by telephone. It is likely to include:

- Your own and any joint buyer's full name and address.
- Your mortgage lender's name and address.
- The amount of funds you intend to borrow.
- Your mortgage account number or reference number.

- The address and agreed price of the property you intend buying.
- Any 'included' fixtures, fittings or appliances.
- Whether the property is freehold or leasehold.
- The vendor's estate agent details (for your solicitor).
- Your solicitor's details (for the vendor's estate agent).
- Landline telephone, mobile phone, fax and e-mail details of all involved.

WHAT HAPPENS BEHIND THE SCENES?

The purchase cannot begin until your solicitor and the vendor's solicitor are communicating with each other. So, the first important task is for each side to swap contact details. You can check this has been done by telephoning the estate agent *before the end of the first week* and asking whether details have been issued and, if so, how they were issued (fax or e-mail are faster than mailing by standard post). Your solicitor will then send a standard confirmation letter to the vendor's solicitor and ask them for a draft purchase contract.

Unfortunately, your solicitor is now reliant on the speed and efficiency of the vendor's solicitor to reply within a reasonable period. In turn, the vendor's solicitor is reliant on the vendor supplying prompt and accurate information about where the property title deeds are being stored. The title deeds need to be delivered to the vendor's solicitor before a draft contract can be drawn up. While these matters are being dealt with, your solicitor may write seeking confirmation of the mortgage offer from your lender, which will help save time later. If your solicitor has not contacted you *by the end of the second week*, telephone them to ask whether a draft contract has been received and, if not, find out whether the vendor's solicitor has been quizzed about the overdue document.

The problem here is that most solicitors won't institute a local search until a draft contract has been received. Local searches usually take about four weeks from start to finish. So, every week that receipt of a draft contract is delayed means a further week has to be added to the local search period. If receipt is delayed until the fourth week, the addition of the local search period means that purchase completion cannot possibly occur until at least eight weeks have elapsed – and *every* delay also increases the opportunities the vendor has to withdraw from selling (perhaps finding an alternative buyer who is prepared to pay the asking price or more). It is therefore crucial to reduce the risk by ensuring the draft contract stage is achieved at the earliest point in time.

STANDARD PRE-CONTRACT ENQUIRIES

Your solicitor will eventually receive the following documents from the vendor's solicitor:

♦ **Office copies of title to the property (now termed 'official copies')**
These will have been obtained from the Land Registry and should include a map detailing the property boundaries. Further details will include information about the registered owner, a description of the dwelling and confirmation about any outstanding loans or mortgages charged against it. The official copy will also include particulars about restrictive

covenants and easements. A restrictive covenant usually limits the use or alteration of a property, for example, by preventing a business being conducted on the premises or adding an extension without consent. An easement describes rights of way over a property or the right you have to use someone else's land or vice versa, for example, for drainage.

◆ **A draft contract**
This is issued in duplicate and contains details and descriptions about the property, its title number, the price and deposit to be paid. Other information relates to standard Law Society procedures for completion and penalties for any breach of contract.

The vendor's solicitor will also send a completed preliminary enquiry form, which will contain answers to a variety of standard questions about the property, such as whether there have been any boundary disputes with neighbours. The form will also include a **very important** statement by the vendor confirming whether they are aware of any matters adversely affecting the property. If the vendor falsifies this statement, they can later be held liable for misrepresentation.

Your solicitor will examine all these documents and instigate local search enquiries (providing they are satisfied the purchase transaction is *likely* to proceed – otherwise they will halt proceedings, so you don't incur search fees).

LOCAL SEARCHES
Your solicitor will send a form to the local authority

(where the property is located) requesting local search information. This procedure will disclose road development and planning proposals, pending or granted, which may have a negative impact on the property. Other searches are likely to explore the affect of coal, salt, tin or china clay mining, which are pertinent for certain areas of the country, and check for any tree preservation orders affecting the property.

Some local authorities reply promptly, while others can be exasperatingly slow. There are two optional methods of collecting local search data that significantly speed up the entire process:

- In 2002, the government encouraged local authorities to sign up to the National Land Information Service (NLIS). This system was devised to speed-up property searches through the deployment of high technology. Most local authorities using it have reported searches are usually completed within hours, rather than weeks, as was previously the case. It is anticipated that all local authority public services will be online by 2005. To take advantage of NLIS, solicitors need to be capable of accessing the system – so when considering a solicitor, ask whether they use NLIS as part of their standard conveyancing service.

- Local search information can be obtained 'in person', making it possible for the whole procedure to be completed in a day. Ask your solicitor whether a *personal search* service is available. This involves a member of the solicitor's staff visiting the local authority and getting hold of the information 'by hand'. Two discouraging aspects are that you may have to pay for the staff member's time and also for an indemnifying insurance policy, just in case anything is missed when they collect the data.

LISTING INCLUSIVE FIXTURES AND FITTINGS

Items that are to be included in a property purchase cause more problems than almost anything else. Careful cataloguing of fixtures, fittings and appliances at the outset can prevent difficulties later. It is not enough just to record an appliance as a 'washing machine', because this provides the vendor with an opportunity to swap the shiny new device you saw at the point of viewing for any rusty old contraption. A full description is needed and it should include the manufacturer's name, model number, colour, size and condition. These details must be passed on to your solicitor at the earliest stage, so they can be included in the purchase particulars.

The same comprehensive description should be given to carpets, curtains, light fittings, wardrobe units *and* items in the garden. Many a new buyer has moved into a house with a garden initially described as 'well stocked with plants', only to discover the vendor subsequently takes most of them with him.

FROM DRAFT CONTRACT TO ENGROSSED CONTRACT

Once all aspects of the purchase are agreed between the two parties and all relevant documents and investigations of title at the Land Registry have been completed, a final version of the contract is drawn-up ready for signing. This is known as the 'engrossed' contract.

THE SOLICITOR'S PRE-EXCHANGE MEETING

'Exchange of contracts' is an important stage in the purchase, because it signifies the point when both seller and buyer become committed to the transaction. Up until exchange of contracts, either party can withdraw without penalty – but buyers who withdraw *after* exchange have to pay compensation to the seller (depending on the prior terms agreed). The penalty usually involves the deposit paid on the day contracts are exchanged, which is typically 5% to 10% of the property price.

Most solicitors will arrange a pre-exchange meeting with their clients. This is a **final** opportunity to discuss important aspects of the purchase and raise any outstanding doubts or concerns about the property. At the end of this meeting, your solicitor will ask you to sign the contract ready for exchange.

EXCHANGE OF CONTRACTS

The solicitors on both sides will agree a date when contracts are to be exchanged. At the same time, a completion date will be decided and deposit funds transferred to the vendor's solicitor. The seller now holds the purchaser's signed contract and the buyer holds the seller's signed contract. 'Completion' is the date when transfer of ownership is concluded and this might occur a week or so after exchange of contracts or (more commonly these days) on the same day. A delay between exchange and completion is beneficial, because it allows the solicitors time to deal with a number of final but necessary procedures. It also gives buyer and seller time to organise themselves and prepare for moving.

Matters that your solicitor will probably have to attend to during this period include:

- Reporting to the mortgage lender that property title investigations have been completed and that there are no matters endangering the security of the property. At the same time, your solicitor will ask the lender for mortgage funds to be transferred ready for the completion date.

- Sending a 'transfer form' to the vendor's solicitor for signing. This clearly identifies the parties involved, the dwelling and the price. When it is returned, the buyer also signs it and the form is then sent to the Land Registry for registration of title after completion.

- If it has not already been done, your solicitor will perform a Land Registry search to ensure no changes to the register can be made between exchange of contracts and completion.

- Arranging for the buyer to sign the mortgage deed, which will then be sent to the Land Registry when the property is registered.

- Arrange for 'requisitions on title' to be sent to the vendor's solicitor. This is usually dealt with by post and describes in detail how completion will occur.

Matters resolved through this document will include the agreed method for balance transfer and how keys and legal papers are to be exchanged.

GETTING ADVANCE NOTICE OF COMPLETION DATE

Your solicitor will inform you about the completion date as soon as it has been agreed. Unless arrangements have already been made in advance, it is worth contacting the vendor or their estate agent to find out:

◆ The time the vendor expects to vacate the property on completion day (this is usually midday).

◆ Where keys to the property can be collected from. It is not usual for the vendor to hand them over in person. Arrangements are more commonly made instead with the estate agent or solicitor.

◆ Once agreed, it is very rare for completion dates to be changed. However, delays can occur if postal strikes, computer system failure or some other unavoidable hiccup frustrates conclusion of the purchase. The good news is that when they do occur, such delays hardly ever last more than 24 hours.

GAZUNDERING

This is **not** a tactic I would recommend purchasers use nor do I believe it is a fair and equitable way for property transactions to be made; nonetheless, gazundering is a legal practice and occurs more frequently than many might think. Gazundering is when a purchaser reduces their offer at the very last minute and usually a day or two before exchange of contracts. The vendor is invariably devastated, because they know weeks of potential marketing for an alternative buyer have been lost and the likelihood is they are already committed to moving. They are forced into making a difficult decision – either they accept the reduced offer and allow the sale to proceed or they return to square one and start looking for a new buyer.

GAZUMPING

Purchasers are 'gazumped' when the vendor accepts a higher offer from another potential buyer, despite the fact that a verbal agreement on price had already been made and negotiations were thought to be concluded. Buyers can reduce the risk of gazumping by:

♦ Asking the vendor's estate agent for a written undertaking to remove the property from sale for a period of at least six weeks, while the legal process gets underway. Under normal circumstances, this should be enough time to reach exchange of contracts.

♦ Maintaining a cordial relationship with the vendor and keeping them up to date with information. Vendors become understandably anxious when they are kept in the dark and may look for an alternative buyer, as an insurance policy, in case you back out of the purchase. Once found, an alternative buyer might offer more than you have and the vendor could decide to accept it.

It may be reassuring to note that first-time buyers are much less likely to be gazumped than others because they have no property to sell and, as there are fewer complications, they can usually achieve exchange of contracts much earlier.

UNDERSTANDING 'COMPLETION'

Most people believe that completion is an instantaneous process, but matters involving property are never that simple. The success of the procedure depends on various agencies and individuals communicating efficiently with each other. First, your solicitor will send funds to the vendor's solicitor by telegraphic transfer and this is where the first complication can arise.

The vendor's solicitor will await confirmation from their bank that the money has been received before they will authorise keys to the property to be released. It is not unusual for the person at the bank, who has been charged with making the telephone call, to be out to lunch or busy attending to other matters – thus causing a delay. Buyer and seller are left wondering what is going on and concern and confusion can quickly set in.

Eventually matters are resolved and the vendor's solicitor forwards the signed 'transfer', the Land Charge Certificate and other relevant documents to your solicitor. Completion is effected and, with a little luck, you get the keys and move into your new home. This is sometimes where the second complication arises because, having arrived at your new home, you might find the vendor has yet to move out. Having a flask of coffee and some lunch provisions at hand should distract you long enough to get your feet in the door so, always go prepared!

After completion, your solicitor will still have a number of matters to attend to. These will include:

- Formal registration of your title with the Land Registry.

- The payment of stamp duty land tax, if applicable.

- Receipt of a Land Certificate from the Land Registry, which officially confirms your ownership of the property (a Charge Certificate will be issued instead of a Land Certificate, if the property has been bought with a mortgage).

- Sending the Charge Certificate to the mortgage lender along with search results and any other pertinent documentation, which they will keep as security against the loan.

- Drawing-up an account of service costs and disbursements.

YOUR SOLICITOR'S COSTS

Most solicitors issue a final account statement and their invoice within a couple of weeks of completion, though this depends on when the above matters are attended to. You then have 30 days to make payment in full. Property deeds are usually retained by the lender or, if there is no mortgage, stored free of charge by the solicitor (but always get confirmation of this in writing). Solicitors will often store your deeds safely and without charge, hoping you will use their services again when you next decide to move.

WHAT IS THE HOME INFORMATION PACK (HIP) LEGISLATION?

There has been extensive publicity about the planned introduction of the 'Home Information Pack' (previously called the 'Seller's Pack') in 2006. Although this major piece of legislation will affect vendors far more than buyers, it is important that you are aware of its implications.

Government suggests that HIPs will improve the house-buying process and reduce the time it takes from an offer being accepted to completion of the purchase. There has been considerable debate about whether HIPs will work and the National Association of Estate Agents firmly believes the legislation, as it stands, has serious flaws. Nonetheless, the government is determined to introduce it, following a consultation period. The main elements of HIPs are that from 2006:

◆ Sellers of residential properties in England and Wales, or their agents, will be required to make a Home Information Pack available **before** marketing their home for sale, and to make a copy of the pack available to prospective buyers on request. The pack will include standard documents and information for prospective buyers.

◆ Sellers are likely to have to provide the following documents in the 'Pack':
  – terms of sale;
  – evidence of title;
  – replies to standard preliminary enquiries;

- copies of planning, listed building and building regulation consents and approvals;
- copies of warranties and guarantees, if the property is new;
- guarantees of work carried out at the property;
- replies to local searches;
- a 'Home Condition Report' based on a professional survey of the dwelling, including an energy efficiency assessment.

♦ The sellers of leasehold properties are also likely to have to provide:
- a copy of the lease;
- most recent service charge accounts and receipts;
- building insurance policy details and payment receipts;
- regulations made by the landlord or management company;
- memorandum and articles of the landlord or management company.

The cost of supplying the 'Pack' will be borne by the vendor and this is expected to be between £300 and £700, though some of this would normally have been incurred in any event further into the sale process. The main element of contention is the provision of a 'Home Condition Report', as many believe the accuracy of it will be severely undermined if a buyer cannot be found within a reasonable time, thus negating the value of having such a report at all.

Estate agents and solicitors have been aware of the legislation for some years and are gearing themselves up for the 2006 commencement date. Some high street names have suggested they intend subsidising production of part of the 'Pack' to attract clients, though sellers are still likely going to have to bear some of the expense. Recent political commentators have stated that the government may consider a gradual introduction of HIPs, rather than cause potential chaos by full instigation on a set date.

Recommended websites

www.keyguide.co.uk
This is a useful and informative guide to the different rules and procedures for buying property in Scotland.

www.tradingstandards.gov.uk/fife/homebuyers.pdf
This colourful booklet (produced by Fife Council) comprehensively describes the laws and procedures affecting buyers of *newly built* property in Scotland. It is a useful guide, offering sound and concise advice.

www.wilsonsolicitors.demon.co.uk
A great little site – check on 'conveyancing' for a detailed overview of the entire process.

22

Delays and Problems

Most property purchases run smoothly and reach completion without a hitch. However, a few suffer from what may at first seem insurmountable problems, which understandably cause exasperation and panic. Delays and difficulties are frequently outside the buyer's immediate control but, given time and a good deal of perseverance, even the most challenging of situations can often be resolved.

GETTING CAUGHT IN A CHAIN

First-time buyers tend to believe they cannot get caught in a chain, because they have no property to sell. Sadly, this is not true. Their purchase is the fuel that activates the chain and all the sales and purchases further along it are interdependent on each other – so if one stops, all of them stop. The first-time buyer's purchase may thus be obstructed by a transaction several links along the chain.

Being able to proceed or not depends on whether the next vendor up the chain is prepared to sell; but they might have to withdraw, if their own purchase is blocked. Chains don't just operate from the bottom up; sometimes they also work from the top down and from any point in between. It is imperative that buyers find out:

- What the problem is?
- Where the problem is along the chain?
- Who is causing it?

Solicitors may help, but they rarely have the time or inclination to get too involved, so much of the investigative work may fall on you. Once you have identified the stumbling block you can assess whether a remedy is practical or possible. Breaking the chain may sometimes be the only way forward, as this limits transactions and reduces the number of people involved. For example, if the people whose home you are buying cannot move because their own purchase has collapsed, you could ask them whether they have considered renting as a temporary solution, so their sale can proceed.

Agreeing a completion date is a common cause of problems, particularly with a long chain. When all transactions are interdependent on each other, all parties need to be flexible enough about dates so their moves are able to coincide. If just two people become intractable the whole chain of transactions can fall apart, so try to remain as adaptable and accommodating as possible to improve the likelihood of success.

WHEN THE OWNER'S SOLICITOR FAILS TO REPLY

Once an offer has been accepted, there is usually a torrent of calls from the estate agent and legal exchanges between solicitors. But this can quickly decline into a period of uneasy silence. If the vendor's solicitor fails to reply to your own solicitor's enquiries or repeatedly makes verbal excuses for not replying by letter, you can be fairly certain a problem exists. This may be something quite trivial, such as the vendor waiting for a response from their mortgage lender. Or it could be something more ominous, such as another buyer making a higher offer for the property.

In any event, it is imperative you urge your solicitor to find out what the problem is, so it can be resolved. If the delay continues for more than two or three weeks without satisfactory explanation, you are probably right to feel suspicious. It may be better to resign this transaction to the background for the time being and begin looking for an alternative property, just in case things don't work out the way you had originally planned.

EXCHANGE OF CONTRACTS GETS DELAYED

Under normal circumstances and assuming your solicitor doesn't cause hindrance, vendors should be able to reach the 'exchange of contracts' stage within eight weeks. However, this is an important point in the legal process because it commits both sides to proceeding, so if there is going to be a problem, this is when it is most likely to occur.

Usually, the exchange of contracts also involves the exchange of money. A deposit of between 5% and 10% is usually paid to the vendor's solicitor. So, just as you will pay a deposit to your vendor, the vendor may also have to pay a deposit to the people they are buying from. Unfortunately, if they have secured a mortgage of 90%

or more, it suggests they don't have a great deal of savings to fall back on and the deposit may prove difficult to raise. The question your solicitor will need to ask is: 'Given enough time, is it likely the vendor will find enough for the deposit and, if not, is it their intention to withdraw their property from sale or move out to alternative accommodation?'

If they are likely to find the money eventually, it is far better that 'completion' is delayed rather than exchange of contracts. Completion does not have to occur immediately nor even within several weeks of exchange. So, if the vendor needs time to find the additional funds, ask if exchange of contracts can take place and suggest that a longer period is given to complete.

THE VENDOR DECIDES AGAINST SELLING

Vendors can occasionally decide to withdraw at the penultimate moment of a sale. This is devastating news for the unwary first-time buyer, but they shouldn't despair, because there is every chance the vendors will change their minds again, given a short time to contemplate the issues involved. It may be, for example, they were *always* uncertain or apprehensive about selling, but never voiced it to their agent or solicitor. For some, a house represents stability and leaving it can be a very traumatic experience.

Regardless of the circumstances and reasons for hesitation, if owners are given enough time to consider the situation rationally, a sale may eventually proceed. During this period of uncertainty, buyers should maintain close contact with the vendor's estate agent and ask for regular updates about how matters are developing. If things look bleak, this time could be used productively to view alternative properties.

DEALING WITH SOLICITORS WHO ARE TOO SLOW

Unlike estate agents, whom most instinctively distrust, people tend to bestow demigod status on solicitors. We assume their initial promise of 'a fast, efficient and professional service' will bear fruit as the purchase gets under way, but can be taken by surprise when it fails to materialise. There are both competent and incompetent individuals in all walks of life and the legal profession is no different. Although most solicitors are very capable and skilled in their field, some can also be abrupt, cantankerous, overbearing and full of their own importance; others can be indecisive and slow to act, lacking in both knowledge and experience.

The latter group are likely to cause you considerable problems, because they will delay your purchase and frustrate the vendor, their agent and solicitor. If you genuinely believe your conveyancer is taking too long to complete tasks, ask to speak to a senior partner and voice your concerns. Always remember you are the paying customer and have a right to demand nothing short of a courteous, able and professional service.

ALLOWING FOR SEASONAL PROBLEMS

The legal process is invariably slower during Christmas and New Year, though many solicitors try to bring exchange of contract and completion dates forward, if they can. The other major problem occurs during the peak spring selling season, when conveyancers can become swamped with clients and paperwork. Since it is nigh impossible to arrange a purchase outside these periods, all you can do is assume things will be more sluggish and patiently wait for completion to occur.

ENCOUNTERING PERSONAL PROBLEMS

There are occasions when a difficult personal event can coincide with a property sale and, under such circumstances, a buyer may need lots of tolerance and compassion. For example, separation and divorce often means the shared property will be considered a partnership asset and will have to be sold so its value can be realised. Such situations can be financially and emotionally draining for the parties and legally complex too, because both husband and wife are likely to have separate solicitors acting for them.

Even worse is the scenario where a vendor dies part way through the sale process. The surviving partner or next of kin is likely to have far more on their mind than disposal of the property and, as a result, exchange of contracts and completion will have to wait. Quite apart from the emotional turmoil caused by such events, the legal situation also demands a period of contemplation. The deceased's last will and testament must first be dealt with and any inheritance settled, before anything can be sold. These situations rarely prevent a sale from proceeding, but they can cause a delay of several weeks and sometimes months, particularly when there is a coroner's inquest.

THE CHANGE FROM RENTING TO OWNERSHIP

The biggest difficulty in moving from renting to home ownership is getting the timing right. Many try to plan it so that tenancy expiry coincides perfectly with a purchase completion, but this is rarely successful.

Assured shorthold tenancies (ASTs) have a fixed term (usually six or twelve months) and, if you are planning to buy a property, it is better to wait until the fixed term has ended and a **periodic shorthold tenancy** has begun. This type of tenancy runs from month to month (or the periodic nature of rent payments) and begins automatically upon expiry of an assured shorthold term (assuming a new AST has not been entered into).

To end a periodic shorthold, tenants usually only need give one month's written notice (including a full rent period) to their landlord. This makes it easier to plan the end of tenancy to fall within a couple of weeks of the purchase completion date, rather than trying to forecast what may happen months ahead when a fixed AST term expires.

DEALING WITH A DEPOSIT SHORTFALL

The range and amount of expenses involved when buying a house can take some by surprise. The earlier parts of this book will have prepared you better than most but, even so, you may find there are insufficient funds remaining to pay the deposit on exchange of contracts. If this is the case, tell your solicitor at the *earliest* opportunity, because he may be able to negotiate a reduction with the vendor.

Recommended websites

www.adviceguide.org.uk
The Citizens Advice Bureau website has an entire housing section, offering concise information and guidance on all property-buying issues.

www.goodmigrations.co.uk/avoid.php3
This page from Good Migrations explains some of the main pitfalls when buying a home and offers advice on how to avoid them.

www.themovechannel.com/howto/find/off-plan-problems.asp
Buying new property before it has been built (called 'buying off-plan') presents its own set of problems. This page from The Move Channel explains the main implications.

Preparing for Completion Day

Completion day is usually demanding enough for those who are organised, but it can be chaotic and exhausting for those who are not. There is often precious little notice given of completion and, since it is likely to occur within two weeks of exchange of contracts, the more you can sort out beforehand the better. Your solicitor should tell you when it will take place, but don't rely on it, otherwise you could find yourself having to arrange everything the day before it happens. Use this valuable time productively to plan and prepare as much as you can.

ACQUIRING FURNISHINGS

Buyers often build up a stock of furnishings for their new home before they move and, although the desire may be to buy new, financial restraints usually confine first-time buyers to second-hand items. Unfortunately, relatives and friends may also exploit this situation to offload unwanted and occasionally useless pieces that would otherwise be assigned to the local tip. So, beware those who feign generosity by offering junk.

It is best to make a list of the *essential* items you are going to need in your new home from day one, such as a bed, wardrobe, cooker and fridge; then set about asking friends and relatives if they know of any 'going cheap'.

This way you can inspect an item before accepting it and also plan where it can be stored.

A mistake made by many novice homemakers is to collect too much furniture for the space available or acquire large single items that simply won't go through the entrance door or up the stairs. Always check the dimensions of bulky objects beforehand and, if you need to, make a special visit to the property to confirm they will fit.

USING A REMOVAL FIRM OR DOING IT YOURSELF

If you have managed to collect an array of furnishings, now is a good time to plan how they will be collected from their various storage locations and transported to the property. Anyone with large amounts stored or those that have been renting an unfurnished property might have to employ a removal firm to do the job. Shop around for the best quotes and confirm they are free to undertake the task on the proposed completion day.

If you only have a small number of items, you could try asking the vendors whether they have any space to store them. They might have already emptied a spare bedroom or dry garage and invite you to use the space in advance of moving in. This is helpful to you, because it reduces the workload on completion day; it can also be helpful to the vendors, because they will be reassured to know you intend proceeding with the purchase. However, remember to inform your contents insurer and check the policy covers such an arrangement.

The final alternative is to hire a van and do the job yourself, which is what most first-time buyers do. If you don't currently hold a full driving licence, you will need to ask someone who does to help you on the day – it is also a good idea to get another couple of friends or relatives to help fetch and carry.

ARRANGING TO COLLECT THE KEYS

As explained earlier, keys to the property are likely to be handed to the estate agent or solicitor when the vendor vacates. Arrangements should have been made in advance of completion day, but it is always worth double-checking the day before to make certain nothing has changed. If keys are already in the agent or solicitor's hands, confirm they are **all** the keys for the property. The bunch should include (as appropriate) keys for:

- entrance doors
- garage
- garden shed
- patio and conservatory doors
- cellar doors
- window locks
- garden gates
- alarm system
- exterior meter cupboards
- communal entrance doors (for apartment blocks).

Some leasehold developments also have electronic or manually-operated security entrance doors and car park gates. Ask the estate agent for code numbers in advance of moving and also confirm they are in possession of any electronic 'beeper' devices, which are sometimes used for automatic access.

COPING WITH CHILDREN AND PETS

It may be endearing to have the entire family, including young children and pets, move into the new home at the same time – but rarely is it ever practical. More often, someone has to spend the whole day supervising and taking care of them, which means there will be one less pair of hands available for moving and organising furnishings. If possible, arrange in advance for a relative or trusted friend to look after toddlers, cats and dogs – then throughout the following day, you can give them your undivided attention to help them settle in.

DEALING WITH IMPORTANT SECURITY MEASURES

Moving day itself can be hectic and with so much activity going on, it is easy to forget there may be opportunistic thieves standing by to exploit the situation. Always appoint one 'helper' to stand guard over the open van tailgate and property entrance door. If there are insufficient numbers to supply separate security:

✗ Don't stack boxes outside.

✗ Don't leave furnishings unattended.

✗ Don't leave the removal van unlocked while carrying items into the house.

✗ Don't unlock more than one entrance door into the property and always close the door as you enter through it.

✗ Don't allow unfamiliar faces into your house (thieves have been known to say they are from the gas or electric company or even that they are a neighbour offering to help you move in).

✓ Be extra careful of local youths observing you.

✓ Be extra vigilant if you unload during darkness.

✓ Keep your mobile phone switched on and with you at all times.

✓ Remove the 'For Sale' sign as soon as possible, as this advertises the fact that you are new to the area and probably have possessions still boxed and 'ready to go'.

✓ Check security lights operate properly (if there aren't any – consider their installation a priority task).

✓ Check that all exterior doors have at least five or seven-lever locks (if you are concerned about who may have keys, change the locks as soon as possible).

✓ Check that all ground floor windows have robust locking devices.

✓ Check that the security alarm functions properly and, if code activated, change the code (the instruction manual should explain how to do this).

✓ Make sure that valuable items, including jewellery, chequebooks, bank and credit cards, are all placed somewhere secure.

It is **very important** you arrange contents insurance **before** completion day and check that you will be covered either by the removal firm, van hire company or through a separate policy while transporting your furnishings. If you have existing insurance, write to the company in advance explaining when you intend changing address – at the same time, ask whether a special policy or an extra premium is required to cover accidental breakage or theft while your possessions are in transit.

OBTAINING MANUALS AND INSTRUCTIONS

A day or two before completion, remind the estate agent (or vendor if you have their telephone number) you need the manuals for hot water, heating and alarm systems and for all included appliances. If any are reported missing, ask the vendor to write down a set of simple operating instructions that can be left in the property.

FINAL MORTGAGE CHECKS

Your solicitor will check whether mortgage funds are available for completion but, for your own peace of mind, it is always worth checking preparations for release of the balance with your lender a few days beforehand. If your lender reports that funds will be delayed due to an unforeseen snag, completion will also have to be postponed, so let your solicitor know straight away.

A SCHEDULE OF EVENTS

There will be a gradual build up of activity, appointments and events prior to moving and, to help reduce an equal build up of stress, it is useful to devise a schedule to help remind you what needs doing and when. A good tip is to attach an A4 sheet of paper to your fridge and jot down 'things to do' as they arise, then transfer these to a more organised schedule at the end of each day or week. It is also useful to keep an organised record of contact details for all the agencies, companies and individuals you have had dealings with during the buying process. A simple address book kept specifically for this purpose is ideal. Some of the tasks you should plan to undertake include:

◆ Setting up a new account with a bank conveniently located to where you will be living. This is important if you want to receive cheque books and guarantee cards in advance of moving. You will also need to supply the new details to utility companies and your mortgage lender for direct debit payments.

◆ Registering with a new doctor at a local health centre.

◆ Arranging for your children to be inducted into a new school.

◆ Organising new buildings and contents insurance.

◆ Changing the address on important documents such as a driving licence, car registration, TV licence, investment schemes, pet chip registration, credit cards, loan agreements other than the new mortgage, hire purchase agreements, and so on.

◆ Making arrangements for mail to be forwarded.

◆ Registering with a new dentist.

◆ Changing the postcode security marking on valuable possessions.

- Changing your details with Internet and mobile phone providers.

- Making sure that your employer is primed with the new details so that payment slips are sent to your new address and salary is paid into your new bank account.

- Stopping deliveries of newspapers and terminating regular services provided by window cleaners, etc.

MAKING SURE OTHERS CAN CONTACT YOU

There are so many ways that people can communicate these days, but only if they have the appropriate contact details. Make sure significant agencies and individuals, such as your solicitor and mortgage lender, have up-to-date e-mail addresses, landline and mobile telephone numbers, fax number and postal address. If you have given a mobile telephone number, make sure your phone is kept charged and switched on – you would be amazed how many buyers and sellers provide details of an inoperative telephone number.

Finally, if you are due to work away or are about to go on holiday, let your solicitor and the vendor's estate agent know your departure and return dates – also let them know whether they can contact you by alternative means during this period, such as through a different office or hotel telephone number.

THE DAY BEFORE COMPLETION

This is the last chance you have to check with your solicitor that everything is going according to plan and the only opportunity you may have to put any outstanding questions about the property to the vendor. It is also a good idea to pass on your details to the gas, electricity, water and telephone companies and check that services are connected. This is particularly important if the property has stood vacant for any length of time or when it is a home on a new development.

Completion day itself is likely to be a hectic, nerve-wracking, exciting and exhausting, physical and emotional roller-coaster. Try to get a full night's sleep so you can be up bright and early in the morning, have time for a hearty breakfast and be prepared for the day's events.

Recommended websites

www.b4u-pay.com/your_moving_checklist.htm
A great checklist of essential 'moving' tasks, which have been broken down into time periods from six weeks before moving to the moving day itself.

www.bbc.co.uk/crime/prevention
This website is packed full of good sensible advice and information about crime prevention. It includes details about the best type of door and window locks to use, the value of burglar alarms and advice on a range of easy crime-beating property boundary installations.

www.serviceforce.co.uk
If you need a replacement instruction manual for an AEG, Electrolux, Parkinson Cowan, Tricity Bendix or Zanussi appliance you can download it from this site.

24

Completion Day

This is it. The day you have worked so long and hard for has finally arrived – you are about to move into your new abode and become one of the UK's seventeen million property investors. If you have absorbed the information and followed the advice so far in this book, you will be ready to accept the responsibilities, contentment and financial rewards that home ownership can bring.

PREPARING A FOOD AND DRINK HAMPER

One of the worst things about completion day is, despite being primed and ready to go, there is usually a great deal of time spent waiting – for telephone calls – for removal vans and helpers to arrive – for the sellers to move out. This can all be made that little bit more tolerable with a hamper packed with 'comfort snacks', sandwiches, hot and cold drinks, plus a newspaper, magazines or a favourite book to help pass the time. Even if the day starts early and never eases off, the pre-prepared goodies will be very welcome, once you and your helpers get the chance to sit down and relax.

KEEPING ESSENTIAL DOCUMENTS NEARBY

It is very easy to misplace essential documents during the turmoil of moving, so keep everything together in a single box file. You may be asked to refer to certain items or quote reference numbers as the day progresses and contact names and telephone numbers should always be readily at hand. Your folder should include:

- mortgage details

- survey report

- legal papers and letters from your solicitor

- solicitor's contact details

- utility (gas, electricity and water) reference numbers and contact details

- a copy of *Yellow Pages* and a local newspaper (for emergency tradesmen)

- a local map or A–Z guide

- vendor's contact details

- vendor's estate agent details

- a copy of the original property marketing brochure

- the full address of the property, including its postcode

- a copy of the lease (if appropriate)

- managing agent contact details (if appropriate)

- a breakdown of the services provided by the managing agent (if appropriate)

- research information, such as details of local shops, health centre, nearest cash-point, bus and train time-tables, and so on

- telephone numbers for local taxis

- contact details of any favoured plumbers and electricians.

CONTACTING YOUR SOLICITOR

The vendor's solicitor will inform your solicitor when the final balance of funds has been paid into their account. Once payment has been verified your solicitor will telephone you, giving you the authority to move. This process relies on several agencies working in quick succession and, unfortunately, because they have to deal with scores of other property transactions on the same day, matters might become drawn out.

If you haven't heard anything by midday, telephone your solicitor to get an up-to-date estimate of when completion is expected to occur. They should be in a position to confirm when the transfer of mortgage funds was made or is due to be made and the approximate time it will take for the vendor's solicitor to confirm receipt. If something hinders transfer beyond mid-afternoon, completion might have to be postponed until the following day when the banks open again for business.

CONTACTING THE VENDOR

If there is a delay, keep the vendor informed of what is causing it and how it develops during the day, as this will help them feel more at ease. Once completion has taken place, telephone them again to find out what time they anticipate vacating the property, so you can begin moving your possessions.

If there is only a short distance between where you are currently living and where you are moving to, there is no need to act until you get confirmation that the vendors have actually vacated. However, longer distances involve more planning and, in such cases, it may be worth starting to move as soon as your solicitor confirms completion has taken place. Arriving on the vendor's doorstep might also encourage them to move a little faster.

COLLECTING KEYS AND MOVING IN

When you collect the keys from the vendor or their estate agent or solicitor, make certain you take possession of every key for the property. If any appear to be missing, ask for them straightaway and make sure you obtain them, because once the vendor has departed it may not be so easy to get hold of them.

Before you move your possessions into the property, walk around the exterior and interior to check that inclusive fittings, fixtures, furnishings and appliances are where they should be and that water, gas, electricity and telephone are available. If any items are missing, telephone your solicitor; if services have been disconnected, telephone the appropriate utility company to arrange connection.

TAKING METER READINGS

There are two things you should do as soon as you get the keys. These are:

- Identify the location of water stop taps, gas mains cut-off valve and the electrical fuse box, in case of emergency.

- Take meter readings for gas and electricity (and also for water, if metered). The readings should be issued to the appropriate utility company as soon as possible and checked against any bills when they arrive.

It is also useful to undertake a full security check of the property before it gets dark. Make sure that all interior and exterior lights work, that any alarm system operates properly and doors and windows all have adequate locking devices.

DEALING WITH DOGS, CATS AND THE KIDS

Young children and pets are totally dependent on you to provide a safe, loving and happy home. Moving from one place to another can be upsetting for them, but there are a number of measures that may help:

Dogs

- Before you allow your dog into the dwelling, position his bed and favourite toys in the room you intend him to sleep in. The sight of familiar things with their familiar smells will help reassure him that all is well.

- Check the garden area to make sure it is safe and that he cannot get through gaps in fencing or under gates. Then allow him to roam freely, as this will help him identify his territory.

- Nervous dogs will drink excessively during the first few days, so make sure there is always lots of clean fresh water available.

- Feeding your dog as soon as he enters the house will help establish confidence that 'the pack' is staying together.

- Remember to change his name and address tag as soon as you move.

- If your dog is identity-chipped, change the registration details as soon as possible after moving. PETLOG can be contacted on 0870 6066751.

- If your dog finds it difficult to settle and appears distressed, ask your vet about a DAP (dog appeasing pheromone) plug-in device. These emit a scent similar to the calming odour released by a mother to her puppies and can be very effective in reducing stress.

- Moving your own possessions into the new house before your dog goes into it will help considerably, because these are objects and smells he is accustomed to.

- There may be a few 'accidents' over the coming days, which is hardly surprising given the change of environment. Don't scold your dog, as this may only exacerbate the situation. He might have forgotten where the door is or can't find it quickly enough to let you know he needs to go out – be patient, remind him where the exit is and praise him whenever he 'asks' to go.

- With so much activity going on in the new home, your dog can become nervous and fretful. To help calm him, it is important to try to keep to established routines. Try to feed and walk him at the same times as you have always done.

- Dogs are incredibly adaptable and, given lots of TLC and a little time, your pooch will quickly identify the strange surroundings as his new home.

Cats

- Cats tend to be more territorial than dogs, so keep your cat indoors for at least a couple of days, so he has the opportunity to explore it fully and can become familiar with the layout.

- As with dogs, make sure your cat's name and address tag is changed and introduce him to the property *after* installing his bed and your own possessions.

- Before he goes out for his first adventure in the new neighbourhood, feed him half of his normal meal. This will encourage your cat to return for the second half when he gets hungry. If you can, supervise his first outing until he seems confident about the area.

- If the distance between your previous home and the new one is relatively short, your cat may attempt to travel back to it. It is difficult to avoid this and all you can do is be aware of it and check your old neighbourhood, if he fails to return home when expected. Warning your old neighbours and other people he may call on is also a useful precaution – make sure all these people have your new address and telephone number.

Children

- Regardless of age, some children can react badly to moving home and particularly when they feel they have had little choice in the matter. This is a phase that can be alleviated by involving them as much as possible in the build up to moving and during the move itself.

◆ Losing friends and favourite play areas can be traumatic. Try to encourage children to keep in contact with their pals by telephone, letter or e-mail and arrange regular visits whenever possible.

◆ When you introduce yourself to your new neighbours, make sure you take your children with you. This can help establish new relationships, particularly if the neighbours have children around the same age.

◆ Allow your children to have some say in planning the layout and decoration of their new bedroom. This can help them become aware there are some advantages to moving.

◆ Make sure younger children have the opportunity of visiting their new school several times before they start full-time. Accompany them on bus routes with their newfound friends until they become confident of undertaking the journey without you.

Recommended websites

www.helpiammoving.com/advice/pets.html
A page full of advice about how to move with all kinds of pets including dogs, cats, fish, guinea pigs and hamsters.

www.lawlersremovals.com/pdf-docs/moving_with_children.htm
Practical and sensible advice about moving with children is presented in this short and readable article by Lawlers.

www.parentlineplus.org.uk/data/parents/changsch.htm
Good advice about how to settle children into a new
school and details of how to order the *Changing Schools*
publication free from Parent Plus.

25

Essential Tasks After Moving In

In amongst the excitement of moving in, it is all too easy to put off tasks that are crucial for you and your family's safety, security and well being. This chapter deals with a number of elementary issues best dealt with during the first few days. Once these inspections and chores are completed, you can relax and enjoy your new home with confidence.

GETTING THE 'SOLD' SIGN REMOVED

The 'sold' sign is a clear indicator to would-be thieves that you have recently moved into the property and probably have lots of valuable new possessions still in their boxes. Thieves also know that most new occupiers give scant regard to improving security until after an incident has occurred, which means your property may currently be a significant target.

As a first step towards thwarting local criminals, contact the estate agent and request they remove their 'sold' sign from your garden at the earliest possible opportunity.

CHECKING THAT UTILITY COMPANIES HAVE YOUR CORRECT DETAILS

Prior to taking up occupation, you will have informed the appropriate gas, electricity and water companies of your impending move. You will also have contacted them again to give them meter readings on the day you moved in. When your first bills arrive, inspect them carefully to make sure your personal details and the meter readings are recorded correctly. Any discrepancies should be reported without delay and a new bill requested from them, incorporating the amendments.

MEETING THE NEIGHBOURS

Good neighbours are extremely useful as they can help you settle into the property and augment your integration into the local community. Moreover, they will keep an eye on your new home while you are at work or away on holiday. Meeting the neighbours and establishing a rapport with them should therefore be undertaken as soon as possible.

One of the easiest ways of achieving this is to invite them to your house-warming party or a summer evening barbeque. If time is short and this seems like too much to organise, just knock on their door one afternoon and introduce yourself. Remember this could be the first step in creating a long-term friendship with mutually beneficial rewards, so don't be shy, they will be just as curious about you as you are of them.

INFORMING OTHERS OF YOUR NEW ADDRESS

Letting all your friends know that you have moved is the easiest part of this process, because all you need do is refer to your address book and send each one a letter or postcard. The hardest part is making sure other individuals, agencies and institutions are informed.

These will include:

- The council tax department of the local authority.
- Your GP, dental practice, optician and health centre.
- Your employer.
- The benefit agency (if appropriate).
- Your Internet provider.
- Any existing loan or hire-purchase provider.
- Credit card companies and your bank.
- Satellite television subscription provider.
- Appliance warranty and all insurance policy companies.
- Investment and savings scheme providers.
- The Inland Revenue tax office.
- Vehicle license registration office.
- Your pet's veterinary practice.
- Any clubs, associations or groups you belong to.
- Magazine subscription departments.
- Regular service providers (such as a preferred local garage that attends to your car).

TESTING APPLIANCES AND INSTALLATIONS

One of the first and most important systems you will need to become familiar with is the property hot water and heating installation. Read the manual or instructions thoroughly before testing. If a manual is not available, you should ask someone qualified and experienced, such as a CORGI registered engineer, to check the system and guide you through its operation. Next, check that all other appliances work, including:

- oven and hob
- washing machine
- alarm system
- dishwasher
- waste-disposal unit
- kitchen and bathroom extractor fans
- shower unit
- power sockets and light switches
- fusing system
- fan-heaters
- smoke alarms
- door bells
- intercom and main entrance auto-door openers (for apartment blocks).

FIXING NEW LOCKS ON ALL DOORS AND WINDOWS

This job is so often overlooked by first-time buyers, despite the fact that it is one of the easiest and most significant tasks they should perform after moving in. Buying your new home is likely to be the biggest investment you will ever make – so it makes good sense to protect it. Every opening window should have a top and bottom lock and ideally hinge bolts as well, to prevent the frame being forced. Economic window locks can be purchased from all good hardware and do-it-yourself stores.

The easiest way of changing an entrance door lock is to measure the existing one and replace it with another with the same dimensions. This avoids having to alter the opening in the door or in the doorframe – the new lock is simply slotted into the same aperture and secured into position. There are a great variety and quality of locks available and, as the popular saying goes, you tend to get what you pay for. Make sure replacements are at least five lever or, even better, seven lever insurance locks.

ENSURING THE GARDEN IS SECURE

The next most vulnerable area of your property open to intruders is the garden. Check that gates leading to the rear of your home have substantial bolts and that fences are secure and intact. Consider planting thorny bushes up against boundary walls, which will discourage anyone who might attempt to climb over them. You might also plan to install exterior lights, triggered by movement detectors, as these are excellent deterrents.

Finally, examine the exterior aspects of your home from a potential burglar's point of view and prepare a list of jobs that, once completed, will improve the defence of your property. For example, could someone hide behind bushes while attempting to break in? If so, trim them down to a more appropriate height or remove and replace them with smaller plants.

CHECKING FOR ANY OBVIOUS DAMAGE

Although your survey will have identified any need for major repairs, it will be down to you to find minor defects – and this is best done purposely by inspection, rather than waiting until they become obvious. For example, a radiator that drips every now and then is easily fixed, but if it is left too long it may develop into a burst that floods your new home while you are out at work. Imagine the damage that could be caused – and all for the want of a spanner and a few minutes' work.

Newly built homes have a set procedure to deal with minor defects, called a 'snagging list'. Any problems, such as a faulty heating system or a window that won't open properly, should be reported to the developer *in writing* as soon as they are discovered. When builders are still working on the estate they may suggest you report faults verbally and direct to the site foreman, but this means you will have no proof of ever having reported it, should animosity or a dispute later develop between you. *Always* put enquiries, requests and complaints in writing and keep a copy as evidence, which you can later refer to.

INSPECTING THE LOFT OR CELLAR

These areas are sometimes disregarded during the first few hectic days of moving in, but they are ignored at your peril. The loft needs checking for leaking pipes, over-flowing or inadequately lagged water tanks, missing insulation and wind-damaged roofing felt. Lofts also sometimes contain discarded boxes and other debris left behind by the previous owners. Cellars should be checked for dampness, rodent infestation, leaking sub-floor pipes and unsecured cables.

SETTING UP STANDING ORDERS AND DIRECT DEBITS

Most household bills can be paid by monthly standing order or direct debit from your bank account, which helps to reduce the time and inconvenience of having to pay quarterly bills as they arrive. This method also helps you to budget more effectively, because the monthly amounts remain constant, whereas many quarterly bills vary. Standing orders are regular payments of fixed amounts you instruct the bank to make on your behalf. Direct debits are authorised by you, but consist of varying monthly, quarterly or annual amounts requested by the billing company. Charges and fees that can be paid using these methods include:

- council tax
- gas
- electricity
- water
- television licence
- ground rent
- management fee or service charge
- telephone
- mortgage repayments
- contents and buildings insurance premiums
- regular transfers from one bank account to another (for example, as savings for a holiday fund)
- life assurance premiums
- car insurance.

If you wish to set up regular monthly payments, consult the relevant company or authority and ask for a bank mandate form. A few banks also offer a specific 'household' account (sometimes at an additional charge) from which they will arrange all regular bills to be paid. Ask your bank whether they offer this service and whether fees are charged for managing it.

ACQUIRING A TELEVISION LICENCE

If you use or install television receiving equipment in your home to receive or record television programme services, you are required by law to have a valid TV licence. The term 'equipment' includes video recorders and personal computers with broadcast cards installed. There are very few exceptions and, if you are caught not having a licence, you are committing a criminal offence and can be prosecuted and fined up to £1,000. The Licensing Authority reports that their detection methods are extremely efficient, catching 1,200 offenders every day of every week.

Those aged 75 and over are entitled to a free licence and registered blind people are eligible for a 50% discount on the usual charge (currently £121 for colour and £40.50 for black and white). First-time buyers who previously lived in their parents' home take note: even if the TV you have brought with you was purchased as a gift by your parents or was originally covered under your parents' licence, you still need to obtain your own licence when you move the set into your new home.

Licences can be obtained at all post offices and by direct debit or credit card by telephoning 0870 241 6468. Payment can also be made online and further information on licensing is also available on the website at *www.tv-l.co.uk*

PARTY NOW – DECORATE LATER!

There is a certain truth held dear by all owner-occupiers – the more you adorn your home with new furnishings bought with your own hard earned cash, the less likely you are to hold wild parties for you and your friends. It may be slightly disheartening to learn that in buying your own home, you are growing up and maturing into a responsible adult. These are not your parents' or your landlord's possessions, they are *yours* – and you will have an irresistible desire to take good care of them.

So, if you want to have one last fling, plan a huge house-warming party in the first few weeks of moving in and **before** you begin decorating, laying new carpets or buying new furnishings. Then it won't matter that much if things get damaged or red wine is spilled on the carpet, because most things will probably be replaced sooner or later.

Recommended websites

www.inspectorhome.co.uk
When 85% of newly built homes are reported to have snagging defects, it may pay you to employ a professional to check your new house within the first two-year builder's warranty. This company provides a 450-point check and makes sure houses are finished to an acceptable standard.

www.neighbourhoodwatch.net
This is the site of the Neighbourhood Watch Scheme and an excellent source of home security information. If a scheme doesn't exist in your neighbourhood, starting one may be a good way of getting to know your new neighbours.

www.ukenergy.co.uk
Compare the price of gas, electricity, telephone and digital television services from different suppliers, and then switch to save money.

26

Dealing with a Financial Shortfall

Levels of personal debt have soared amongst people in the UK for the last decade. This is partly due to a greater than ever desire for hi-tech and luxurious material goods and an increased reliance on credit to pay for them. But for owner-occupiers, the higher levels of property-related debts are sometimes unintentionally acquired through elements outside their control, such as rising interest rates or the loss of steady employment. In these situations, the burden of repaying a mortgage debt can quickly turn into an overwhelming problem. The home becomes a millstone and any chance of enjoying what it has to offer is lost under a cloud of worry and fear.

Negative equity is the worst-case scenario for them (having a property worth less than the mortgage debt *and* not being able to afford repayments). Many sit and agonise but do nothing to help resolve the situation, until it is too late. The lender then repossesses the house, sells it below value and adds selling expenses to the outstanding mortgage debt. This does not solve the problem from an owner's point of view – it merely exacerbates it. They lose the one asset that could otherwise have propelled them forward.

Dealing with mounting and increasingly unaffordable debts at the *earliest* opportunity means the worst-case scenario can often be avoided and a happier outcome achieved. This chapter offers advice and lists sources of useful additional information on how to overcome a financial shortfall. Mortgage arrears must never be brushed under the carpet, ignored and allowed to grow. They should instead be treated as a temporary hiccup whose cure involves rapid and direct action.

PAYING YOUR MORTGAGE DEBT FIRST

All credit falls into the following categories:

- **Secured** – usually means the credit amount is 'secured' against the value of your home and the property can be repossessed and sold to help pay off the loan, if you default on payments.

- **Unsecured** – usually means your home has *not* been secured against the credit and the property cannot be repossessed, if you fail to make payments.

If your income fails to meet your outgoings, the roof over your head should **always** be considered *the* priority, so make sure you keep up your mortgage and any other 'secured' repayments above all other expenses. Secured payments are sub-divided into:

- **First charge** – means the lender is first in the queue before other lenders when it comes to repossessing your home, if you don't meet repayment instalments.

◆ **Second (and subsequent) charge** – means the lender can only repossess your property if the 'first charge' lender decides not to do so or is entitled to any remaining funds after the 'first charge' has deducted outstanding arrears.

Even if you cannot meet the full monthly payment, pay whatever you can afford while looking at ways in which your other outgoings can be reduced. Always inform the lender in writing **as soon as you know you are struggling**. Tell them:

◆ Why you are finding payments difficult.

◆ How much you can afford to pay each month (but see Debt Dos and Don'ts on page 363).

◆ When you expect to resume full payments and pay off any arrears.

Lenders who subscribe to The Mortgage Code (a voluntary code of practice) will help you to devise a financial plan to help overcome difficulties and pay off mortgage arrears. They are also obliged to examine *all* other alternatives before they consider repossessing your home.

CLAIMING WELFARE ASSISTANCE

You may be able to claim financial help through income support, working tax credit or income-based job seeker's allowance. Contact a Citizens Advice Bureau or a local Department for Work & Pensions (DWP) office for further information. If you are able to claim benefit, the

DWP will normally pay some or all of the interest element of your mortgage, but none of the capital. Unfortunately, the rules generally prohibit any help being offered until after the first 39 weeks of a claim.

There are a number of restrictions when receiving state assistance in these circumstances. For example, the mortgage interest rate used to calculate benefit is set at a standard rate by government and will not be the actual rate you may be paying; and you can only claim for interest on the first £100,000 of your mortgage.

SUBMITTING AN INSURANCE CLAIM

If you took out a mortgage payment protection policy, now is probably the right time to submit a claim. Some lenders insist on first-time buyers having this type of insurance, because they realise repayments during the early years can be difficult and particularly when interest rates rise sharply. Problems can also occur at the end of fixed-rate periods, when payment amounts sometimes increase as they become aligned with current rates.

CHECKING OUT 'MORTGAGE RESCUE SCHEMES'

Lenders are not all the same. Some are sympathetic to the problems that first-time buyers encounter – others less so – but most will be prepared to help wherever they can. If you have tried every possible means of meeting your repayment obligations, but are still finding it impractical, it is worth asking whether your mortgage provider runs a rescue scheme.

These take various forms with some providing more drastic solutions than others. For example, your lender may offer to buy back your property or part of it and allow you to continue living there as a rent-paying tenant. If your lender doesn't run such a scheme, ask whether a local housing association or the local authority can help. For more information contact the Housing Corporation on (020) 7393 2000 or see *Yellow Pages* for your local authority's contact details.

EXTENDING THE TERM

Most mortgages are for 25 years or less, but some lenders will provide longer terms and this may be a solution worth considering, because extending the term will reduce the monthly repayment amount. However, this option is unlikely to be available for endowment mortgages or those that have only recently begun.

PAYING INTEREST ONLY

You could ask your lender if you can pay just the interest element of your mortgage as a temporary measure. This is only likely to be available to repayment mortgage clients and you should also be aware that such arrangements may not make a great deal of difference, because monthly payments are mostly made up of interest rather than capital in the first few years.

RELINQUISHING POSSESSION

If you have already explored, considered and rejected or have been denied all the above possible remedies *and* have given thought to increasing your income through obvious alternatives (such as renting the property or taking in a lodger), then relinquishing possession may be the only remaining solution. This should be considered a last resort, because it involves handing back the keys to the lender so they can sell it. The problem is they may take months to dispose of the property and during this time you will continue to be liable for mortgage payments. Even worse, they will probably add their estate agent's and solicitor's costs as well as some interest to the arrears and then sell the property at below market value. If the amount obtained through selling doesn't match the mortgage sum (plus added interest and expenses), you could potentially find yourself without a property, but still with an outstanding loan. Rather than hand the property back to the lender, it would probably be wise to keep control of both charges and selling price by disposing of it yourself.

BEWARE OF DEBT MANAGEMENT COMPANIES

Just about the worst thing you could possibly do is get another loan to consolidate your existing debts, which is exactly what many debt management companies do for you *and* charge you a fee for the privilege. In fact, such arrangements may expose you to more uncertainty by turning several 'unsecured' credit arrangements into a single 'secured' loan – although the total monthly amount may reduce, there are far greater implications should you default on payment. Before even thinking about debt consolidation, seek comprehensive advice and information from agencies mentioned in the paragraph below.

GETTING HELP AND ADVICE

The Consumer Credit Counselling Service (CCCS)' is a registered charity that offers free and confidential advice to anyone in serious debt. Call (freephone) 0800 138 1111 or write to Consumer Credit Counselling Service, Wade House, Merrion Centre, Leeds LS2 8NG.

National Debtline is a free, confidential and independent helpline for people with debt problems. It provides specialist advice, backed up with self-help material that will be sent to you free of charge. Call (freephone) 0800 808 4000 or write to National Debtline, The Arch, 48–52 Floodgate Street, Birmingham B5 5SL.

DEBT DO'S AND DON'TS

Do's

Do be very cautious of commercial lenders who present themselves as 'debt advisors'. They may suggest the best plan is taking out another loan to consolidate your debts – but this may not be the best solution to your problems. Get independent advice from the CCCS or National Debtline before considering what you should do.

Do take remedial action to deal with a rising debt problem by talking to an experienced and informed advisor, rather than wasting time worrying about it in isolation.

Do resist the temptation to spend your way into more debt. Retail therapy may be comforting, but it is only appropriate for those who can afford it. If you feel the urge to use credit cards – cut them up!

Do remember that debt can be resolved through careful and resolute financial planning. There is *always* an answer, but you will probably need to consult a specialist and independent advisor to identify it.

Don'ts

Don't ignore your debt problem - it won't go away. The longer you postpone taking remedial action, the bigger the problem is likely to become.

Don't try to borrow your way out of trouble by using extended loans or credit cards to pay for existing liabilities. This only increases the amount of debt over a longer term and makes the problem harder to deal with in the future.

Don't give creditors information about other creditors (unless you are legally bound to do so), as this may compromise your position and restrict the options open to you. Get professional advice first from the CCCS or National Debtline.

Don't present your mortgage lender with a revised payment plan unless you are 100% confident you can achieve it. It is crucial that any offers of payment are honoured, otherwise the lender may consider you too high a risk and unreliable. Any payment plan should be devised with the assistance of the CCCS or National Debtline.

Don't be too proud or too embarrassed to get help. The agencies mentioned understand how easy it is to get into debt and are likely to have dealt with others in a similar situation hundreds of times before. Get the help you need to solve your debt problem – so you can get on with enjoying life.

Recommended websites

www.cccssecure.co.uk
This is the site of the Consumer Credit Counselling Service, which contains a wealth of information, help and advice for anyone worried about debt.

www.debtadvicebureau.org.uk
Good common sense advice and information from a not-for-profit organisation. This bureau is run by unpaid volunteers and offers a free debt management service.

www.nationaldebtline.co.uk
This is the site of National Debtline and contains an impressive range of professional information and advice, including access to an Information Pack that can be downloaded.

Appendix

Mock Credit Reference Report
Supplied by
Experian Limited

**Our reference: 00000000/A1
(Please quote on all correspondence)**

Consumer Help Service
PO Box 8000
Nottingham NG1 5GX

12 September 2003

RR00000

Mr E Somebody
Flat 2
186, High Street
Anytown
Midshire
AX12 34CB

Dear Mr Somebody,

Your Credit Report

Please find enclosed a copy of your credit report which contains all the information we hold about you at the addresses shown on page 1. We have included a leaflet explaining the different types of information that may be contained in your report and the steps you should take if you have any questions. Please use this leaflet to answer any questions you might have.

If you need to contact us in order to query any of the information recorded, please remember that it is essential you quote the reference number at the top of this page. Please also quote the number of each item you are querying (these are printed directly to the left of the item to which they relate for example, E1, C4, P2, etc).

Most of the information we hold about you has been provided by organisations with which you presently have a financial relationship or those with which you have had a financial relationship in the past.

If you have any questions about the information they have given to us you may like to contact these organisations and we need their authorisation to make any changes to our records.

Please note that information may be printed on both sides of each sheet of paper.

Consumer Help Service

*P.S.
The quickest way to get help with your report is to go to our website at www.experian.co.uk. You can click on Consumer Advice and access our on-line Consumer Help Service*

12 September 2003   Page 1 of 7   Reference: 00000000A1

These are the names and addresses you provided when making your application for a report and the names and addresses we have searched.

Main Applicant:

Name: MR EDWIN SOMEBODY

Date of birth: 17/07/1947

Present: FLAT 2, 186, HIGH STREET, ANYTOWN, MIDSHIRE, AB12 34CD

Other: 1, CITY ROAD, SOUTHTOWN, MERSEYPORT, CD43 AB21

Electoral Roll Information

Further information about the electoral roll is given in the explanatory leaflet. The following names are confirmed on the electoral roll at the addresses quoted, from and until the dates shown.

Present Address

E1 Local authority ANYTOWN LA

186, HIGH STREET, ANYTOWN, MIDSHIRE, AB12 34CD

Flat 2

| SOMEBODY EDWIN | From 1996 | to present |
| SOMEBODY ANNE | From 200X | to present |

Flat 1

| ANYBODY JUDITH | From 1995 | to present |

Other address/es

E2 Local authority ANYTOWN LA

1, CITY ROAD, SOUTHTOWN, MERSEYPORT, CD43 AB21

| SOMEBODY EDWIN | From 1982 | to 2000 |
| SOMEBODY ANNE | From 1982 | to 2000 |

Association/Alias

Details of any individuals with whom you have a financial connection are shown below. A financial connection can be due to a joint account, a joint application, a joint judgement, or from information you have provided to us. If you have been known by any other name (for example, a maiden name), this information may also be recorded below. For further information please refer to our explanatory leaflet.

L1 MR EDWIN SOMEBODY, 1 CITY ROAD, SOUTHTOWN, MERSEYPORT, CD43 AB21

Date of Birth	17/07/1947
Associated with	MR SIMON R SOMEONE Date of Birth 02/05/52
Associated Type	ALIAS
Association created by	BOODLES BANK PLC Date 21/12/01

12 September 2003   Page 2 of 7   Reference: 00000000A1

This section includes detials of court judgements, bankruptcies and individual voluntary arrangements. For further information please refer to the explanatory leaflet.

J1   EDWIN SOMEBODY, 1 CITY ROAD, COUTHTOWN, MERSEYPORT, CD43 AB21

Information type	**BANKRUPTCY ORDER** Date 11/01
Source	LONDON GAZETTE

If you have no record of your annulment or discharge from bankruptcy, please provide us with documentation from the court or Official Receiver and we will amend our records. For further information please see the explanatory leaflet.

J2   EDWIN SOMEBODY, 1 CITY ROAD, COUTHTOWN, MERSEYPORT, CD43 AB21

Information type	**ORDER OF DISCHARGE** Date 11/02
Source	LONDON GAZETTE

Bankruptcy details are kept for six years, even if discharged.

J3   EDWIN SOMEBODY, 1 CITY ROAD, COUTHTOWN, MERSEYPORT, CD43 AB21

Information type **SATISFIED JUDGEMENT** Date 10/97	
	Amount £481 Satisfied 11/00
Court name	SOUTHTOWN Case number ST701043
Source	REGISTRY TRUST LTD

Unless you have paid a judgement you should contact the County Court in question and request a Certificate of Satisfaction. For further information please see the explanatory leaflet.

J4   EDWIN SOMEBODY, 1 CITY ROAD, COUTHTOWN, MERSEYPORT, CD43 AB21

Information type **JUDGEMENT**	Date 09/00 Amount £369
Court name NORTHTOWN	Case number NT401135
Source	REGISTRY TRUST LTD

Unless you have paid a judgement you should contact the County Court in question and request a Certificate of Satisfaction. For further information please see the explanatory leaflet.

J5   EDWIN SOMEBODY, 1 CITY ROAD, COUTHTOWN, MERSEYPORT, CD43 AB21

Information type	**VOLUNTARY ARRANGEMENT** Date 02/01
Source	DEPARTMENT OF TRADE & INDUSTRY

Queries about Voluntary Arrangements should be taken up with the Supervisors of the Arrangement. If you have completed the Arrangement and your report does not yet shown this, you may wish to send us a copy of confirmation from the Supervisor so that we can update our records.

If you have any queries regarding the credit account information recorded below and would like to contact the company concerned yourself, a list of useful addresses is included at the end of your report. An explanation of the status history is provided in the explanatory leaflet.

C1   MR EDWIN SOMEBODY, 186 HIGH STREET, ANYTOWN, MIDSHIRE, SB12 34CD

Date of birth	17/07/47
LENDU MONEY LIMITED	BUDGET ACCOUNT
Started 19/11/02 Balance £344	Credit Limit £360

Status history   00000UU
In last 7 months, number status 1-2 is 0; number of status 3+ is 0
File updated for the period to   03/07/03

C2   MR EDWIN SOMEBODY, 186 HIGH STREET, ANYTOWN, MIDSHIRE, AB12 34CD

Date of birth	17/07/47
GENERAL BANK PLC	CREDIT CARD
Started 19/06/00 Balance £1126	Credit Limited £1300
Status history	00000U00000

In the last 36 months, number status 1-2 is 0; number of status 3+ is 0
File updated for the period to 07/07/03

C3   MR EDWIN SOMEBODY, 186 HIGH STREET, ANYTOWN, MIDSHIRE AB12 34CD

Date of birth   17/07/47
GENERAL BANK PLC   LOAN
Starter 04/06/02 Balance £0   Settled 04/06/03
Status history   000000000000
In last 12 months, number of status 1-2 is 0; number of status 3+ is 0
File updated for the period to 28/07/03

C4   MR EDWIN SOMEBODY, 1 CITY ROAD, SOUTHTOWN, MERSEYPORT, DC43 AB21

Date of birth	17/04/47
Arrangement from	01/99 or 08/02
MOBILE PHONE FIRM RENTAL	
Started 05/07/97 Default £548	Defaulted 06/10/97
	Balance Satisfied
Status history	8

File updated for the period to 19/07/02

Defaulted accounts are kept on file for six years from the date of default, even if they are subsequently marked as satisfied by the lender.

12 September 2003   Page 4 of 7   Reference: 00000000A1

C5 MR SIMON SOMEONE, 1 CITY ROAD, COUTHTOWN, MERSEYPORT, CD43 AB21
MOBILE PHONE COMPANY RENTAL

Starter 27/8/98

Default 15/10/98
Balance £101

Status history
File updated for the period to 7/12/99

8

NOTICE OF CORRECTION, Reference 00000000 – See final page of report

Council of Mortgage Lenders (CML) Information

If you have any queries about the CML information recorded below and would like to contact the company concerned yourself, a list of useful addresses is included at the end of your tile. CML information may be recorded at up to three addresses for each entry i.e. the address, at which the possession or surrender occurred, and the previous and forwarding address(es) of the individual concerned. For further information see page 4 of the explanatory leaflet.

M MR E SOMEBODY, FLAT 2, 186 HIGH STREET, ANYTOWN, MIDSHIRE, AB12 34CD
MORTGAGE YOUR HOUSE PLC
POSSESSION ORDER
File updates for the period to

FORWARDING ADDRESS
16/01/00
24/02/00

Previous Searches

The details shown below are those input by the company when they made the search. The information does not imply that an account is held with the company which made the search. Details of companies, which have searched, are kept on file for 12 months. Further information about Previous Searches is provided in the explanatory leaflet.

P1 MR E SOMEBODY, 186 HIGH STREET, ANYTOWN, AB12 34CD

Searched on 15/11/02

Date of birth 17/07/47 Time At Address
06 years 04 months

Searched by
Application type

HOPE BING AND LAMOUR LIMITED
UNRECORDED ENQUIRY

P2 MRS ANNE SOMEBODY, FLAT 2, 186 HIGH ST., ANYTOWN, AB12 34CD

Searched on 05/01/03

Date of birth 17/07/47 Time At Address
03 years 02 months

Searched by
Application type

LENDU MONEY LIMITED
REVOLVING CREDIT

Linked Addresses

Linked addresses are created from the information provided by either the lender(s) shown below or by yourself. This information will reflect addresses that you have been connected with. For further information please see the explanatory leaflet.

B1   MR EDWIN SOMEBODY
1 CITY ROAD, SOUTHTOWN, MERSEYPORT, CD43 AB21
Linked to: **186 HIGH STREET, ANYTOWN, MIDSHIRE**
Source: **HOPE BING AND LAMOUR LIMITED**
Date of information 15/11/02

B2   MRS ANNE SOMEBODY
1 CITY ROAD, SOUTHTOWN, MERSEYPORT, CD43 AB21
Linked to: **2 ELSEWHERE DRIVE, SOUTHTOWN, MERSEYSIDE**
Source   **LENDU MONEY LIMITED**
Date of information 05/01/03

CIFAS – The UK's Fraud Prevention Service

An explanation of CIFAS can be found in the explanatory leaflet. If you wish to contact the CIFAS member for more information about the details recorded, please use the address provided as part of the individual entry. If you feel that a CIFAS entry is incorrect in any way you can either contact the member directly using the same address or provide us with details of exactly what you feel is incorrect and why and we will contact the member on your behalf. This information exists to help prevent fraud.

F1		
Name used	**MRS MARY JONES**	
Date of birth used	12/09/1967	
Address Used	**1, CITY ROAD, SOUTHTOWN, MERSEYPORT, CD43 AB21**	
Date recorded	08/07/02	
Member name	**WATCHIT TV RENTAL**	
Member's address	Watchit House, Television Road, Tellytown, Southshire XZ98 1VY	
Case Reference	14AY2400	
Product Type	PERSONAL CREDIT CARD	
Type of case	FALSE IDENTITY FRAUD – USE OF FALSE NAME WITH AN ADDRESS	
Reason for referral	DATE OF BIRTH	

GAIN is explained in the explanatory leaflet. If you have any queries about this information contact the company who provided us with the information.

T   Mr Edwin Somebody

Date of birth	17/07/1947
Last know at	1, CITY ROAD, SOUTHTOWN, MERSEYPORT, CD43 AB21
Located at	186, HIGH STREET, ANYTOWN, MIDSHIRE
By:	MOBILE PHONE FIRM
Reference 62623456	On 09/03/00

Useful Addresses

The following addresses are provided should you wish to contact lenders in respect of any Credit Account Information or County Courts in respect of judgement information recorded on your report.

SOUTHTOWN COUNTY COURT: QUEEN'S HOUSE, ROYAL STREET, SOUTHTOWN, U148 7RF

NORTHTOWN COUNTY COURT: 100, VICARY ST., NORTHTOWN, EW67 9RW

LENDU MONEY: MRS VERITY HELPFUL, CUSTOMER SERVICES (DATA PROTECTION), LENDU MONEY, CASH HOUSE, 200 NEARBY ROAD, CLOSETOWN, MIDDLESHIRE, KI14 8XZ

MOBILE PHONE COMPANY SERVICES: MRS SHIRLEY ANSWER, CREDIT UNDERWRITING DEPT, MOBILE PHONE COMPANY SERVICES, MOBILE HOUSE, PARK STREET, NOWHERE LK76 5YH

GENERAL BANK: MR ANDRES QUERY, COLLECTION & LITIGATION DEPT, GENERAL BANK, GENERAL HOUSE, LOCAL ROAD, TOWNSPACE, TG98 4TR

Notice of Correction

Reference: 00000000A1
Page 1

00000000/SOMEBODY. MR EDWIN SOMEBODY WISHES IT TO BE MADE CLEAR TO ANY POTENTIAL LENDER THAT THE INFORMATION IN THE NAME OF MR SIMON R SOMEONE RELATES TO A FORMER BUSINESS ASSOCIATE WITH WHOM HE SHARES A JOINT ACCOUNT. MR SOMEBODY DID LODGE AT THIS PREVIOUS ADDRESS, THE JOINT BANK ACCOUNT IS THE ONLY FINANCIAL CONNECTION THEY SHARE AND ANY FURTHER INFORMATION IN MR SOMEONE'S NAME HAS NO CONNECTION WITH MR SOMEBODY. MR SOMEBODY STRESSES THAT HE HOLDS NO RESPONSIBILITY FOR THE DEFAULTED ACCOUNT IN MR SOMEONE'S NAME AND REQUESTS THAT ANYONE SEARCHING HIS REPORT TAKES THIS INTO ACCOUNT.

12 September 2003   Page 7 of 7   Reference: 00000000A1

Useful Addresses and Contacts

AdviceUK. The independent advice network. 12th Floor, New London Bridge House, 25 London Bridge St., London SE1 9ST. Tel: (020) 7407 4070. *www.adviceuk.org.uk*

British Franchise Association. Sponsored by various high street banks. BFA members follow a code of business practice. Thames View, Newtown Road, Henley-on-Thames, Oxon RG9 1HG. Tel: (01491) 578050. *www.british-franchise.org*

Callcredit. Consumer credit referencing agency. One Park Lane, Leeds, West Yorkshire LS3 1EP. Tel: (0113) 244 1555. *www.callcredit.plc.uk*

Citizens Advice. The National Citizens Advice Bureau for independent, confidential, impartial, free advice. Myddleton House, 115–123 Pentonville Road, London N1 9LZ. Tel: see *Yellow Pages* for your local CAB. *www.citizensadvice.org.uk*

Citizens Advice Scotland. The umbrella body for CAB in Scotland. 2 Powderhall Road, Edinburgh EH7 4GB. Tel: (0131) 5501000. *www.cas.org.uk*

Confederation for the Registration of Gas Installers (CORGI). National watchdog for gas safety in the UK. 1 Elmwood, Chineham Park, Crockford Lane, Basingstoke, Hants RG24 8WG. Tel: 0870 401 2200. *www.corgi-gas-safety.com*

Consumer Credit Counselling Service (CCCS). Free and confidential debt advice. Wade House, Merrion Centre, Leeds LS2 8NG. Tel: 0800 138 1111. *www.cccssecure.co.uk*

Cottage Owners Unite (COUNT). Dedicated to the needs of self-catering holiday property owners. Frogmarsh Mill, South Woodchester, Gloucestershire GL5 5ET. Tel: (01453) 872727. *www.cottageownersunite.co.uk*

Council for Licensed Conveyancers. Regulatory body for licensed conveyancers. 16 Glebe Road, Chelmsford, Essex CM1 1QG. Tel: (01245) 349599. *www.conveyancer.org.uk*

Department for Work & Pensions. Responsible for the Government's welfare reform agenda and working age benefit advice. Room 540, The Adelphi, 1–11 John Adam Street, London WC2N 6HT. Tel: (020) 7712 2171. *www.dwp.gov.uk*

Empty Homes Agency. Charity that campaigns to bring empty properties back into use. 195–197 Victoria Street, London SW1E 5NE. Tel: (020) 7828 6288. *www.emptyhomes.com*

Equifax. Consumer credit referencing agency. PO Box 1140, Bradford BD1 5US. Tel: 0845 600 1772. *www.equifax.co.uk*

Experian. Consumer credit referencing agency. Talbot House, Talbot Street, Nottingham NG1 5HF. Tel: 0870 241 6212. *www.experian.co.uk*

Financial Services Authority. Aims to maintain efficient financial markets and help consumers get better deals. 25 The North Colonnade, Canary Wharf, London E14 5HS. Tel: 0845 606 1234. *www.fsa.gov.uk*

Health & Safety Executive. Responsible for the regulation of most health and safety issues in Britain. HSE Infoline, Caerphilly Business Park, Caerphilly CF83 3GG. Tel: 08701 545500. *www.hse.gov.uk*

HM Customs and Excise. Government department responsible for collecting VAT and other taxes. VAT Central Unit, Alexander House, Southend-on-Sea, Essex SS99 1AA. Tel: (National Advice Service) 0845 010 9000. *www.hmce.gov.uk*

Housing Corporation. Invests public funds in housing associations to create safe and sustainable communities. Maple House, 149 Tottenham Court Road, London W1T 7BN. Tel: (020) 7393 2000. *www.housingcorp.gov.uk*

Housing Ombudsman. The independent ombudsman scheme deals with disputes between landlords and tenants. Norman House, 105-109 Strand, London WC2R 0AA. Tel: 0845 7125 973. *www.ihos.org.uk*

Independent Financial Advisors. For independent financial advice. IFA Promotion Ltd., 2nd Floor, 117 Farrington Road, London EC1R 3BX. Tel: 0800 0853 250. *www.unbiased.co.uk*

Land Registry. Maintains detailed records of land ownership (registers of title) for England and Wales. 32 Lincoln's Inn Fields, London WC2A 3PH. Tel: (020) 7917 8888. *www.landreg.gov.uk*

Mortgage Code Compliance Board. Non-statutory regulator ensuring those taking out a mortgage are informed and protected. University Court, Stafford ST18 0GN. Tel: (01785) 218200. *www.mortgagecode.org.uk*

National Debtline. Free and confidential debt advice. The Arch, 48–52 Floodgate Street, Birmingham B5 5SL. Tel: 0800 808 4000. *www.nationaldebtline.co.uk*

Office for the Supervision of Solicitors. Set up by the Law Society to deal with complaints about solicitors. Victoria Court, 8 Dormer Place, Leamington Spa, Warwickshire CV32 5AE. Tel: 0845 608 6565. *www.oss.lawsociety.org.uk*

Office of Communications (OFCOM). The regulator for UK communications industries. Riverside House, 2a Southwark Bridge Road, London SE1 9HA. Tel: 0845 456 3333. *www.ofcom.org.uk*

Office of Fair Trading. Exists to protect consumers and to ensure business compete and operate fairly. Fleetbank House, 2–6 Salisbury Square, London EC4Y 8JX. Tel: 0845 722 4499. *www.oft.gov.uk*

Office of Water Services (OFWAT). The regulator for the water and sewerage industry in England and Wales. Centre City Tower, 7 Hill Street, Birmingham B5 4UA. Tel: (0121) 625 1300. *www.ofwat.gov.uk*

Registers of Scotland. Scotland's national land and property registers. Erskine House, 68 Queen Street, Edinburgh EH2 4NF. Tel: 0845 607 0161. *www.ros.gov.uk*

Royal Institute of Chartered Surveyors. Worldwide property organisation promoting excellence and safeguarding public interest. Surveyor Court, Westwood Way, Coventry CV4 8JE. Tel: 0870 333 1600. *www.rics.org*

Shelter. UK campaigning charity for homeless and badly housed people. 88 Old Street, London EC1V 9HU. Tel: 0800 800 4444. *www.shelter.org.uk*

Tax Credits. Inland Revenue Tax Credit Office for information and explanatory leaflets. Inland Revenue, PO Box 145, Preston PR1 0GP. Tel: 0845 609 5000 for working families

tax credits or 0845 605 5858 for disabled persons tax
credits. *www.inlandrevenue.gov.uk*

Trading Standards. Investigates consumer related problems. 1
Sylvan Court, Sylvan Way, Southfields Business Park,
Basildon SS15 6TH. Go online or look in *Yellow Pages*
for your local Trading Standards office. *www.consumercom-
plaints.org.uk*

TV Licensing. For information about licenses and how to
obtain one. Customer Service, TV Licensing, Bristol BS98
1TL. Tel: 0870 241 6468. *www.tvlicensing.co.uk*

Index